IMAGES
of America

LAKE LURE

On the Cover: The beach by the lake is perhaps one of Lake Lure's best-known landmarks and is used by both visitors and locals alike. In its early years, the Lake Lure Beach had no fence and was open to anyone. The Town of Lake Lure realized lifeguards were needed, so they built a fence and sold tickets to pay for the expenses. (Photograph by Norman Greig; courtesy of the Greig family.)

IMAGES
of America

LAKE LURE

Jim Proctor

ARCADIA
PUBLISHING

ISBN 978-0-7385-9843-7

Published by Arcadia Publishing
Charleston, South Carolina

Printed in the United States of America

Library of Congress Control Number: 2012949481

For all general information, please contact Arcadia Publishing:
Telephone 843-853-2070
Fax 843-853-0044
E-mail sales@arcadiapublishing.com
For customer service and orders:
Toll-Free 1-888-313-2665

Visit us on the Internet at www.arcadiapublishing.com

This book is dedicated to my wonderful wife, Robin, and in memorial for my mother, Anne Washburn Proctor; my father, Francis Clyde Proctor Sr.; Aunt Fanny; Uncle Bud; and my grandparents, Jim and Tootsie Washburn. I do wish I had inherited their eloquence in the art of storytelling.

Contents

ACKNOWLEDGMENTS

I offer my sincerest thanks to all who have helped me in this educational and fun endeavor. Along with my family's collection of historical photographs, I am particularly grateful to Todd Morse, Randy Balot, Bob Washburn, Jane Noblitt Melton, Ben Butler, Chris Braund, Camp Lurecrest, and the Town of Lake Lure for giving me access to their images. I was very lucky to have this project as an excuse to spend many hours talking to folks near and far about our wonderful and beautiful community. I am, of course, also indebted to all the real historians, past and present, for all the previous works written about Lake Lure, Chimney Rock, the Hickory Nut Gorge, and Western North Carolina. I think every author writing a book about the history of any location in Rutherford County owes a hearty thanks to former county historian Clarence Griffin.

Introduction

Lake Lure, one of the most beautiful lakes in the world, is often billed as the "Gem of the Carolinas." This mountain lake is surrounded by majestic cliff-sided mountains and fed by the idyllic Rocky Broad River. Lake Lure's subtropical climate offers diverse plant and wildlife. Lake Lure's history is not only long and fascinating, it is actually much older than the lake itself.

Lake Lure is in Rutherford County, North Carolina, and was, of course, first inhabited by Native Americans. At the time of Columbus's trips to the New World, this area was near the boundary of the Cherokee and Catawba Indian tribes. Many believe this area was sacred to both tribes. There are many stories and myths about its occupants and how the valley was formed. The valley was actually formed by the mountains and river and is called the Hickory Nut Gorge.

This part of Rutherford County was first settled by Europeans around 1760. The highway through Hickory Nut Gorge is, in fact, one of the oldest roads across the North Carolina Appalachian Mountains. This road allowed the travel and tourist industry to come to Rutherford County. During the late 18th and 19th centuries, many way stations and inns were created to provide meals and lodging to the weary travelers. Though often rough, the early roads in this area were highly regarded by the residents of this remote and sparsely settled region. With the rivers too rough for navigation and the railroads still decades away, the early roads and the stagecoaches that negotiated them provided commercial ties to the outside world.

The route through the Hickory Nut Gorge was favored by the early operators of stagecoach lines. Beginning in 1839, the Great Western Stageline utilized this route on its Salisbury-to-Asheville run. Twenty years later, the Asheville-to-Charlotte United States Mail Line traveled the Hickory Nut Gorge Turnpike, advertised as "the cheapest as well as the most direct route."

James Harris and his sons Dr. John and Zadock Harris were some of the first to be aware of the business potential associated with travel and tourism. They built two of the first inns in Rutherford County and were instrumental in the development and the establishment of the early trade routes. Zadock established his inn in the southeastern part of Rutherford County, while John decided to invest in the more remote but scenic western part of Rutherford County. The Harris Inn near the Rocky Broad River was built sometime between 1782 and 1800.

The entrepreneurial spirit of the Harris family was well known in the county. Around 1834, the family tradition of innkeeping was furthered when Bedford and Elizabeth Sherrill, Dr. Harris's daughter and son-in-law, built Sherrill's Inn at the Hickory Nut Gap, 10 miles to the west of the Harris Inn.

Dr. John Harris knew that the development of good roads was essential for the development of Rutherford County. He and several other prominent men petitioned the North Carolina General Assembly to help with this cause and let them develop a toll road from Chimney Rock to Asheville. This venture was widely praised, and in 1823, the general assembly authorized expenditures to be used "in making and improving the road leading from Asheville by the Hickory-Nut-Gap to Rutherfordton." Dr. Harris was one of the first commissioners of this venture. In a progress report to the general assembly issued in 1830, the commissioners noted that the road had been "recently much traveled" and boasted that it was "destined forthwith, to become the great channel of intercourse between the Western States and the Carolinas." They further stated, "The rich and romantic valley of Main Broad River, heretofore locked up by natural towers of rocks and impassable mountains, is now beginning to develop its resources, and present to the way-worn traveler a good road through an exceedingly rough country, rendered doubly interesting by the bold and majestic mountain scenery, which is not surpassed in height, beauty or grandeur in any portion of the Union." In January 1841, the general assembly reappointed Dr. John W. Harris, Bedford Sherrill, and four other men from Rutherford and Buncombe Counties as "Commissioners for the purpose of making and keeping in repair a Turnpike Road." In this act, the assembly incorporated the commissioners as the Hickory Nut Turnpike Company and empowered it to issue capital stock, set construction standards, and establish rates of toll. The turnpike was completed, and on May 10, 1847, it was given a final inspection and opened to traffic. The Harris Inn was used as the tollgate for travelers going west to Asheville. The first post office to serve the Chimney Rock community was established at the Harris Inn on December 19, 1843, with Dr. Harris as postmaster.

By the 1850s, a visit to Hickory Nut Gorge was a favorite excursion for travelers in the Western North Carolina mountains. Already, the natural wonders of the area, such as Chimney Rock, the Bottomless Pools, Hickory Nut Falls, and the grand panorama of the gorge, were admired.

Along with commercial and tourist travelers, the Harris Inn was host to several noted writers. One of the first was G.W Featherstonhaugh, a noted British writer and geologist, who visited in 1837 and wrote about the Harris Inn. Two decades later, Henry E. Colton wrote two books about his travels in Western North Carolina: *Mountain Scenery, the Scenery of the Mountains of Western North Carolina* (1859) and *Guide Book to the Scenery of the Mountains of North Carolina* (1860). Colton obviously enjoyed his stay at the Harris Inn. He states in his first book, "The traveler, at his leisure, can find no better place to rest his weary limbs, or satiate an appetite acquired in the bracing mountain air. An excellent view of the mountains is obtained from this house [the Harris Inn]. In fact, just here is the beginning of the grandest panorama of mountain scenery which is to be found easy of access anywhere in the West." Colton's second book quotes the stagecoach fare for travel from Charlotte to Asheville on the Sullivan line of stages as $9.

In 1869, Judge George Washington Logan bought the Harris Inn, and it became known as the Logan House. The Logan House continued to be a focal point for travelers, tourists, and writers passing through this region. It was while staying at the Logan House that Frances Hodgson Burnett wrote her play *Esmeralda*. From the inn, one can often see the appearance of a cabin on the rock face of Rumbling Bald Mountain; this, according to the local folks, is "Esmeralda's Cabin," a reminder of Burnett and her play. *Esmeralda* became the longest-running play on Broadway in the 19th century. In 1891, Col. Thomas Turner built another famous inn three miles northwest of the Harris Inn and named it the Esmeralda Inn after Burnett's play.

In 1880, Jerome B. Freeman purchased 400 acres, including Chimney Rock, from the Speculation Land Company. He paid $25 for the entire tract of land. He soon built a trail suitable for horses and foot traffic to the base of the rock. He then installed a ladder to allow tourists to climb to the top of Chimney Rock. Chimney Rock Park was opened to the public in 1885.

At about the same time, Charles Duley Warner, a well-traveled friend of Mark Twain, passed through in the 1880s. He made the acquaintance of Judge G.W. Logan and stayed at the Logan House. Warner wrote that he enjoyed his stay at the inn but not the judge's politics.

In 1881, Ida F. Chunn wrote *The Descriptive Illustrated Guide-Book to North Carolina*, in which she states, "The trip through the Hickory Nut Gap claims manifold attractions; the Pools, Chimney Rock, High Falls, Bald Mountain, etc., in addition to the wild beauty of the route. It is suggested that several days be given to the pass, making the comfortable farm-house (Logan's) near the eastern end of the gap the objective point." Edwin A. Gatchell toured the area in 1886, and the next year, he wrote *The Standard Guide to Asheville and Western North Carolina*. About his trip from Asheville to Rutherfordton, he writes, "Continue your trip to Judge G.W. Logan's Hotel, where you will find a hearty welcome, comfortable quarters, and good fare."

In 1887, the Seaboard Air Line Railway, a major east-west railway, finally reached Rutherfordton. In a published advertisement titled "Mountainous Regions Western North Carolina," the railway encouraged tourists to travel further west. This booklet spotlights the Chimney Rock area. In the beginning paragraph of the booklet, the author states, "I rode horseback for two days through this section and found a number of boarding houses and hotels, all comfortable places, delightfully situated for summer rest, and pure water piped from the mountains above them and magnificent mountain scenery right at their door. These hotels, as a rule, are very clean, with comfortable beds and good cooking, plenty of eggs, chickens, splendid North Carolina ham, all the milk and cream you want and ample supply of fresh vegetables. There being no frost in the Gap, the gardens are very early. Fish are very Plentiful; I got up the second morning I was there and caught enough for breakfast right at my door."

In 1913, author Margaret Worley wrote of her stay in the Hickory Nut Gorge, "Crossing a charming, though somewhat deep and rocky ford of the Broad River, you continue on up the beautiful valley, the mountains draw in about you, and you are at Logan's, a large, old-fashioned farmhouse which was converted to uses of a wayside inn when the road went through to Rutherfordton, connecting the mountains above here with the low country. Logan's is 'in the Scenery,' so they tell you a good many times while there—and unquestionably it is. A beautiful cultivated valley lies about the house enchantingly surrounded by mountains. The mountains of this region, although so individual in form, so picturesque, or so beautiful, are, according to General Logan, worth about a cent apiece, there is so little soil on them."

The 20th century brought many changes for the Hickory Nut Gorge. Due to poor health, Dr. Lucius B. Morse came to visit in the early 1900s. He and his brothers bought the Chimney Rock Park in 1902. Dr. Morse made many improvements to this tourist attraction, and soon, his dream for a much larger development, including a mountain lake, was developed. With several financial backers, Dr. Morse created Chimney Rock Mountains, Inc., and began buying land and options for land around the Broad River below Chimney Rock. Soon, this new development company had acquired over 8,000 acres. The centerpiece of this resort was to be a lake created by impounding the Rocky Broad River at Tumbling Shoals: Lake Lure. The lake's name would come from Dr. Morse's wife, Betty. The impounded water came from the Broad River, Cane Creek, Buffalo Creek, and several other small creeks. Although there were many farms and a church built where the lake would flood, there was no town named Buffalo flooded, as reported in local rumors. The farms above the lake on Buffalo Creek were, however, known as Buffalo. Carolina Mountain Power Company, all of whose common stock was owned by the Chimney Rock Mountains, Inc., was formed, and the construction of the dam began in 1925 under the guidance of Mees & Mees, an engineering firm from Charlotte, North Carolina. Carolina Mountain Power Company owned all the land under the lake, the dam, and the powerhouse. Development of the resort was funded by a $1-million mortgage with the Bird Mortgage Company of Asheville, North Carolina. This mortgage was secured by the property above Lake Lure and later acquired by the United States Fidelity and Guaranty Company (USF&G) of Baltimore, Maryland. The Carolina Mountain Power Company financed construction of the dam that impounded Lake Lure with a $550,000 mortgage with Stroud & Company of Philadelphia, Pennsylvania. This mortgage was secured by the property owned by the Carolina Mountain Power Company, including the land on which the dam was constructed as well as the land inundated by Lake Lure. The dam was completed in September 1926, and the lake began to fill. At full pond, Lake Lure covers approximately 720 acres and has a shoreline of approximately 21 miles. The power plant began operations in 1928 with the sale of electricity to the Blue Ridge Power Company, later bought by Duke Power Company. The hydropower plant has produced electricity every year since, and the current owner, the Town of Lake Lure, continues to contract with Duke Energy for the sale of electricity.

The Town of Lake Lure was incorporated in 1927. The boundaries of the town include all the land owned by Chimney Rock Mountains, Inc., the Lake Lure Development Company, and Carolina Mountain Power Company. The first mayor of Lake Lure was Dr. Morse. The development company constructed the Lake Lure Arcade Building and several small structures. They sold land to the company that built the Lake Lure Inn. The development company built a beautiful school and gave it to the Rutherford County Schools. At this time, several very large homes were built on Lake Lure. The most prominent home was built by the Ward family and later bought by the Haynes family (owners of the Haynes Hosiery mills).

Unfortunately, the plans for a resort development came to a halt in 1929 with beginning of the Great Depression. Both USF&G and Stroud & Company foreclosed their mortgages. Soon after the foreclosures, USF&G established the Lureland Realty Company to dispose of the property that had been secured by the property owned by Chimney Rock Mountains, Inc. By the beginning of 1942, the Lureland Realty Company had sold all the property that had been owned by Chimney Rock Mountains, Inc.

Stroud & Company changed the name of the power company to the Carolina Mountain Power Corporation. William C. Rommell, president of Stroud & Company, operated the Carolina Mountain Power Corporation from 1931 until Lake Lure was acquired by the Town of Lake Lure in 1965. Rommell was most interested in the production of power, and even before his company acquired the lake, he allowed the Town of Lake Lure to operate the recreational facilities and police the lake. In 1963, the North Carolina General Assembly authorized the Town of Lake Lure to issue revenue bonds for the purpose of acquiring Lake Lure. The acquisition was completed on July 26, 1965. The sleepy town of Lake Lure changed very little for several decades. It was most famous for fishing, boating, restaurants, small motels, and rental cabins. With little growth and the trend to consolidate schools, the county closed the Lake Lure School in 1961.

In the late 1960s, a resort was established on the north end of Lake Lure. It was first called The Mountains, then Fairfield Mountains, and eventually Rumbling Bald Mountain Resort. This development became the only resort in Western North Carolina with two championship golf courses. There are now many fine restaurants and great places to stay in Lake Lure. The Lake Lure Inn has been completely remodeled, and the kitchen serves gourmet food. For a second time, Lake Lure has a local school, the Lake Lure Classical Academy: A Challenge Foundation Academy, so local children do not need to travel to other towns for school. Many families have once again found Lake Lure to be a great place to not only visit, but also to live year-round. Certainly one of the greatest modern events was the purchase of Chimney Rock Park and other properties by the State of North Carolina for the new Chimney Rock State Park. The park was established in 2002 by the North Carolina Division of Parks and Recreation. The park continued to grow to nearly 6,000 acres and now includes most of Rumbling Bald Mountain and Chimney Rock Park.

After all these years, Lake Lure is still one of the prettiest lakes in the world and truly is the "Gem of the Carolinas."

One

The Hickory Nut Gorge before Lake Lure

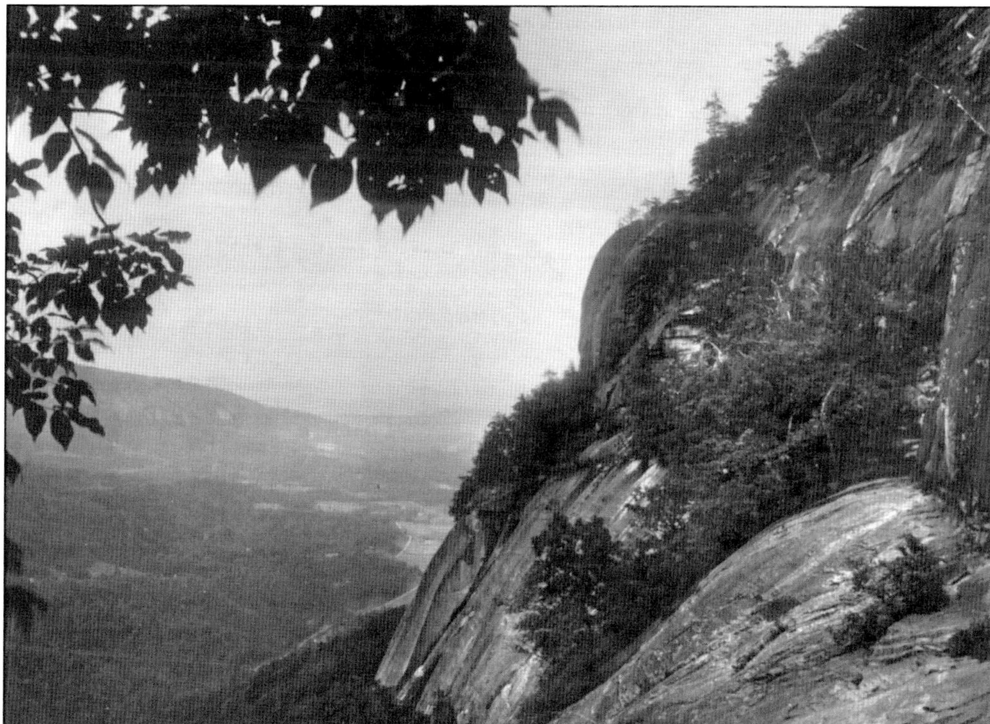

Lake Lure is located in the Hickory Nut Gorge. Before the dam was constructed at Tumbling Shoals in 1925, the peaceful and picturesque valley was first inhabited by Native Americans. European pioneers began settling the Hickory Nut Gorge in the 1700s. This photograph was taken before Lake Lure was filled. (Author's collection.)

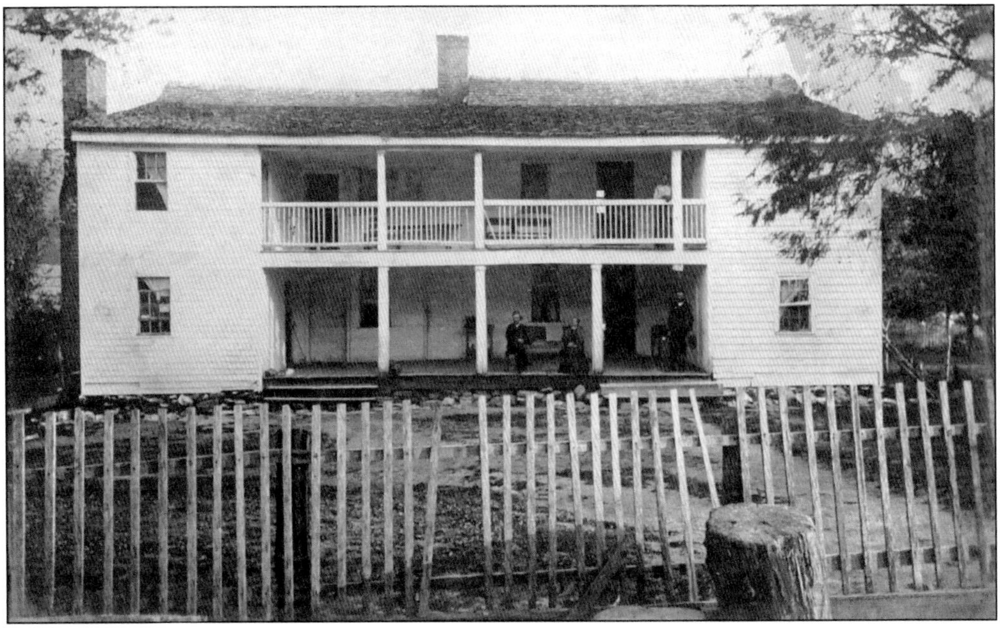

The photograph above is the earliest known image of the Harris Inn (later known as the Logan House and Pine Gables). The inn is the oldest structure in the Hickory Nut Gorge and provided room and board for passengers on the stagecoach line that ran between Rutherfordton and Asheville. The inn was first two log cabins; the oldest was said to be built in the late 1700s. In 1834, the log cabins were boarded over, and side rooms and porches were added. The photograph below shows the side of the inn, several outbuildings, and horse-drawn wagons near the old toll road. (Author's collection.)

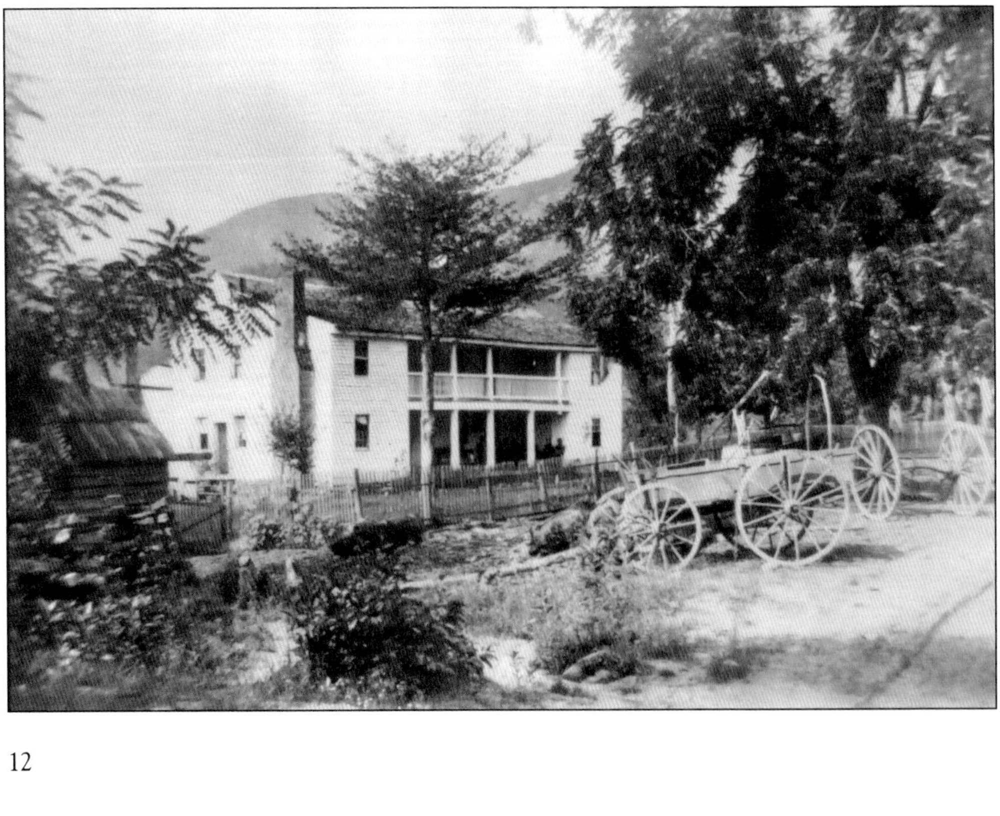

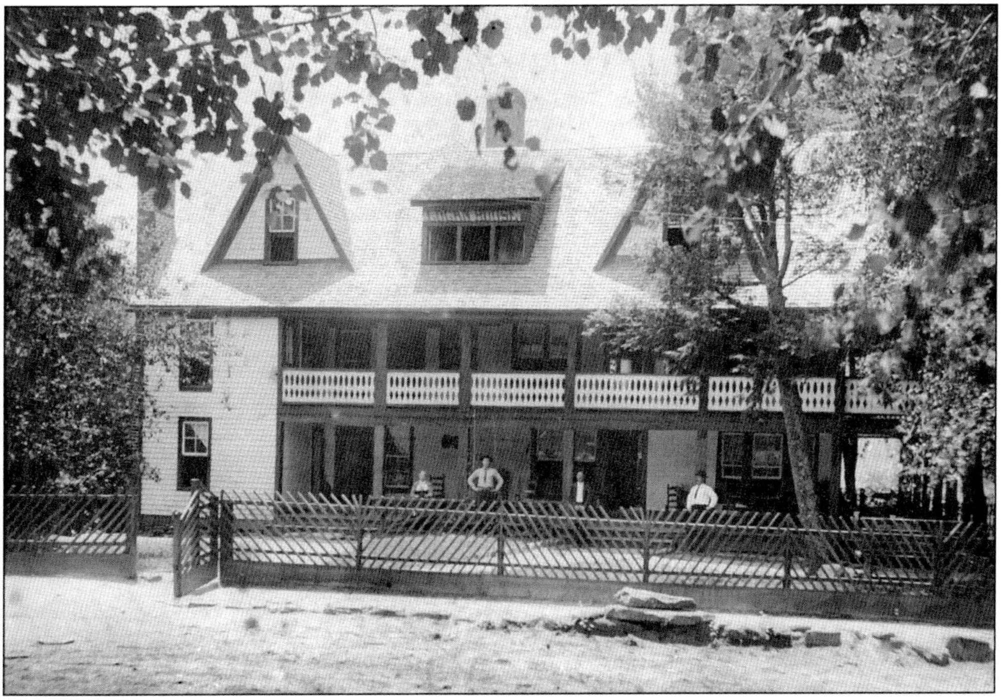

The first post office in the Hickory Nut Gorge was established in 1843 and located in the Harris Inn. Judge G.W. Logan bought the Harris Inn in 1869 and renamed it the Logan House. In 1877, he added a third floor, a wraparound porch, and a major addition on the back. (Author's collection.)

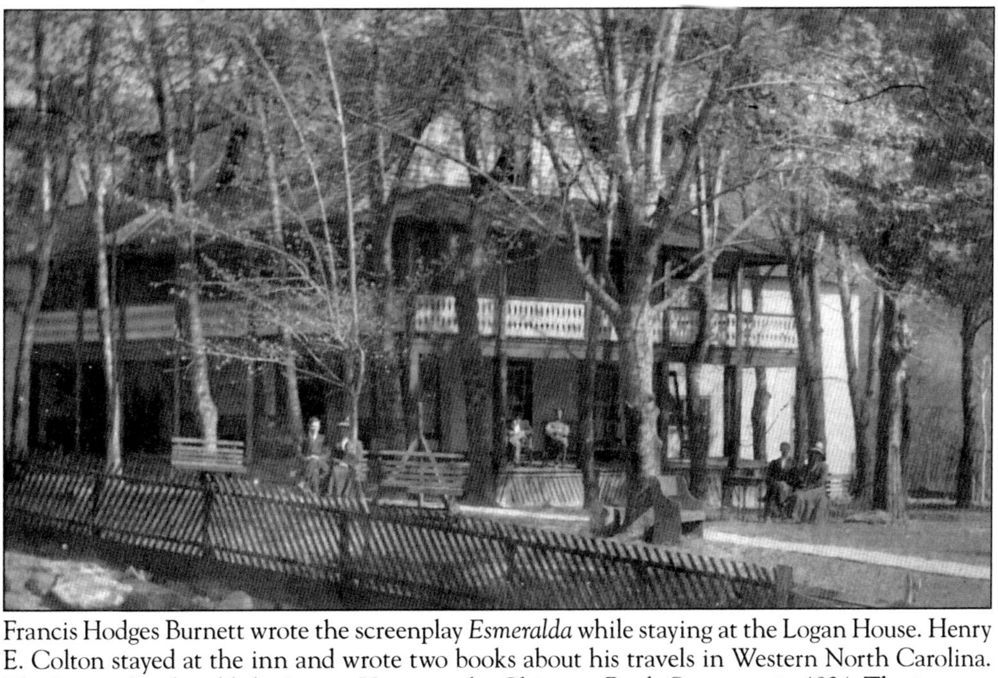

Francis Hodges Burnett wrote the screenplay *Esmeralda* while staying at the Logan House. Henry E. Colton stayed at the inn and wrote two books about his travels in Western North Carolina. The Logan family sold the Logan House to the Chimney Rock Company in 1924. The inn was used for the company's administration building and, for a short time, the Chimney Rock School. (Author's collection.)

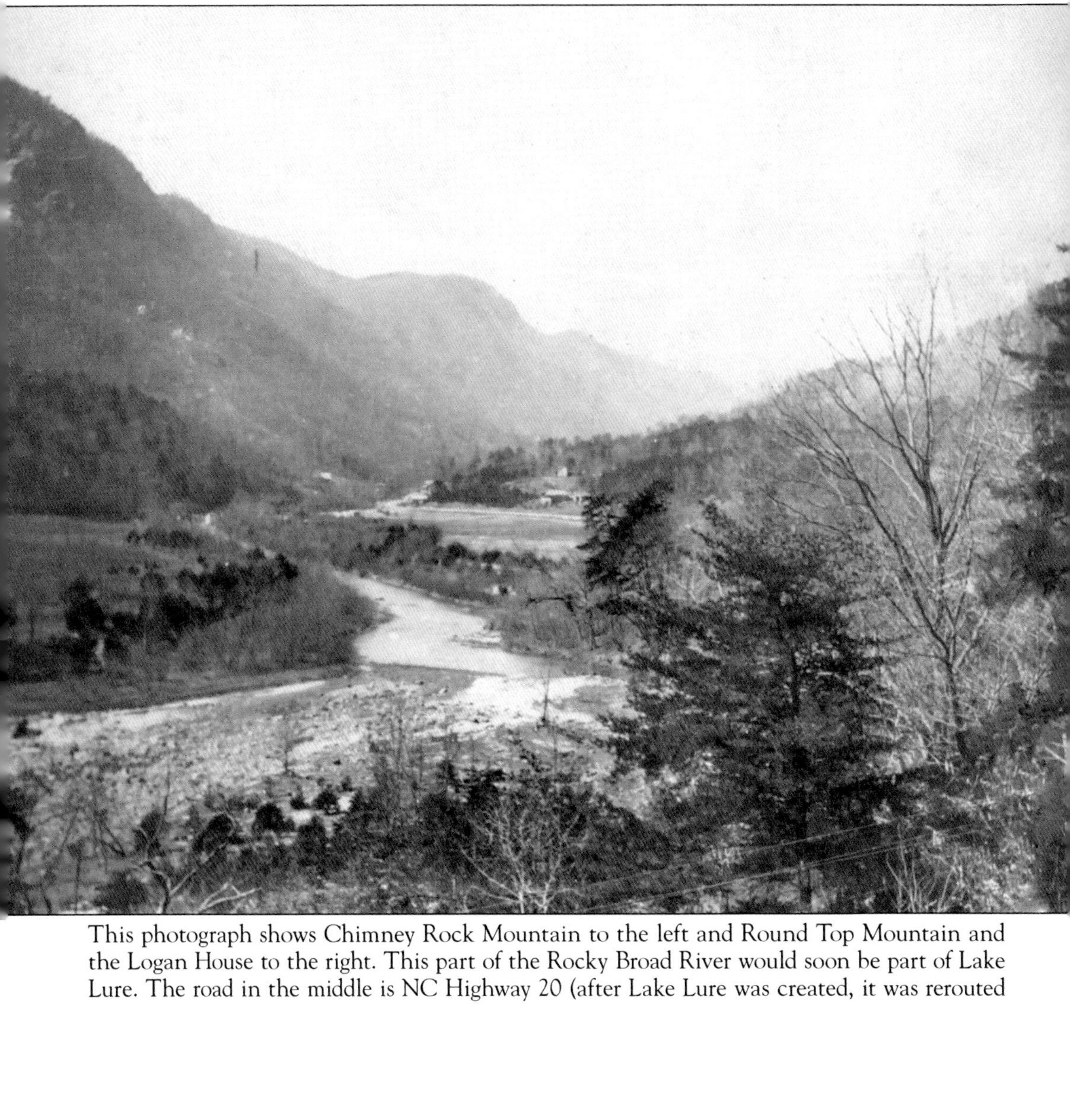

This photograph shows Chimney Rock Mountain to the left and Round Top Mountain and the Logan House to the right. This part of the Rocky Broad River would soon be part of Lake Lure. The road in the middle is NC Highway 20 (after Lake Lure was created, it was rerouted

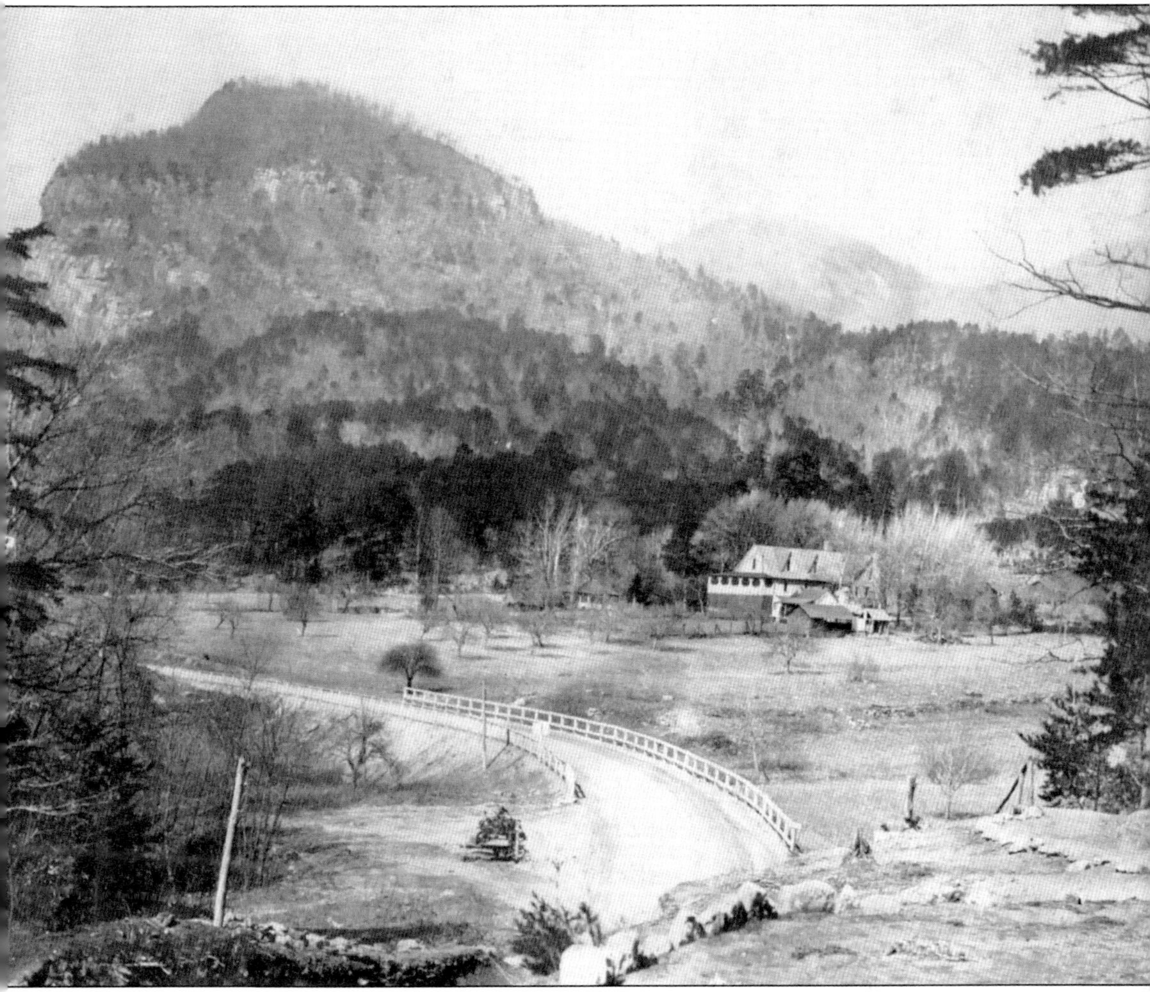

and renamed US Highway 74). In 1913, Boys Scouts from Mecklenburg County camped near the Rocky Broad River behind the Logan House, and for the week, it was called "Camp Reynolds" in appreciation of William A Reynolds. (Author's collection.)

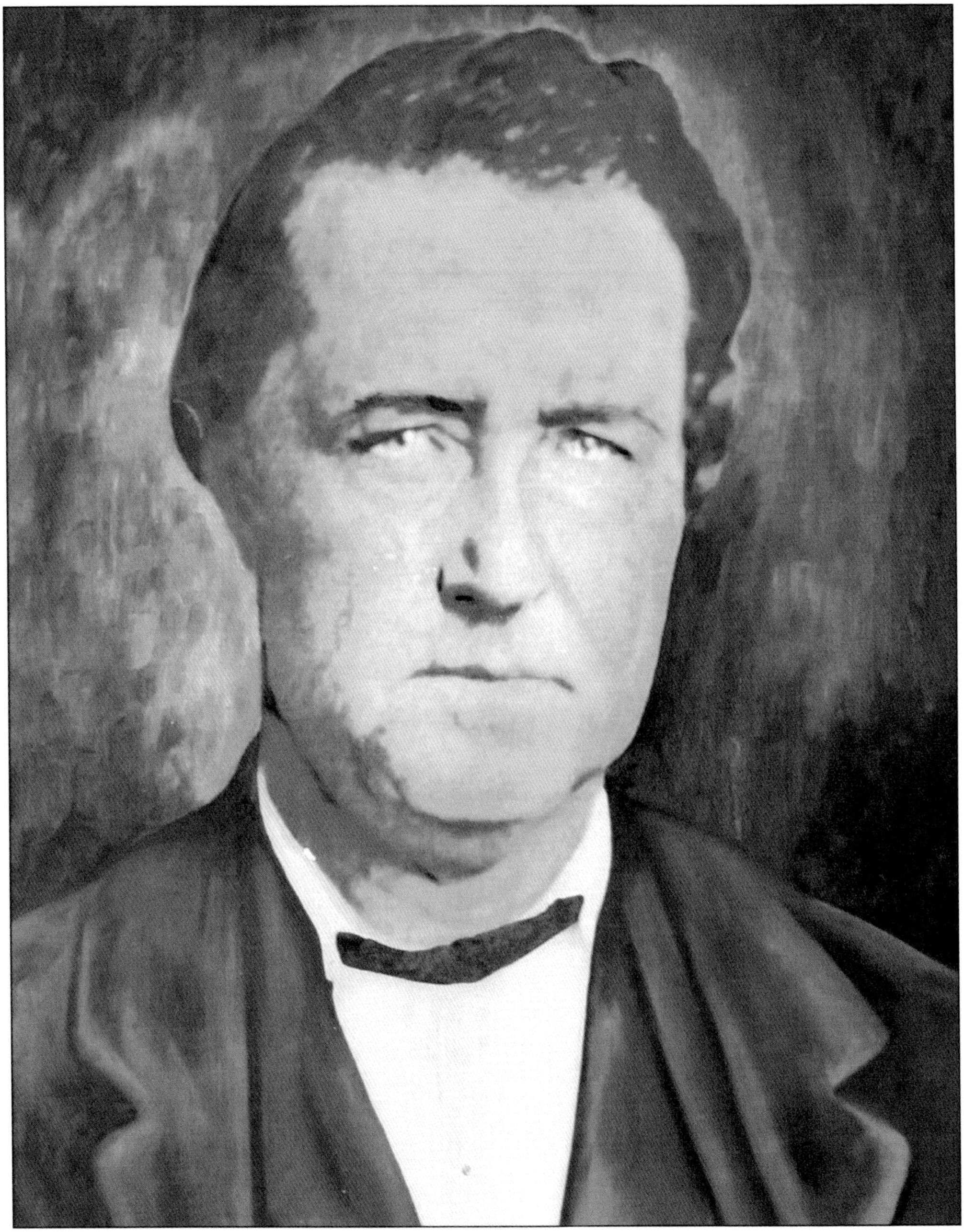

In 1869, Judge George Washington Logan purchased the Harris Inn and renamed it the Logan House. At an early age, Judge Logan became active in the study of law and county politics. He served as clerk of county court (1841–1849), county solicitor (1855–1856), member of the Confederate Congress (1863–1865), delegate from Rutherford County to the state convention (1865), and brigadier general of the division of North Carolina troops. He was also a member of the House of Representatives of North Carolina (1866–1874) and superior court judge (1868–1874). A Whig in politics, Judge Logan was a staunch Unionist during the secession crisis. He is perhaps best known as an uncompromising foe of the Ku Klux Klan and, as such, narrowly escaped impeachment by the North Carolina General Assembly. (Author's collection.)

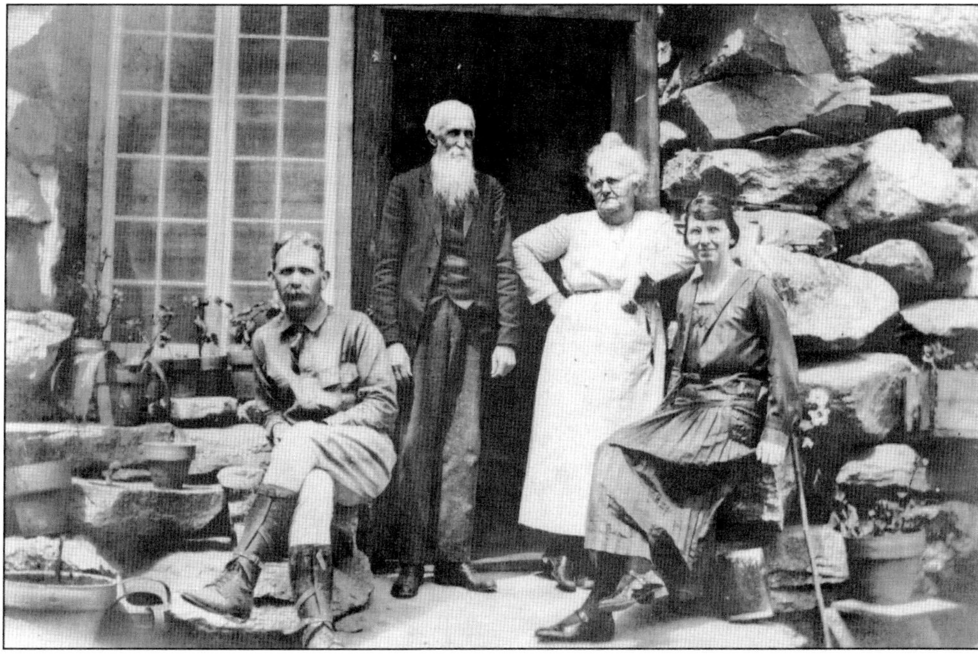

Mr. and Mrs. James Mills Flack, shown here in the middle of this photograph, ran the Logan House for several years in the late 1870s. In 1898, James bought the Mountain View Hotel in Chimney Rock. Their hospitality was famous throughout the region. (Courtesy of the Morse family.)

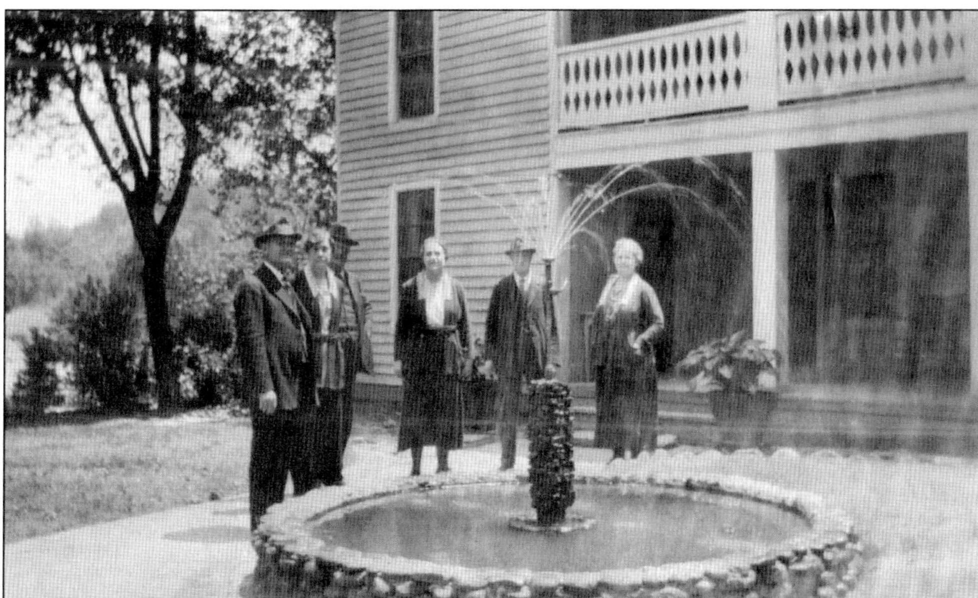

Guests at the Logan House are seen here enjoying a new water fountain. Noted travel author Edwin A. Gatchell toured the area in 1886. About his trip from Asheville to Rutherfordton, he wrote, "Continue your trip to Judge G.W. Logan's Hotel, where you will find a hearty welcome, comfortable quarters, and good fare." (Author's collection.)

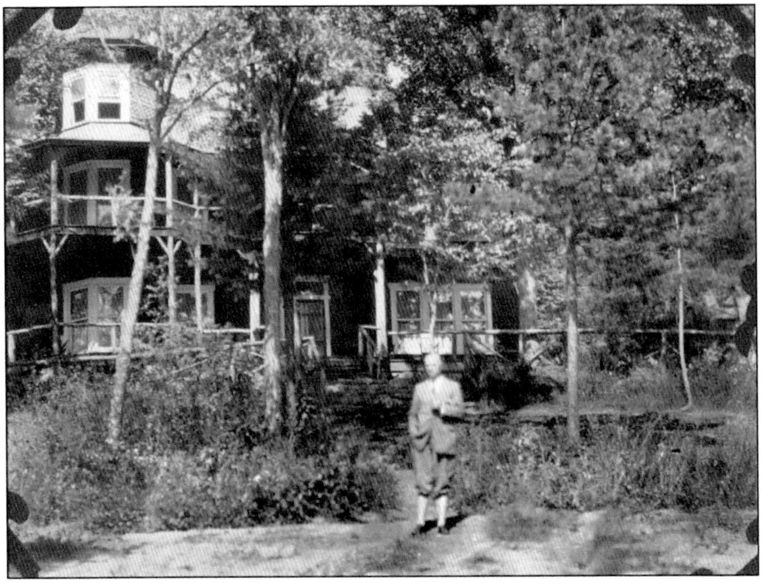

Dr. Lucius B. Morse came to visit the Hickory Nut Gorge in the early 1900s. He moved to Western North Carolina in hopes of curing his tuberculosis. He is shown here in front of his sanatorium near Chimney Rock. He and his brothers bought the Chimney Rock Park in 1902. (Courtesy of the Morse family.)

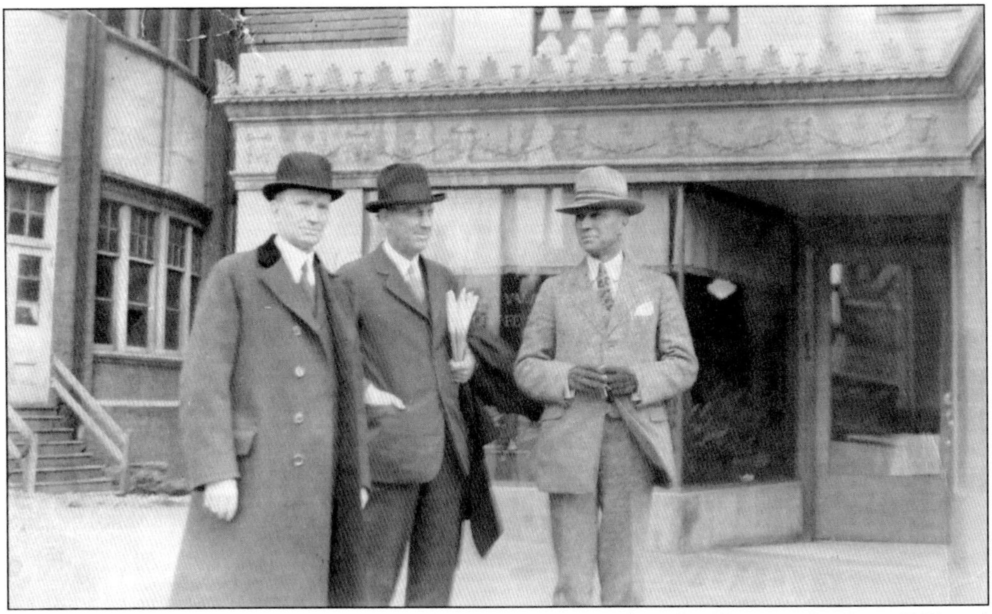

Brothers Hiram Morse, Asahel Morse, and Dr. Lucius Morse bought Chimney Rock in 1902 and soon had plans for a much larger venture. After making many improvements to the park, they set their sights on the creation of a mountain lake resort. (Courtesy of the Morse family.)

Dr. Morse made many improvements to this tourist attraction. This very early photograph of Chimney Rock was taken before a fence was built around the top of the rock monolith. (Courtesy of the Morse family.)

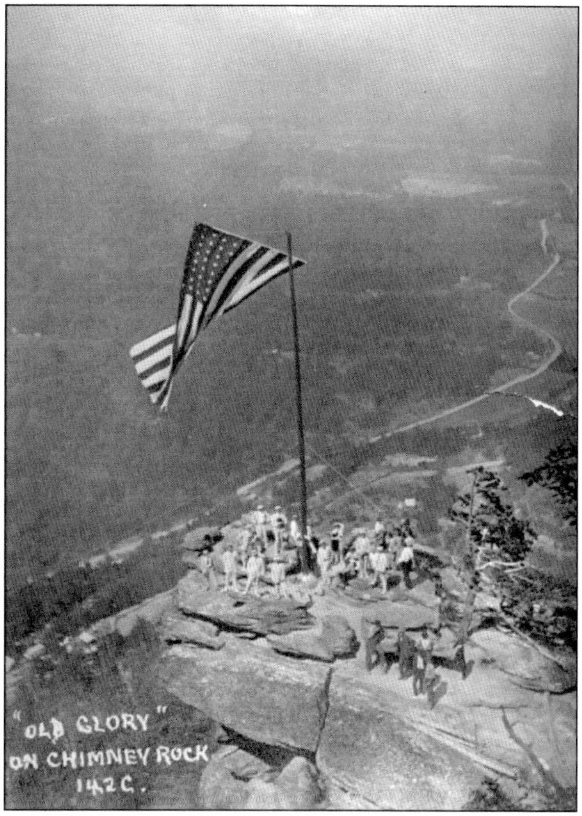

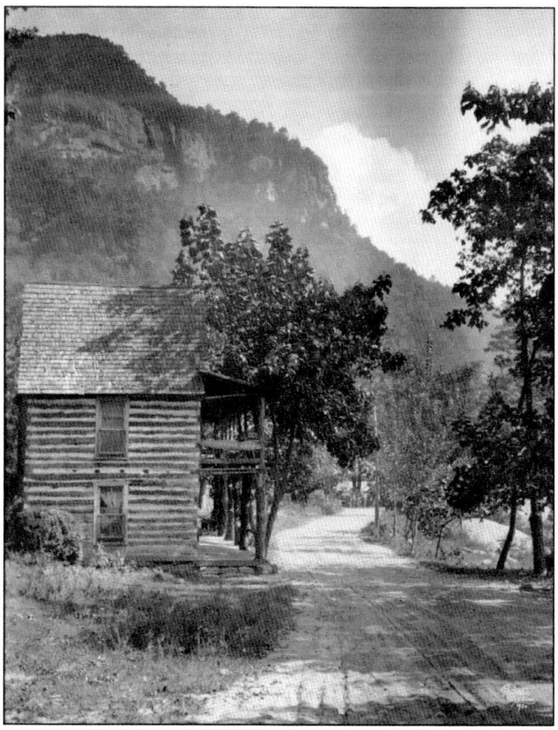

Jerome B. Freeman bought the property that included Chimney Rock in 1880. After he sold the Chimney Rock property to the Morse brothers, he built Freeman Camp, a rustic hotel that accommodated up to 40 guests. At that time, the road was still narrow and hard to negotiate when it rained. (Courtesy of the Morse family.)

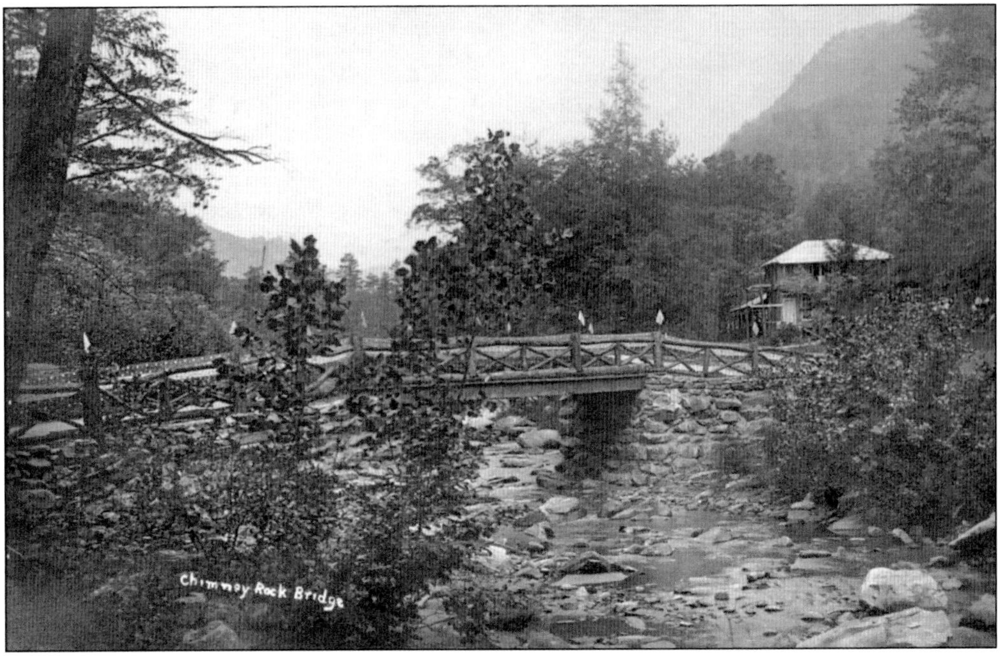

The first bridge built over the Rocky Broad River for a road to Chimney Rock Park was completed in 1916; unfortunately, it washed away during the 1916 flood less than a month after it was constructed. Undeterred by the loss, the Morse family rebuilt the structure with a bridge that would last many decades. (Courtesy of the Morse family.)

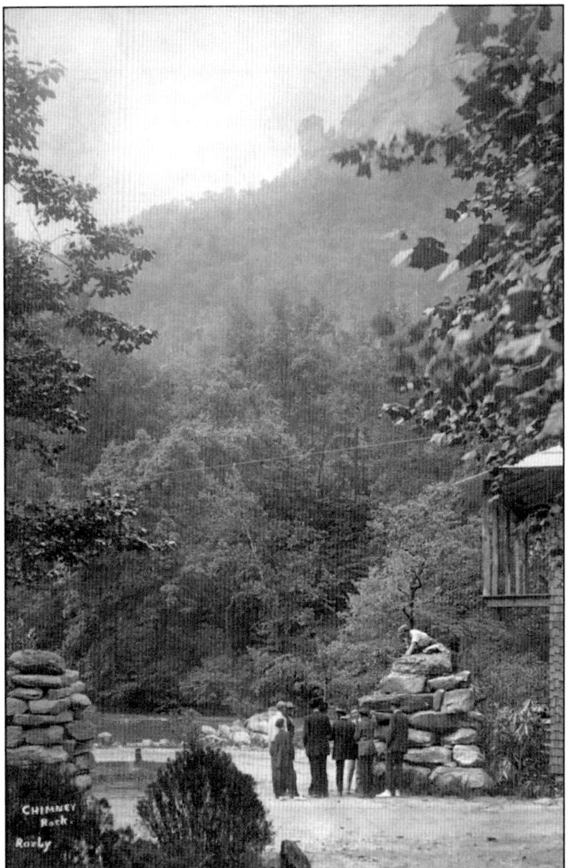

This photograph shows the old entrance to the Chimney Rock Park with Chimney Rock in the background. The rocks and road were mostly washed away during the 1916 flood. (Courtesy of the Morse family.)

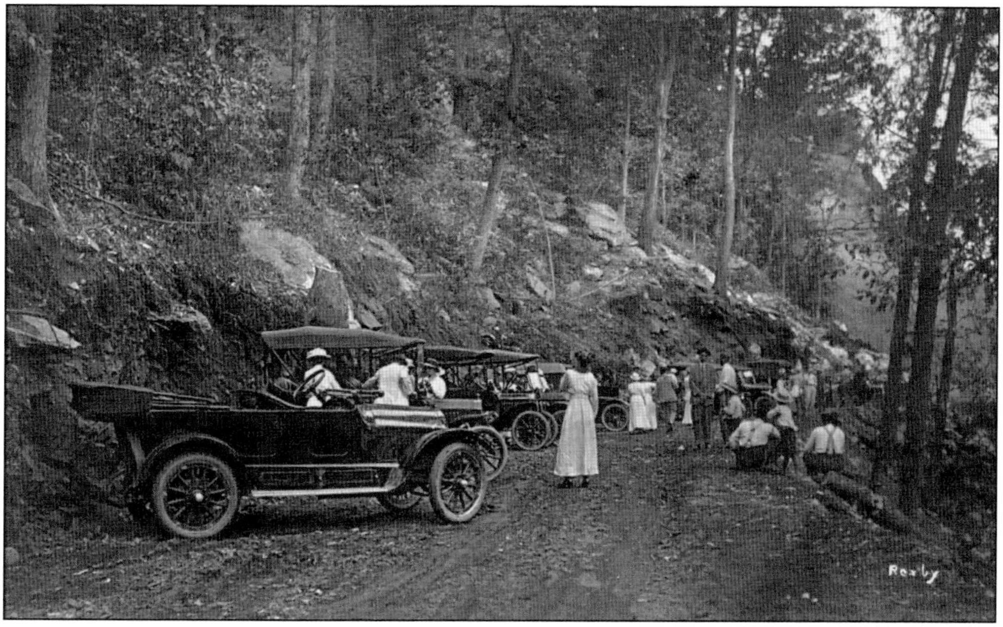

The Morse family knew that the only way for Chimney Rock Park to survive was to build a road up to the rock that was suitable for motorcars. Plans were drawn, and in 1916, the new road to Chimney Rock Park was completed. Horses and foot traffic were still allowed but from then on, most of the visitors came by automobile. (Courtesy of the Morse family.)

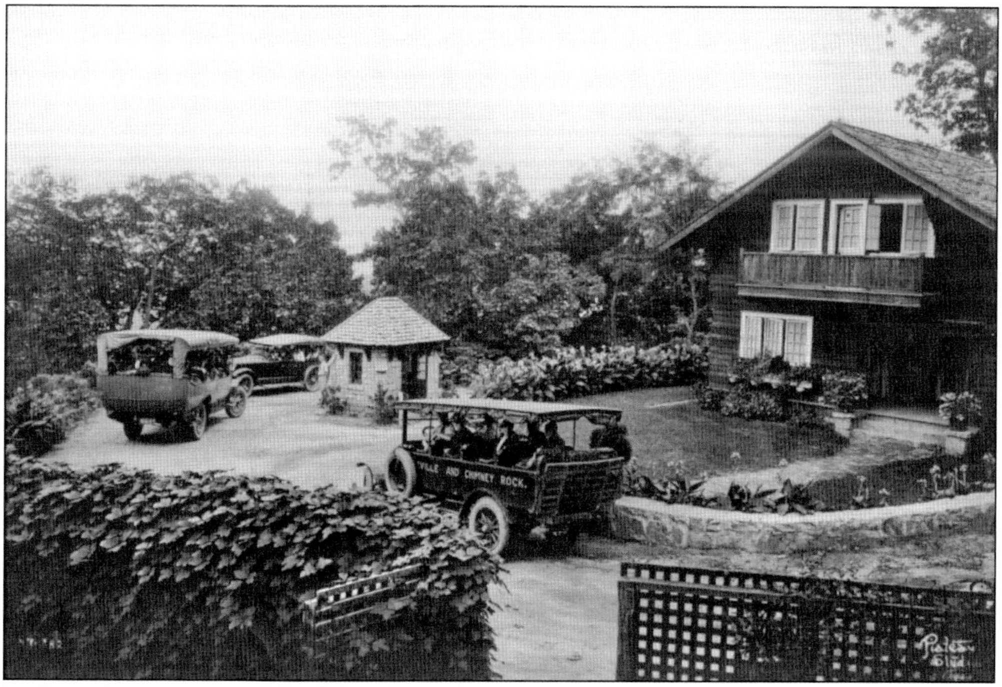

In the early 1900s, most folks did not have their own automobile, and tour buses were often used to carry tourists to Chimney Rock. The gatehouse, built in 1919, was later used as a residence for the owner. The house is now used by the Chimney Rock State Park staff. The entrance road is three miles long and rises 880 feet in elevation. (Courtesy of the Morse family.)

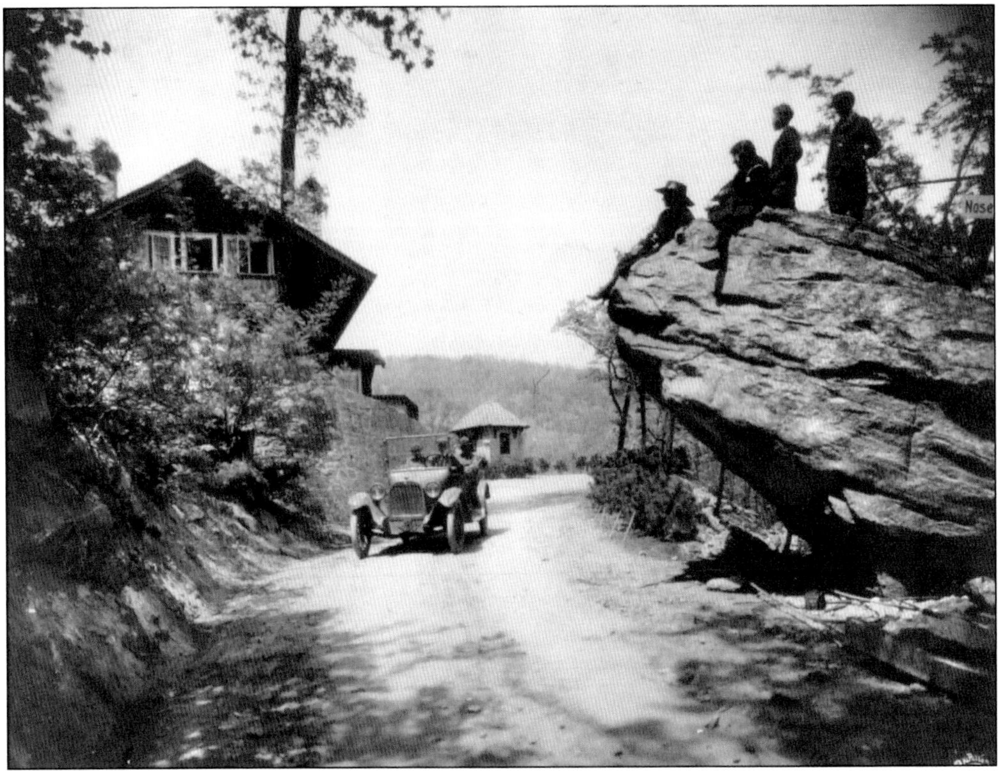

The Morse family knew it was crucial to have a "modern" road to the base of Chimney Rock. The above photograph shows the gatehouse at center and guest cabins to the left. For the construction of the last mile of road, pictured below, a steam drill was used to prepare for dynamite blasts. (Both, courtesy of the Morse family.)

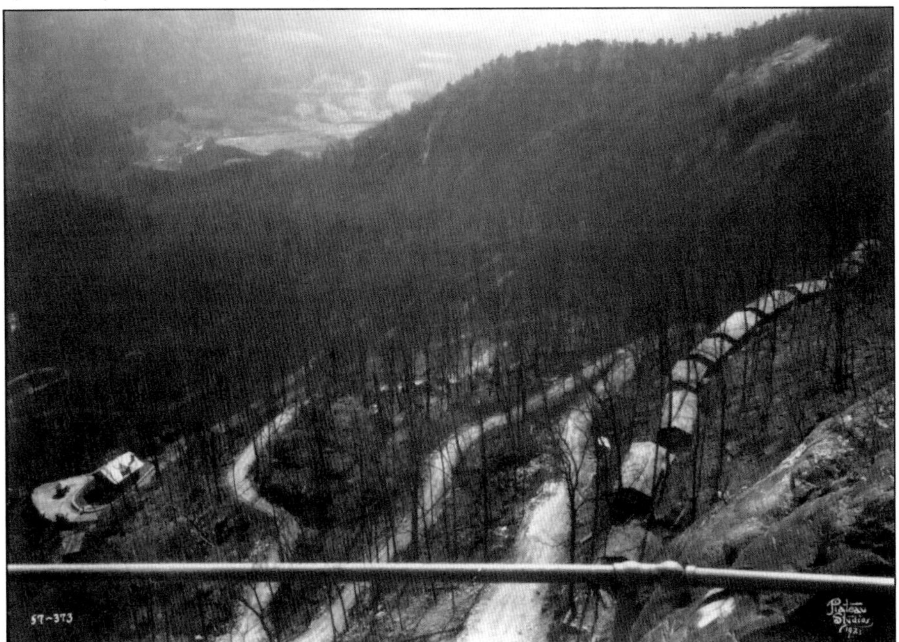

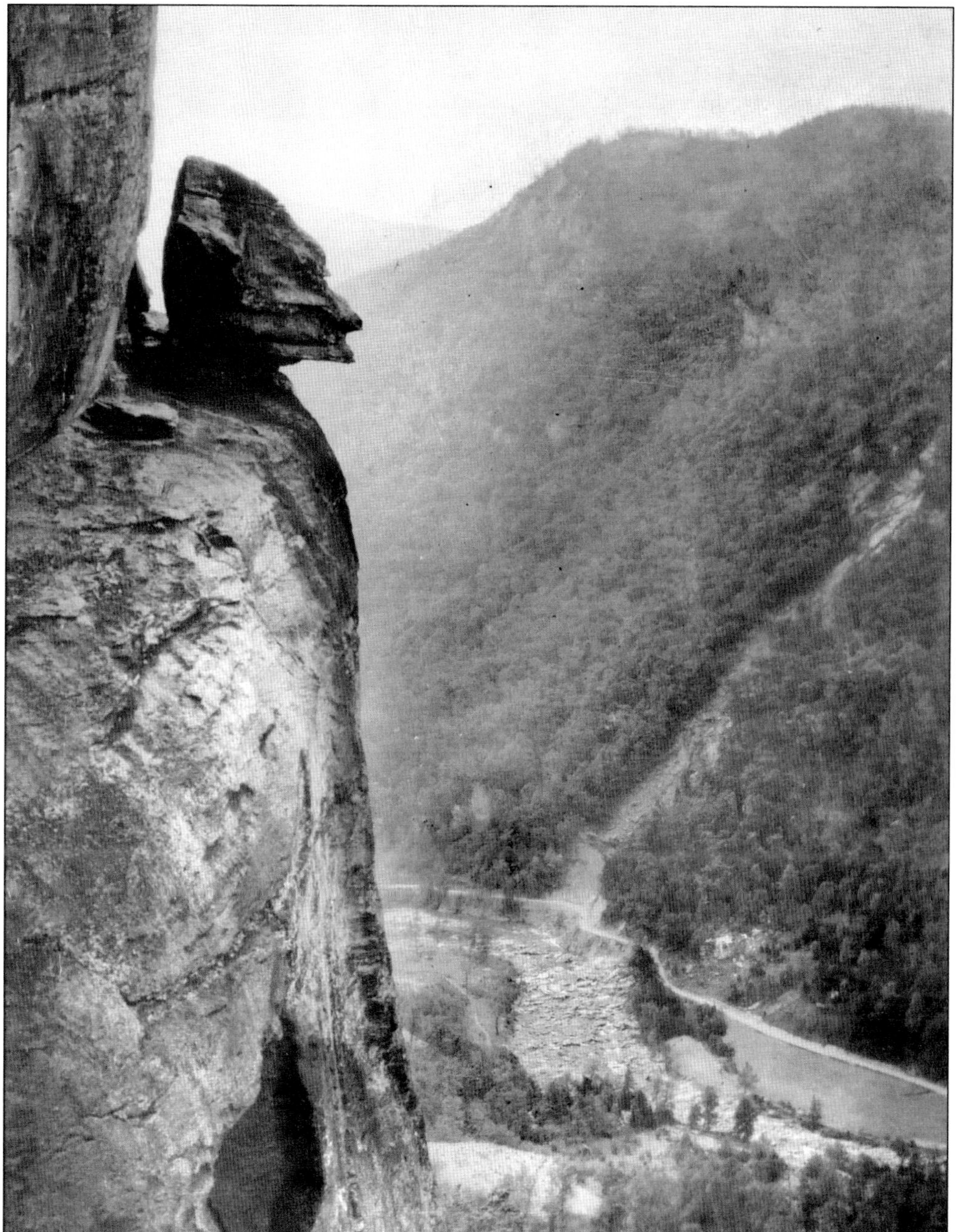

This photograph of Devil's Head at Chimney Rock shows the extensive landslides that occurred as a result of the horrific flood of 1916. (Courtesy of the Morse family.)

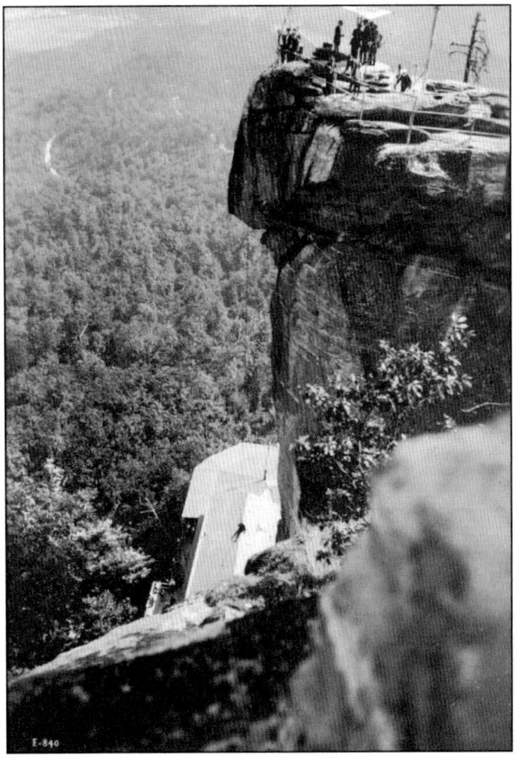

A worker rappels off Chimney Rock. Below the mountaineer is the Chimney Rock Pavilion. The pavilion opened on May 15, 1919. It had a large three-story restaurant that could seat 200 patrons and a large dancing pavilion. The pavilion was soon famous for fried chicken prepared by Mrs. A.M. Grover. (Photograph by Norman Greig; courtesy of the Greig family.)

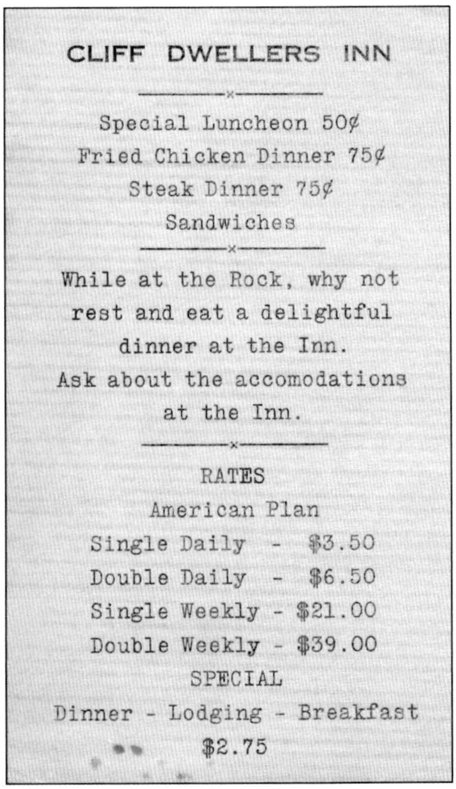

CLIFF DWELLERS INN

Special Luncheon 50¢
Fried Chicken Dinner 75¢
Steak Dinner 75¢
Sandwiches

While at the Rock, why not rest and eat a delightful dinner at the Inn.
Ask about the accomodations at the Inn.

RATES
American Plan
Single Daily - $3.50
Double Daily - $6.50
Single Weekly - $21.00
Double Weekly - $39.00
SPECIAL
Dinner - Lodging - Breakfast
$2.75

In 1920, the Morse family built the Cliff Dwellers Inn. The inn was a series of two- and three-bedroom cabins and a common area called the Club Room. The back wall of the Club Room was part of the granite cliff below Chimney Rock. Here is a menu from the Cliff Dwellers Inn. (Courtesy of the Greig family.)

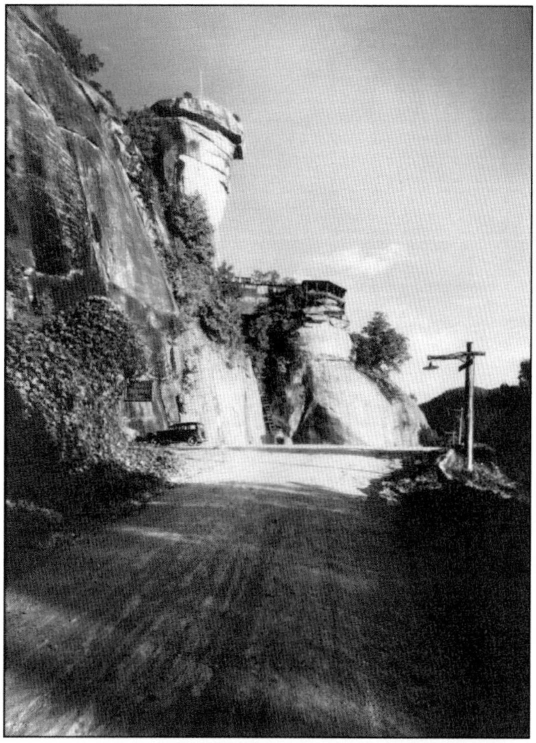

With the pavilion and the Cliff Dwellers Inn, Chimney Rock Park was a destination in itself. Famous for great food and rooms with hot- and cold-running water, the park offered state-of-the-art accommodations. (Courtesy of the Morse family.)

Guilford Nanney rebuilt the trails started by Watt Foster and Jerome Freeman. He then created new trails, including this one located just above the Hickory Nut Falls. Rocks and lumber were hauled by hand and with the help of mules. (Photograph by Norman Greig; courtesy of the Greig family.)

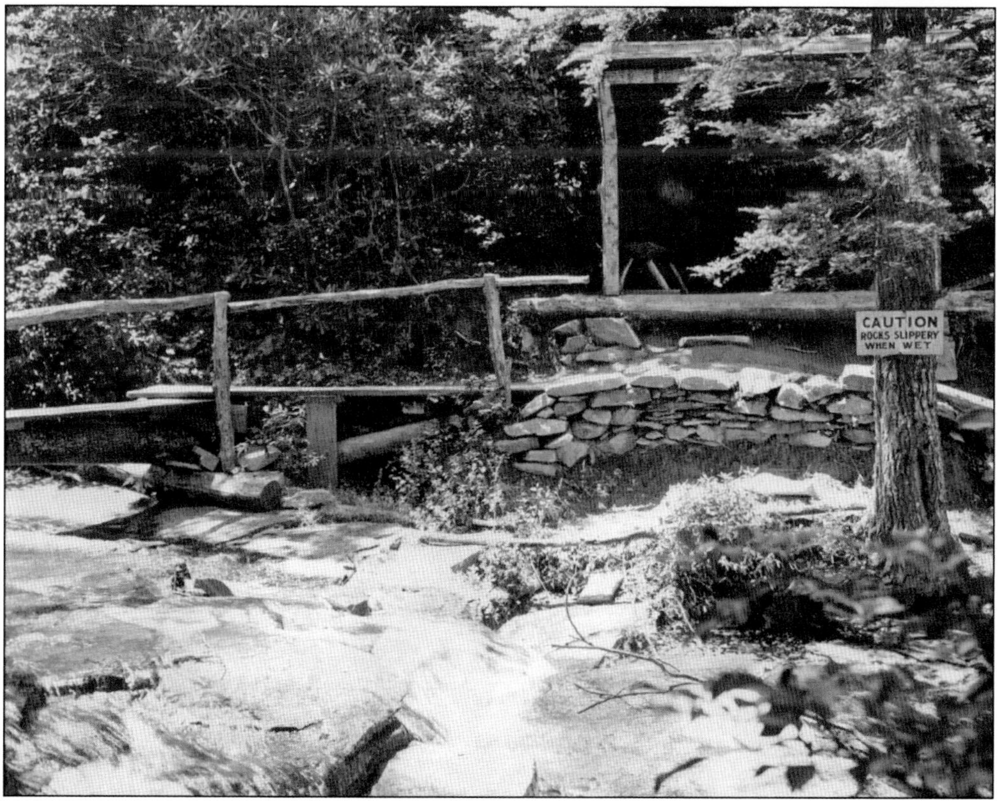

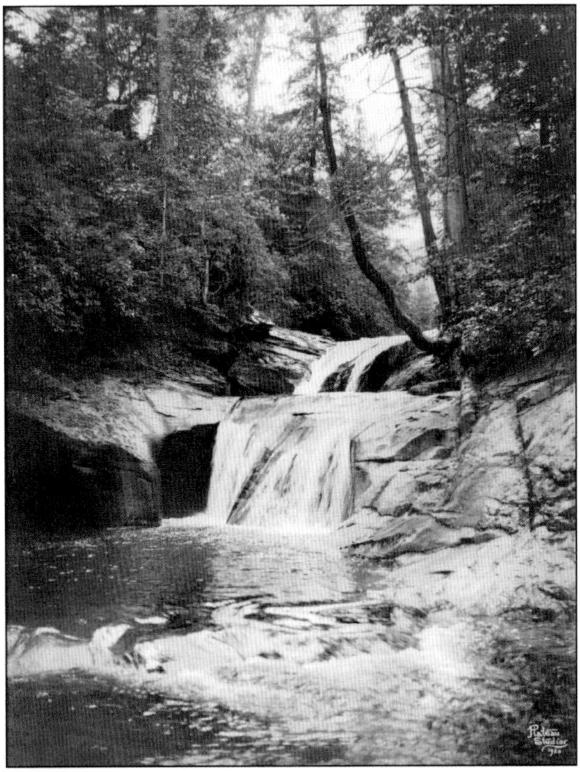

This 1920 photograph shows the Bottomless Pools. There are three pools in solid granite that were originally thought to be bottomless. During the Great Depression, Lee Powers acquired the pools and built walkways so tourists could better enjoy the park. (Courtesy of the Morse family.)

The series of waterfalls above the Hickory Nut Falls remains one of the prettiest places in the world. (Photograph by Norman Greig; courtesy of the Greig family.)

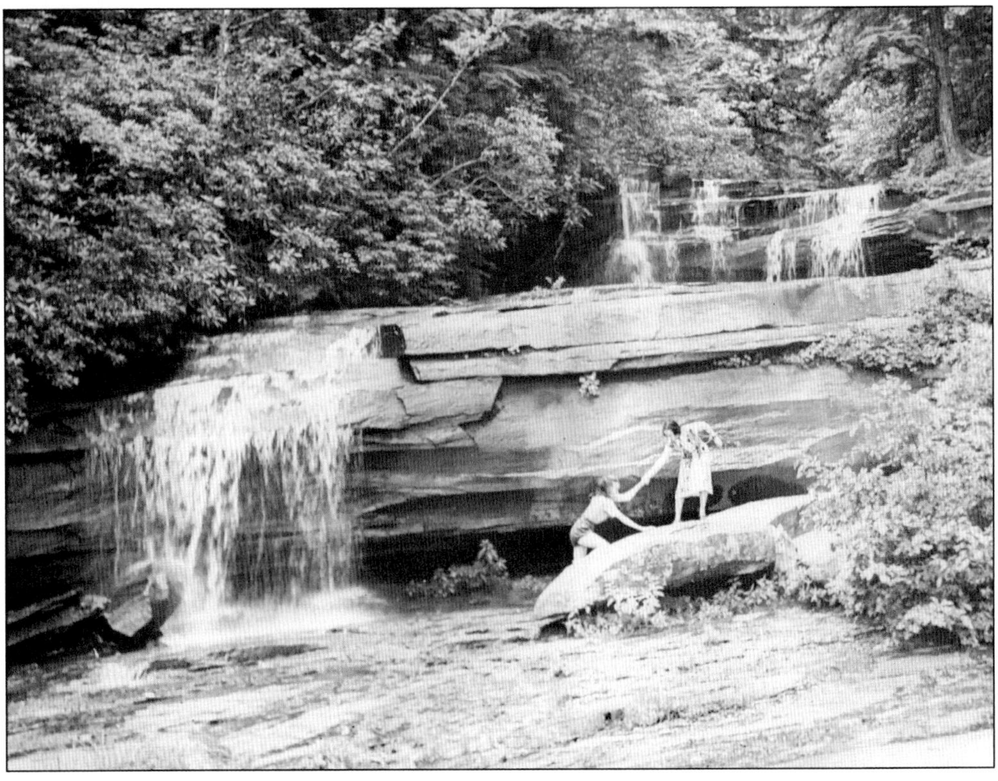

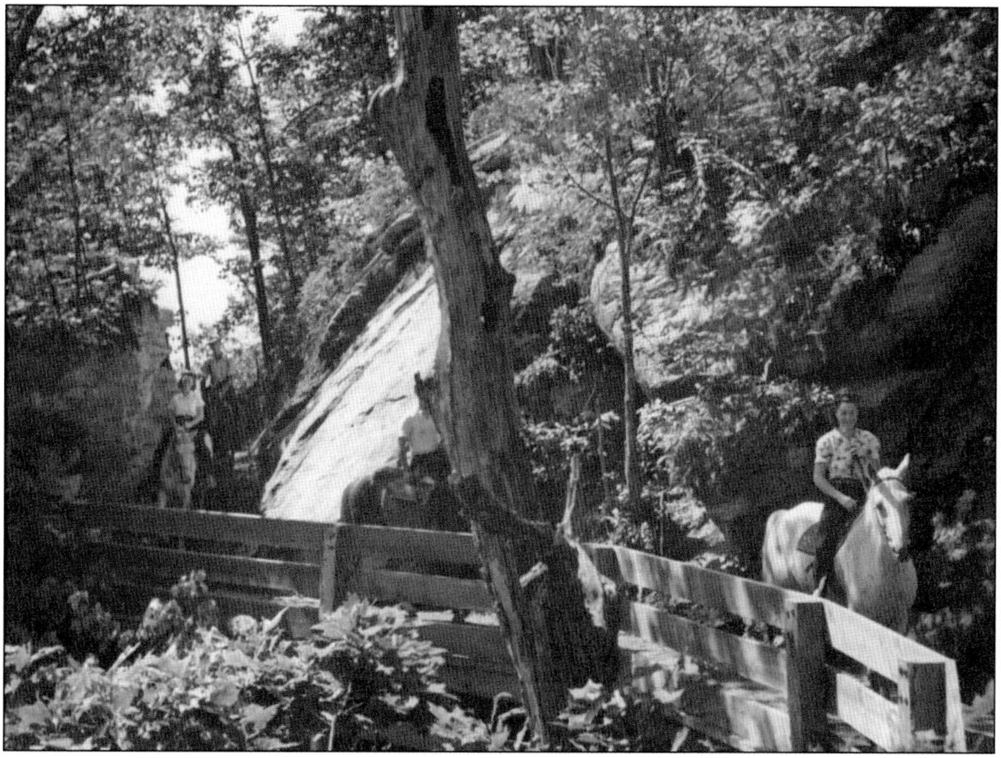

During the park's early years, tourists could travel the trails at Chimney Rock on horseback. The image below shows horses near the steps going to the top of Chimney Rock. (Both, photograph by Norman Greig; courtesy of the Greig family.)

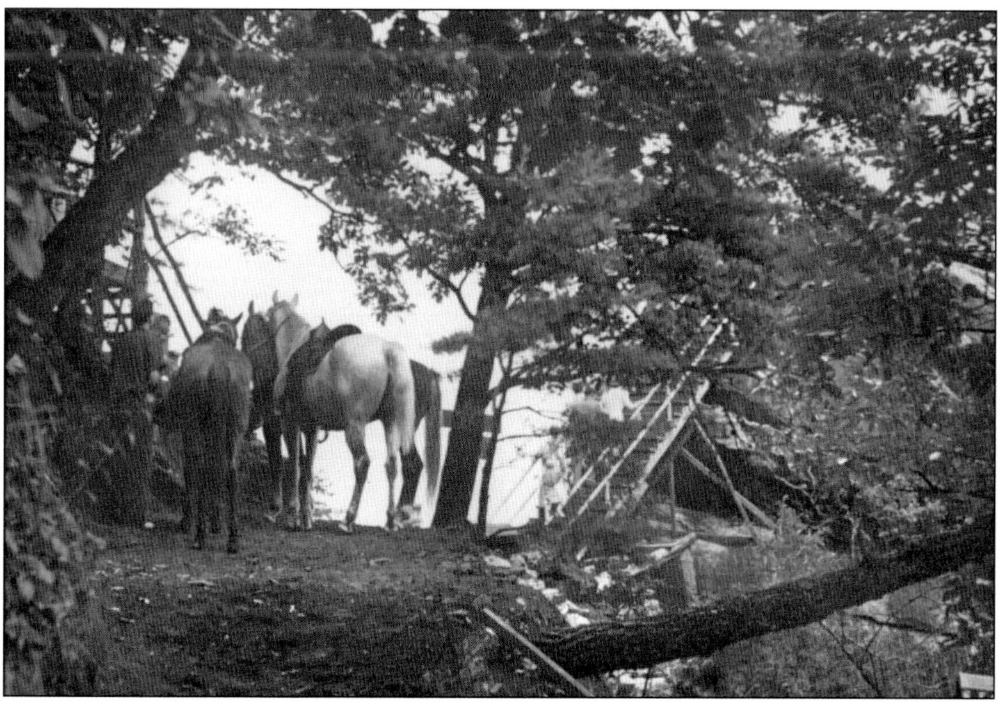

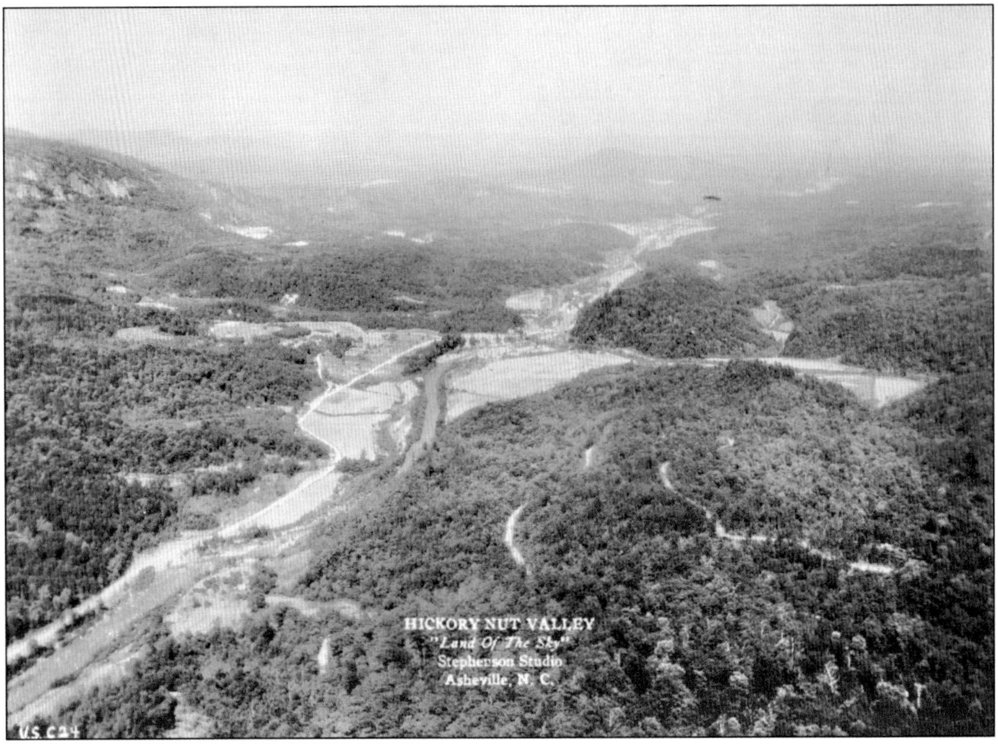

These two photographs show the Eastern Hickory Nut Gorge before Lake Lure was flooded. The Morse brothers were confident their dream could be expanded to encompass the rest of the gorge. In 1923, the brothers and a host of other investors created Chimney Rock Mountains, Inc. The corporation was capitalized at $400,000—the largest corporation granted a charter by the state at that time. (Above, courtesy of Morse family; below, courtesy of the Greig family.)

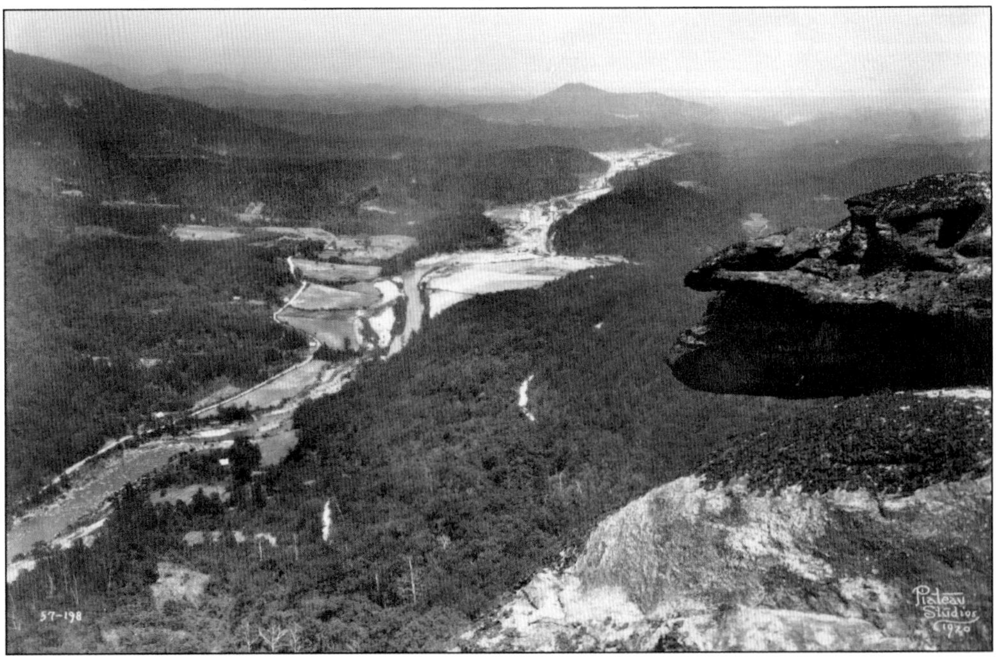

Two

Lake Lure Development to 1965

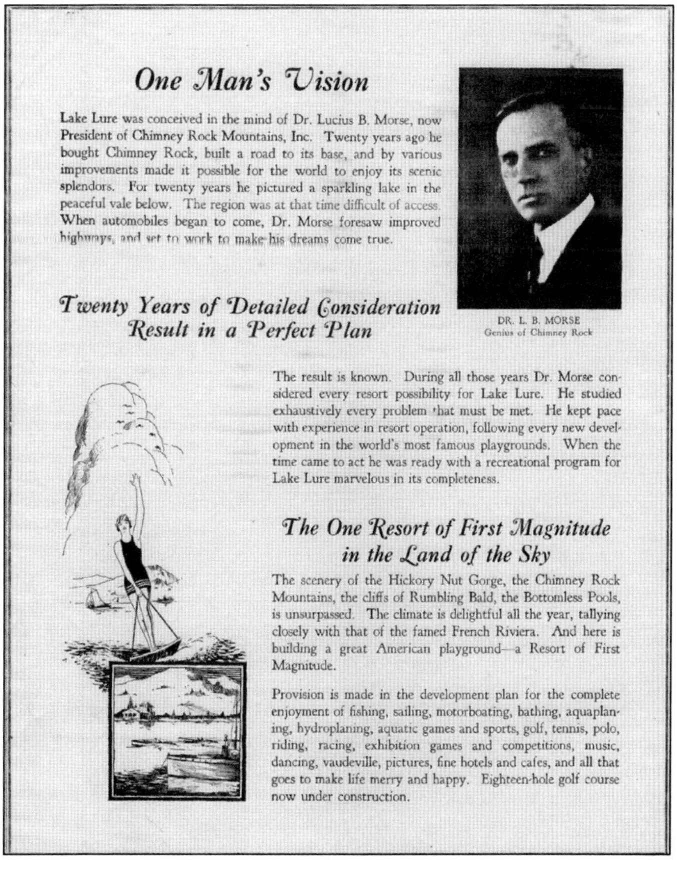

One Man's Vision

Lake Lure was conceived in the mind of Dr. Lucius B. Morse, now President of Chimney Rock Mountains, Inc. Twenty years ago he bought Chimney Rock, built a road to its base, and by various improvements made it possible for the world to enjoy its scenic splendors. For twenty years he pictured a sparkling lake in the peaceful vale below. The region was at that time difficult of access. When automobiles began to come, Dr. Morse foresaw improved highways, and set to work to make his dreams come true.

DR. L. B. MORSE
Genius of Chimney Rock

Twenty Years of Detailed Consideration Result in a Perfect Plan

The result is known. During all those years Dr. Morse considered every resort possibility for Lake Lure. He studied exhaustively every problem that must be met. He kept pace with experience in resort operation, following every new development in the world's most famous playgrounds. When the time came to act he was ready with a recreational program for Lake Lure marvelous in its completeness.

The One Resort of First Magnitude in the Land of the Sky

The scenery of the Hickory Nut Gorge, the Chimney Rock Mountains, the cliffs of Rumbling Bald, the Bottomless Pools, is unsurpassed. The climate is delightful all the year, tallying closely with that of the famed French Riviera. And here is building a great American playground—a Resort of First Magnitude.

Provision is made in the development plan for the complete enjoyment of fishing, sailing, motorboating, bathing, aquaplaning, hydroplaning, aquatic games and sports, golf, tennis, polo, riding, racing, exhibition games and competitions, music, dancing, vaudeville, pictures, fine hotels and cafes, and all that goes to make life merry and happy. Eighteen-hole golf course now under construction.

This is from an early sales flyer promoting the Lake Lure development. (Author's collection.)

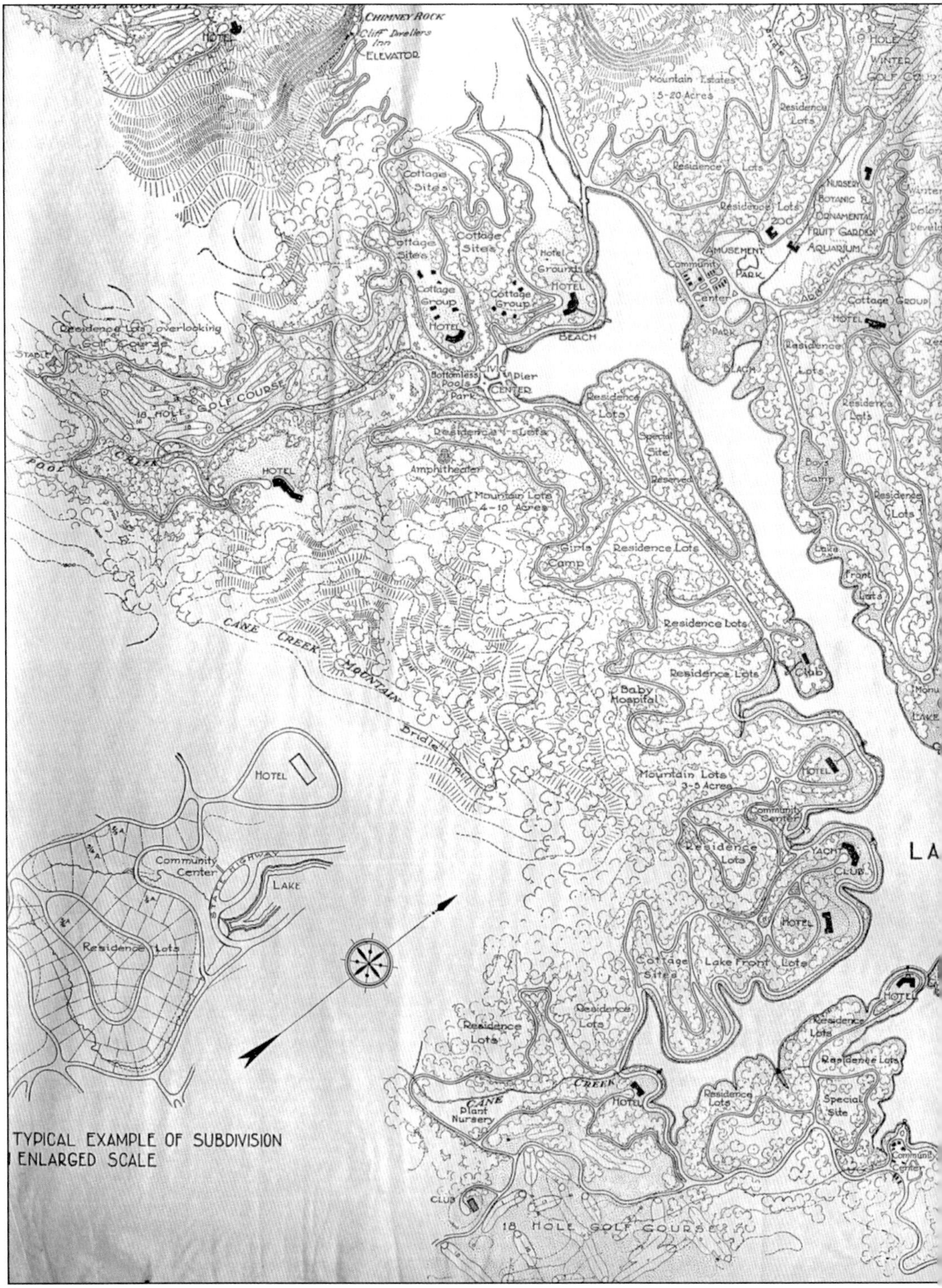

In 1923, the Morse bothers had found enough investors to create Chimney Rock Mountains, Inc. The corporation purchased over 8,000 acres, and plans were developed for a world-class resort. This map shows the grand plans for "A National—All Year—Mountain Lake Resort in the Chimney

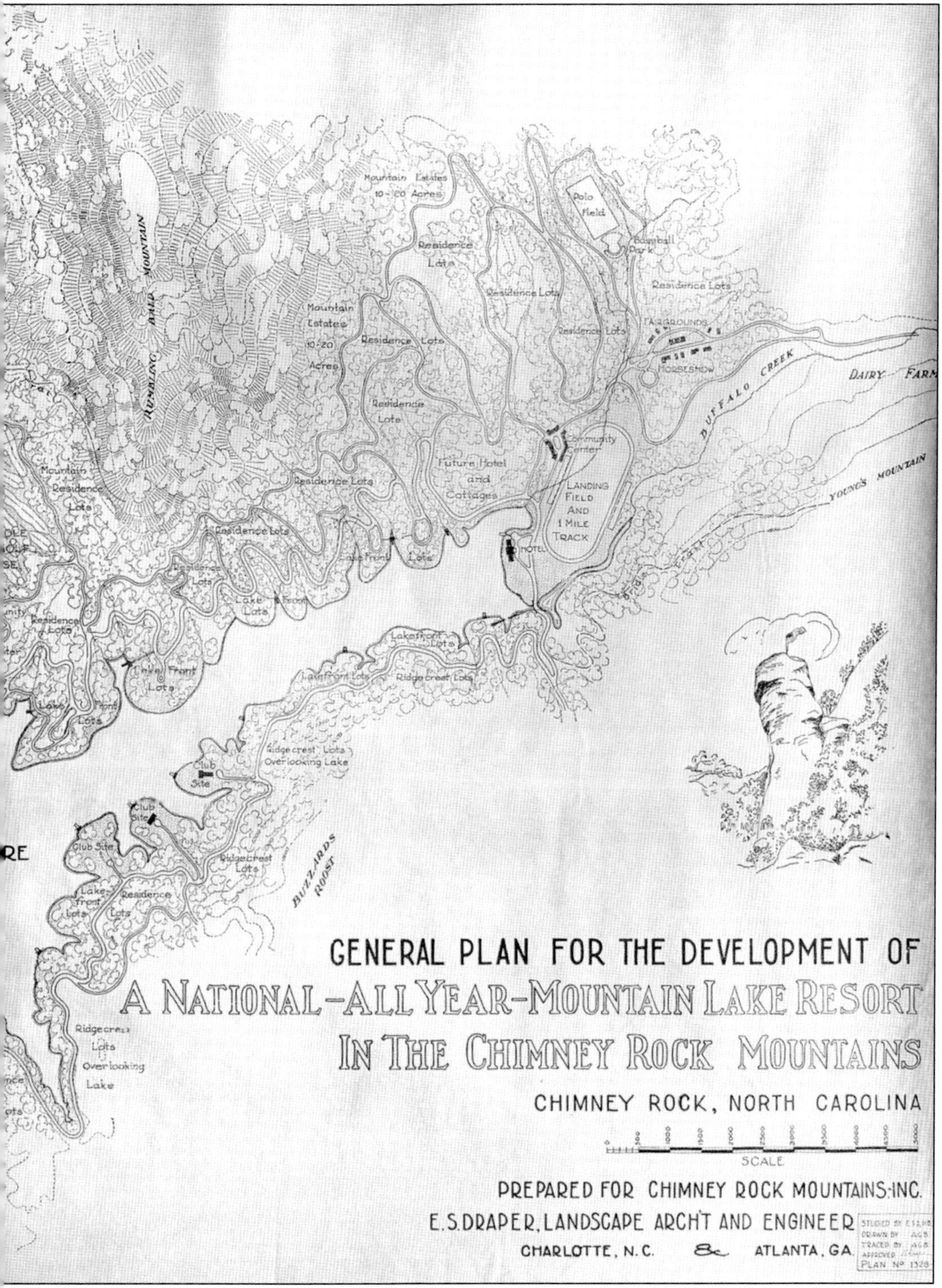

Rock Mountains." These plans included five golf courses, eight hotels, a casino, clubhouses, an amusement park, polo field, landing field, and, of course, Lake Lure. (Author's collection.)

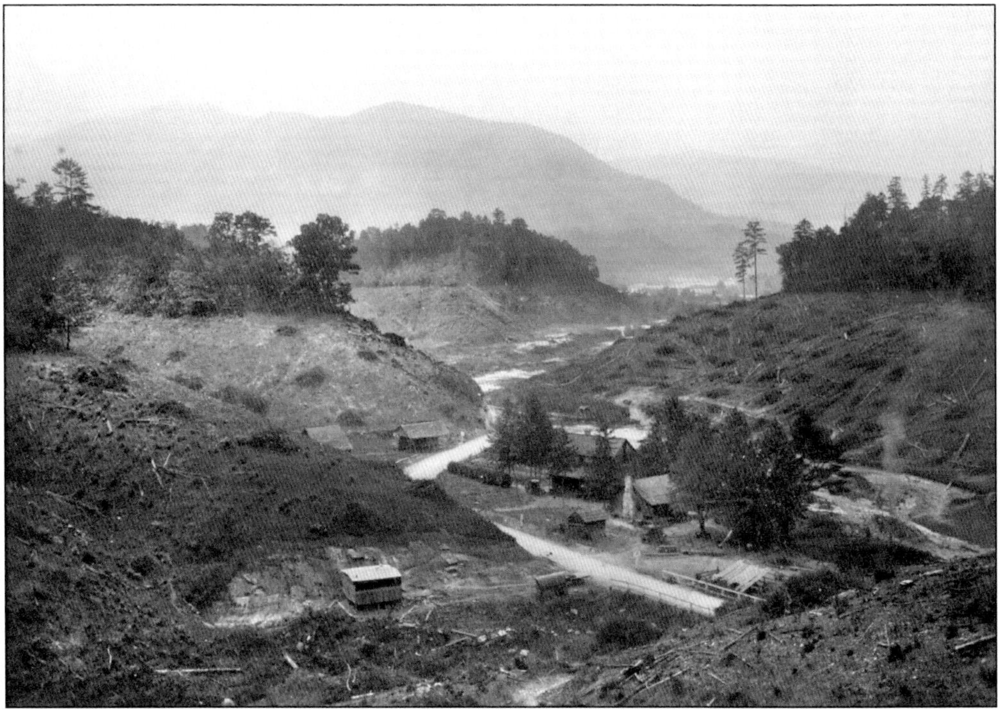

The building of Lake Lure displaced several farms, a store, and a church. Please note, however, there was never a town called Buffalo, as one rumor states. NC Highway 20 was completed only a decade before construction of the lake started. Several miles of the highway would soon be under water, and a new road would be built around the lake. (Courtesy of the Morse family.)

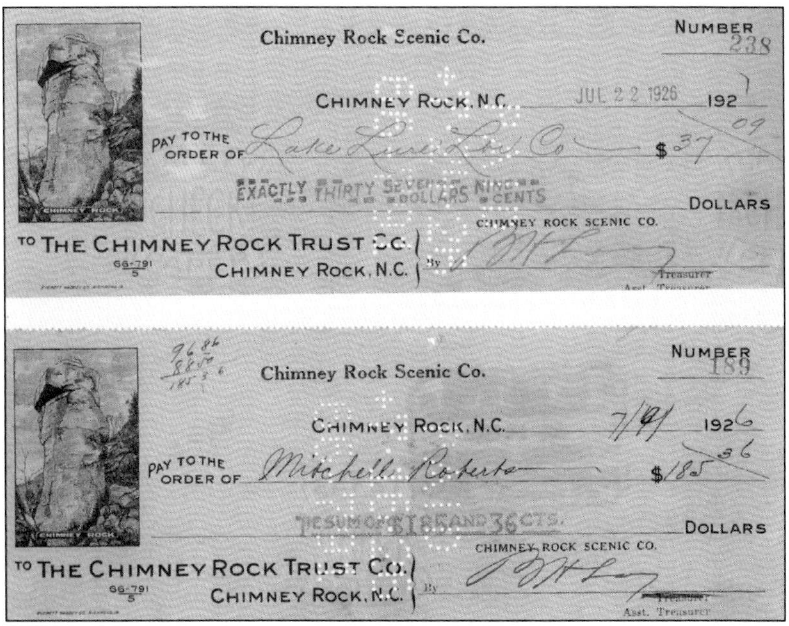

CHIMNEY ROCK
Chimney Rock Scenic Co.
NUMBER 238
CHIMNEY ROCK, N.C. JUL 22 1926 192
PAY TO THE ORDER OF Lake Lure Lot Co $37 09
EXACTLY THIRTY SEVEN DOLLARS NINE CENTS DOLLARS
TO THE CHIMNEY ROCK TRUST CO.
66-791
5
CHIMNEY ROCK, N.C.
CHIMNEY ROCK SCENIC CO.
By
Treasurer
Asst. Treasurer

CHIMNEY ROCK
96.86
88.50
185.36
Chimney Rock Scenic Co.
NUMBER 189
CHIMNEY ROCK, N.C. 7/21 1926
PAY TO THE ORDER OF Mitchell Roberts $185 36
THE SUM OF $185 AND 36 CTS. DOLLARS
TO THE CHIMNEY ROCK TRUST CO.
66-791
5
CHIMNEY ROCK, N.C.
CHIMNEY ROCK SCENIC CO.
By
Treasurer
Asst. Treasurer

The Chimney Rock Bank and Trust Company was created in 1924. J.H. Thomas was the president, J.M. Flack was the vice president, and Carrie Dalton Flynn was secretary. The bank prospered until the Great Depression but was forced to close on February 5, 1930.

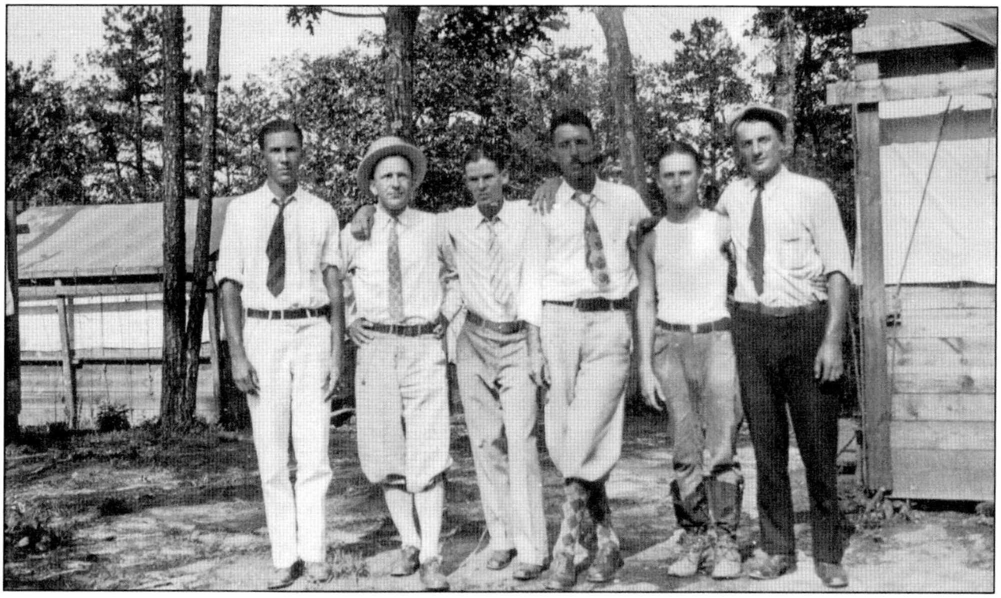

The engineers building the lake and dam lived on-site in a tent compound. The large force of engineers were under the direction of E.S. Draper, a well-known landscape architect with offices in Charlotte, New York, and Atlanta. (Courtesy of the Morse family.)

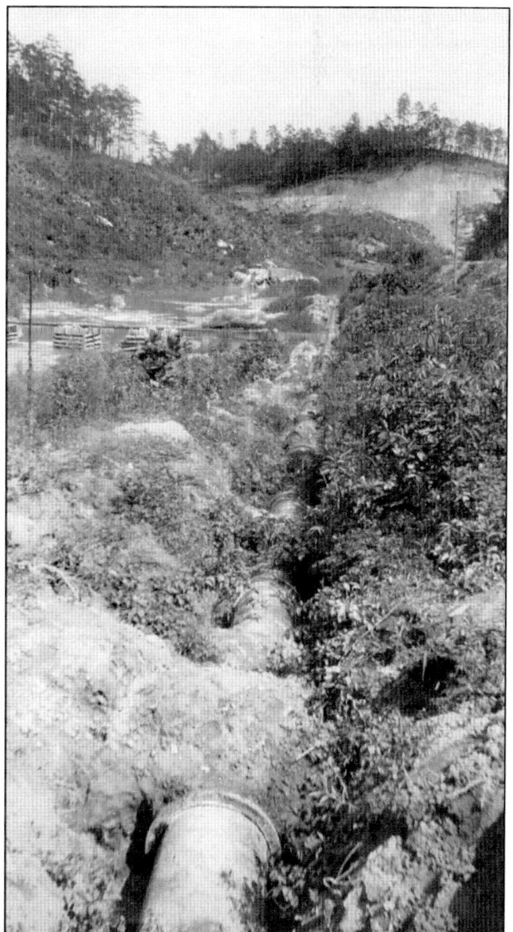

Before Lake Lure was filled, an extensive network of sewer pipes was laid on the ground, on pilings, and in ditches. Hundreds of workers used mules and a steam shovel to dig ditches and install these extremely heavy cast-iron pipes. These pipes have served their purpose for over 80 years. (Courtesy of the Greig family.)

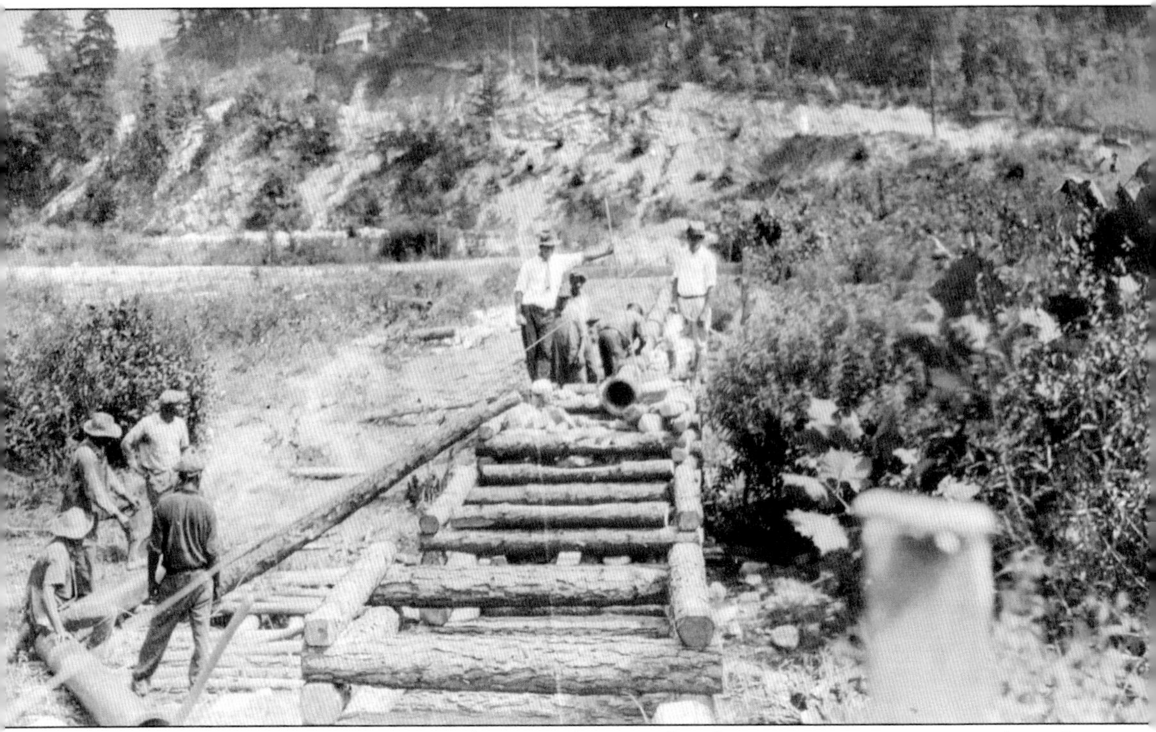

Log platforms were built to support the sewer lines, and rock supports were constructed inside the wood. The logs were easy to find, as the entire flood plain had to be timbered. (Courtesy of the Greig family.)

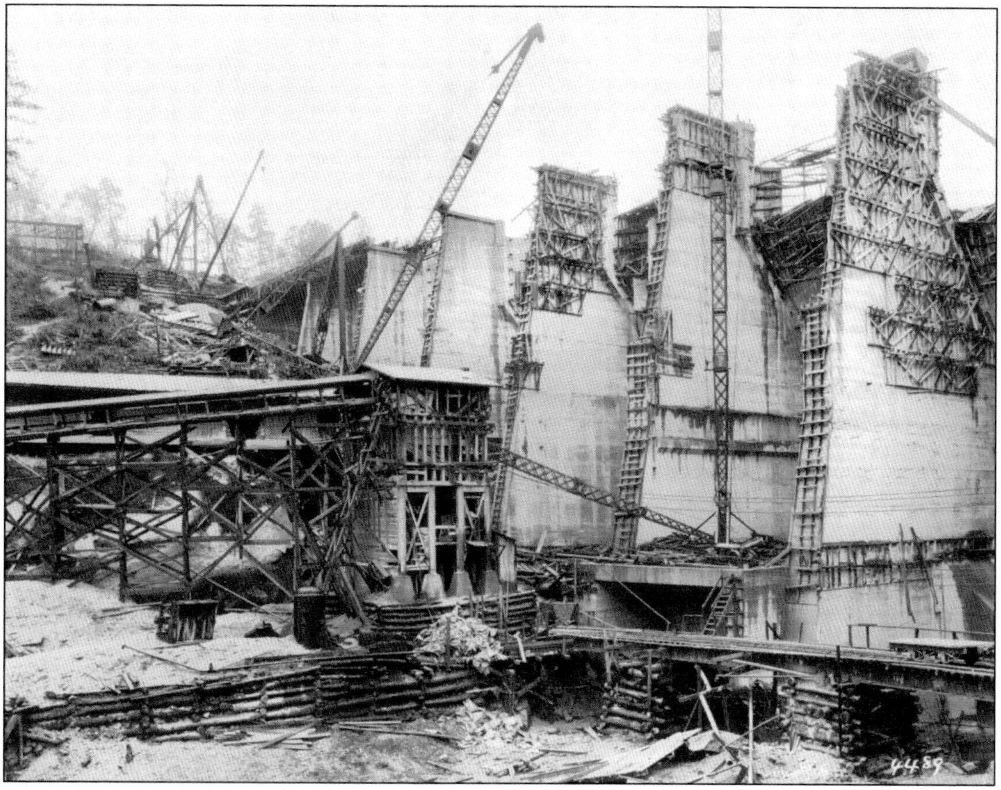

The construction of the Lake Lure Dam used the most advanced construction techniques for its time and was an extraordinary example of what man could do with several hundred cubic yards of concrete, cranes, and massive wooded forms. Note the train track and flatcar at the right of the photograph. The photograph below shows how concrete mixing was a huge operation. (Both, courtesy of the Town of Lake Lure.)

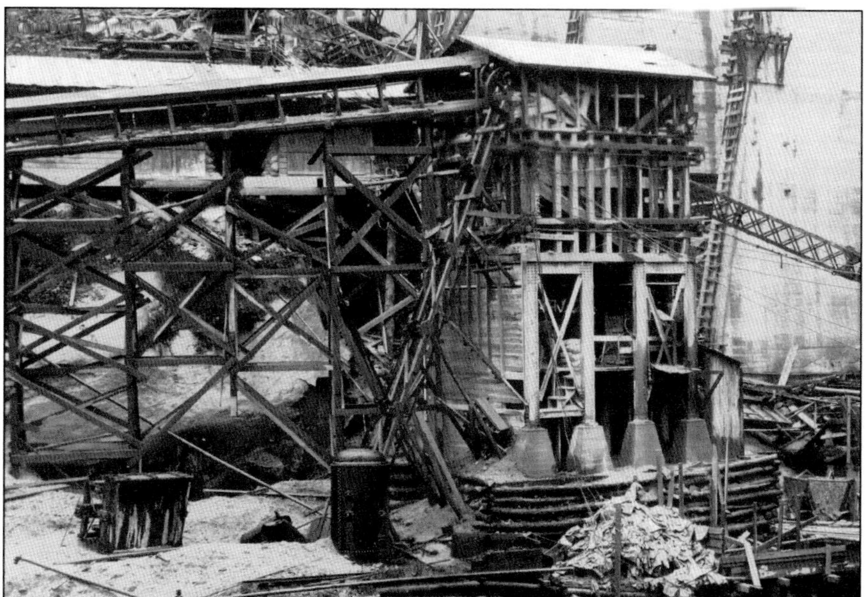

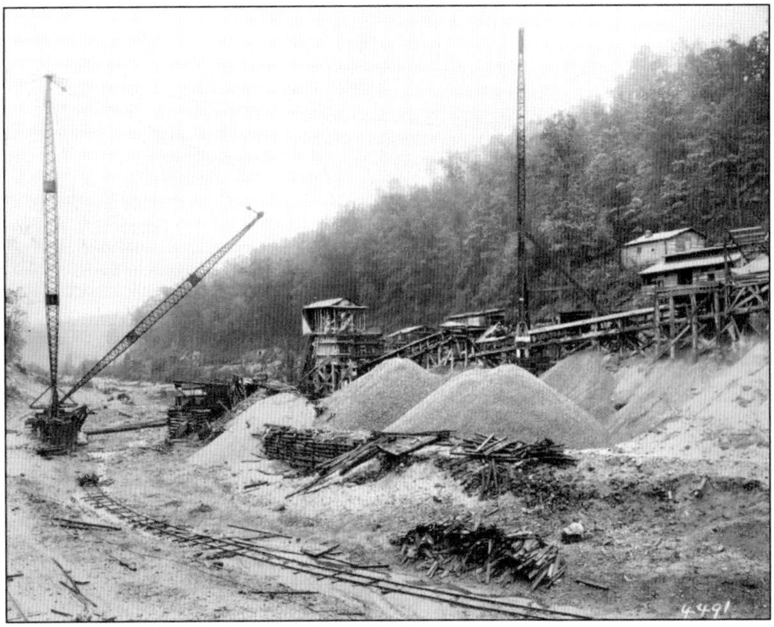

The trees in the entire lake bed were clear cut. There were several large sawmills with huge piles of sawdust in the area soon to be flooded. Temporary train tracks were installed to carry the lumber out to the road. All of these temporary structures were built and then removed before the lake was filled. (Courtesy of the Morse family.)

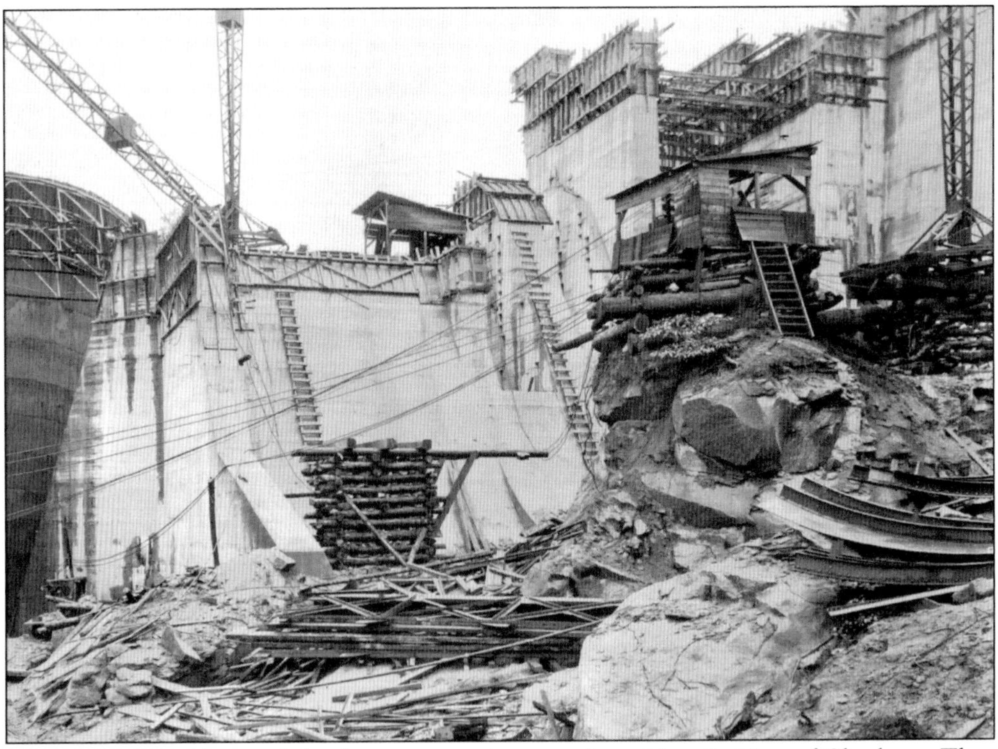

The engineers in charge of the dam construction were from Mees & Mees of Charlotte. They supervised the construction of the mulitple-arch concrete dam. The large cranes were mostly powered by humans, and the wood forms were all placed by hand. (Courtesy of the Town of Lake Lure.)

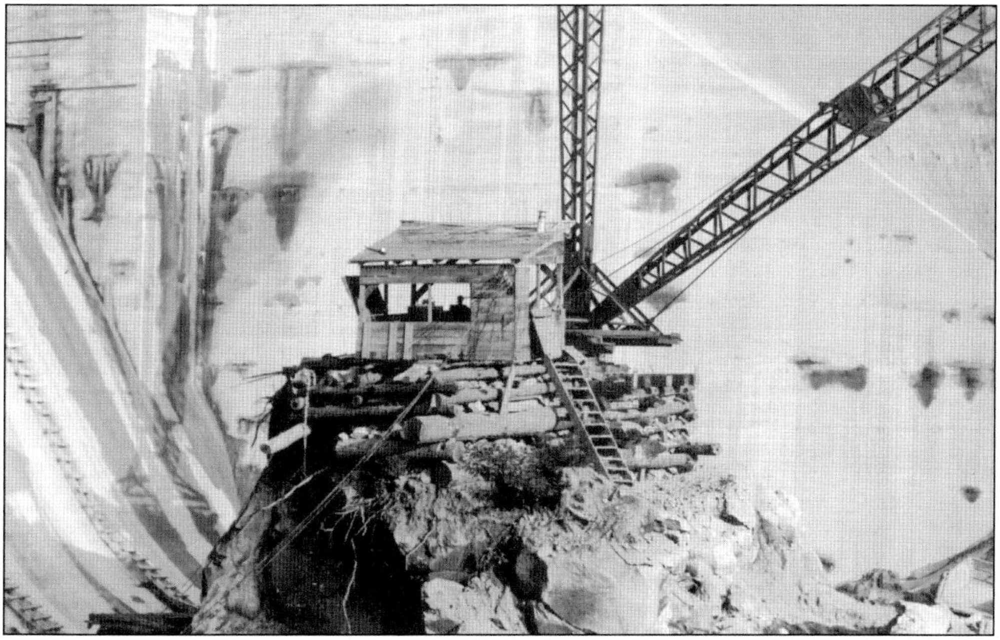

Temporary buildings and an assortment of pulleys were used to operate the cranes at the Lake Lure Dam. This photograph shows how small the crane operator looks in relation to the huge dam in the background. (Courtesy of the Town of Lake Lure.)

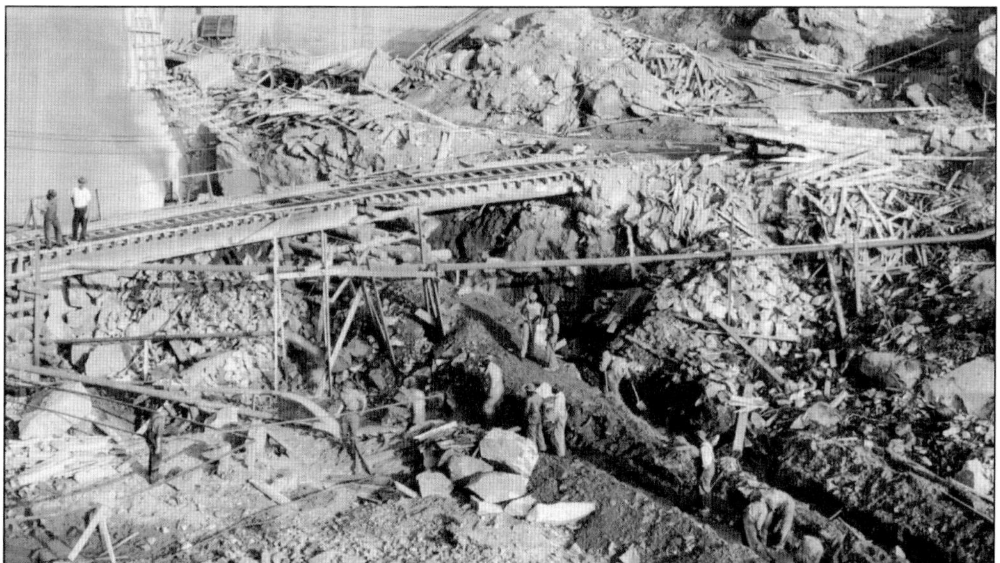

Even with the trains and steam shovels, most of the work was done by hand. This photograph shows several pipes used to remove water that was building up behind the dam as it was being constructed. (Courtesy of the Morse family.)

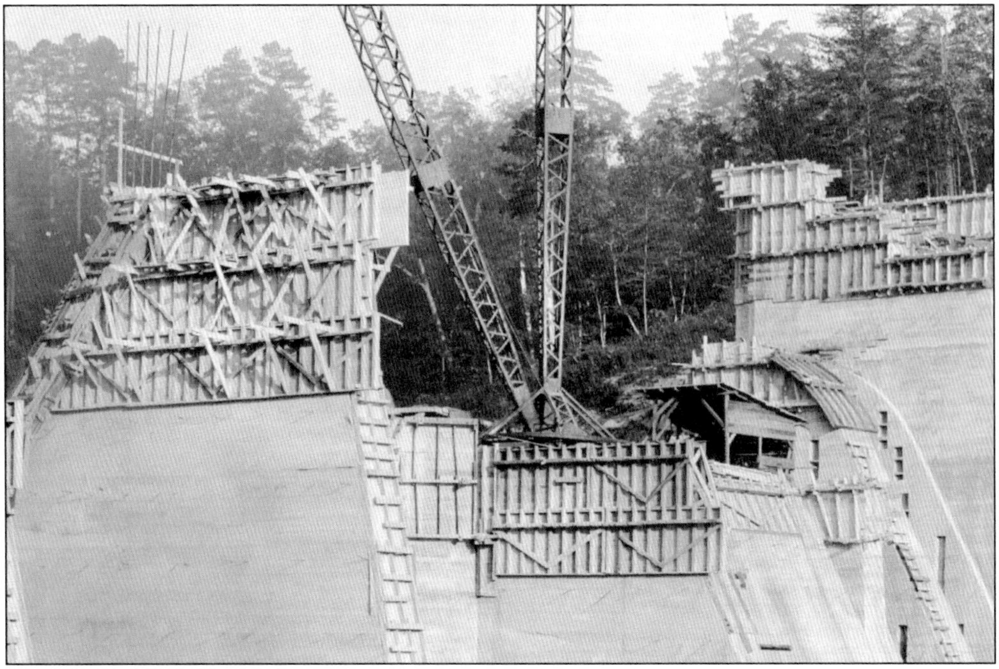

Wood forms were used multiple times and moved with these cranes. Shelters were built and rebuilt as the dam continued gaining height. (Courtesy of the Town of Lake Lure.)

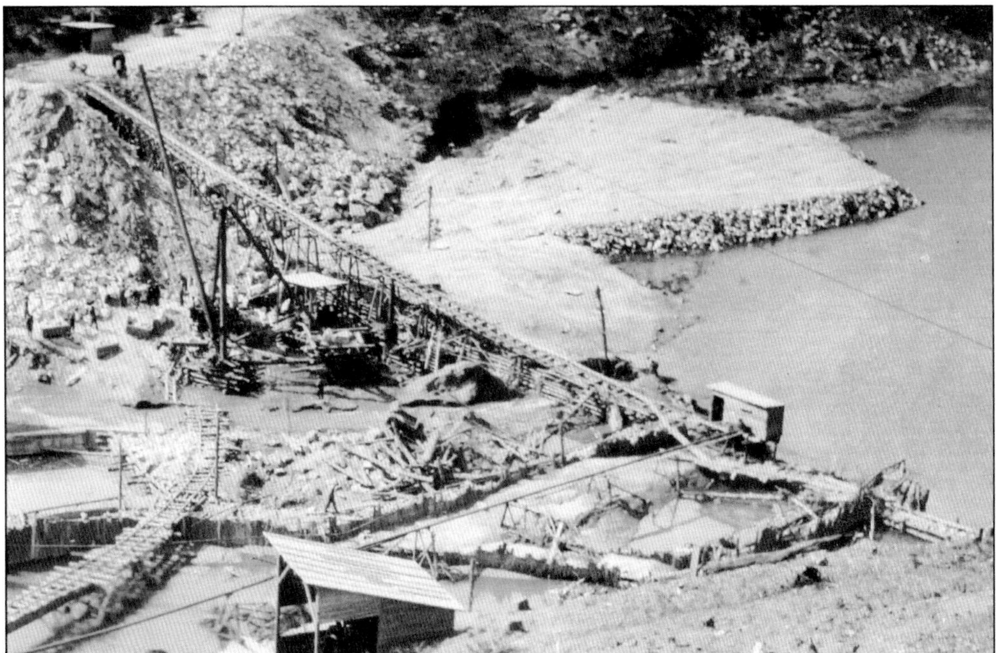

The trains were often pulled by mules. Massive amounts of rock, logs, pipes, and sand had to be moved. As the dam was constructed, the water level rose. After major rain events, some of the equipment was forever buried by the lake. (Courtesy of the Morse family.)

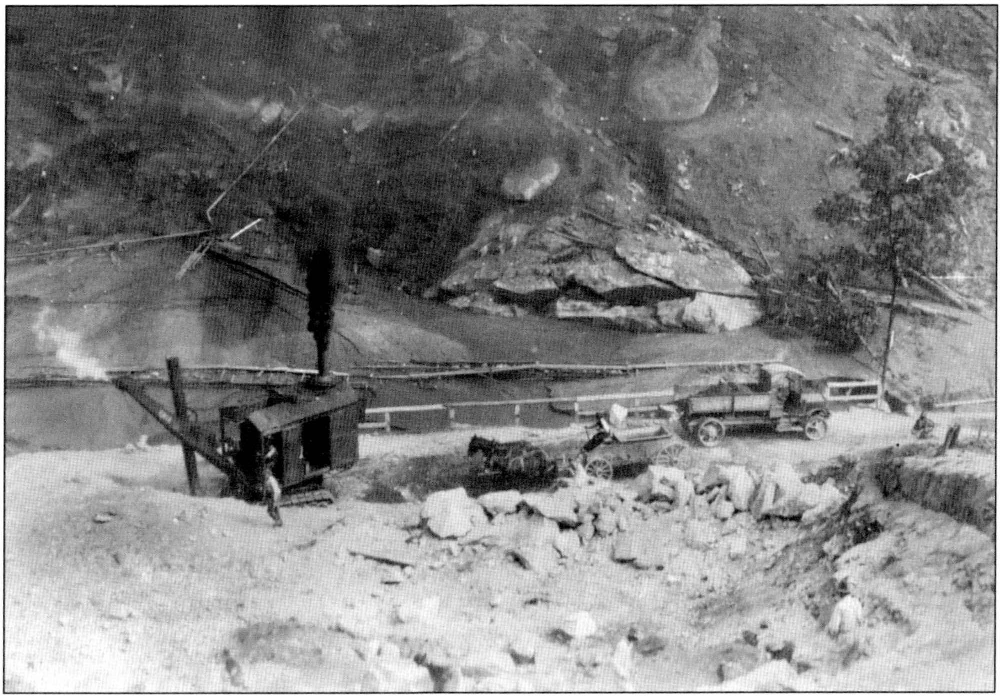

Pictured here is one of only a few steam shovels used to clear the way for Lake Lure. Former mayor Paul Wilson helped operate a steam engine while he was still a young man. A REO truck similar to this one was left to be flooded. It was recovered by Jack Donaldson in the 1980s and is still used in parades. (Courtesy of the Town of Lake Lure.)

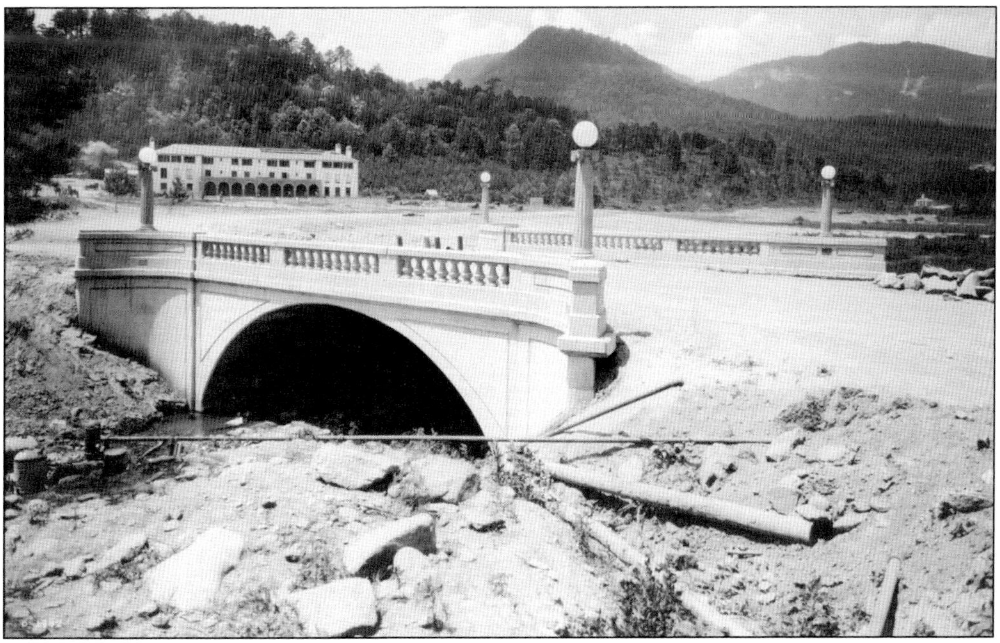

This photograph shows the newly built bridge across Pool Creek with the Lake Lure Inn in the background and the Chimney Rock Baptist Church at far right. (Photograph by Norman Greig; courtesy of the Greig family.)

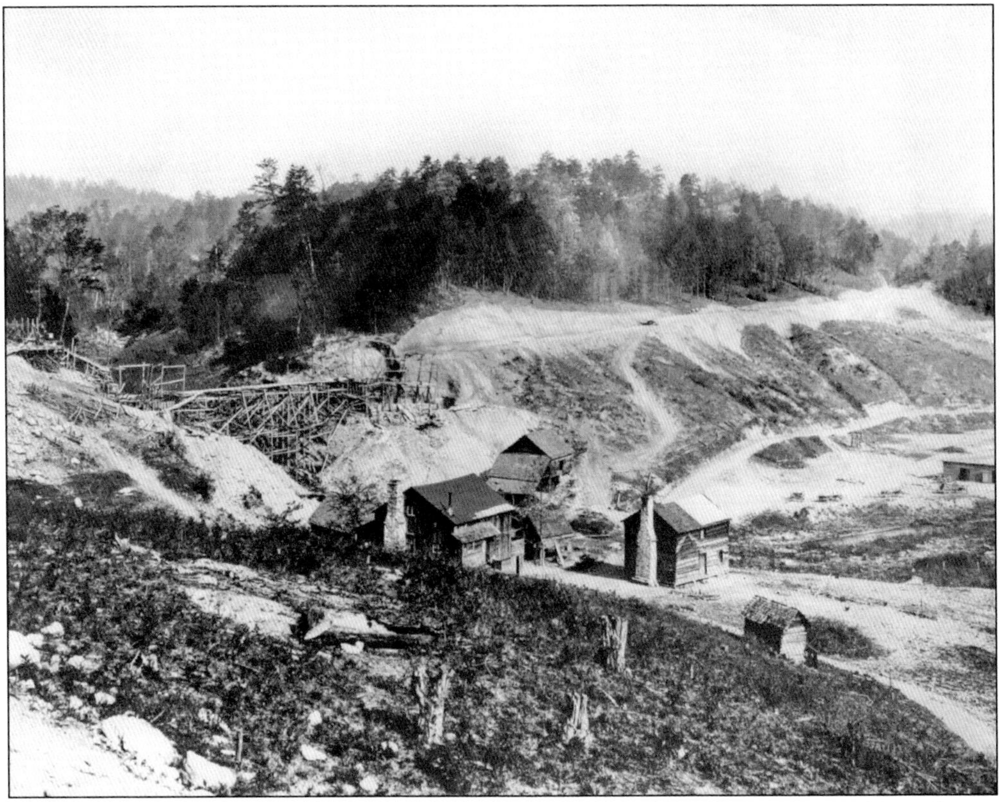

These farmhouses were just below the modern-day Larkin's on the Lake Restaurant. Moonshiners frequented this cove, and the local folks called this area "Drunkards Flats." All the homes and barns were burned or torn down. The only structure left standing was the Baptist church. The Tryon Bay Bridge is under construction. (Courtesy of the Greig family.)

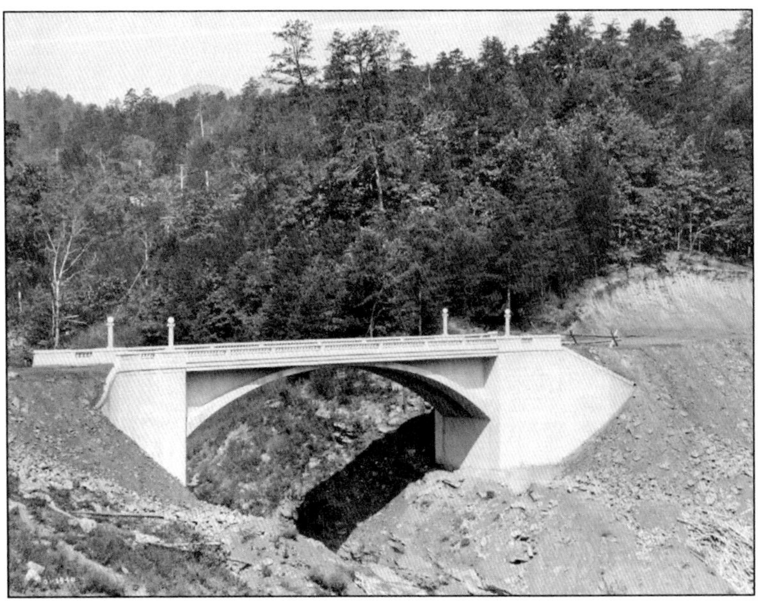

Seen here is the bridge over Cane Creek, now Tryon Bay, just before the highway opened. NC Highway 20 was relocated to higher ground and later renamed US 74. Unlike most bridges in the United States at that time, the new bridges were equipped with modern electric lights. (Courtesy of the Greig family.)

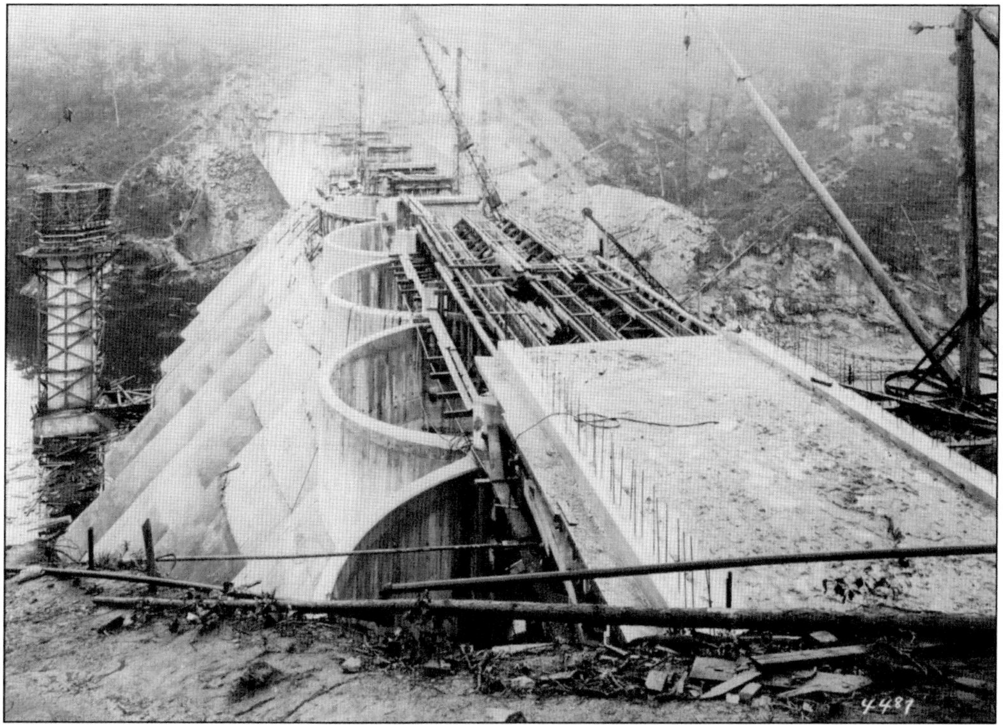

The dam was nearly complete when construction of the road had just started. The total height of the dam is 104 feet tall, and it is 571 feet across. At this point in time, the lake is only 12 feet deep. (Courtesy of the Town of Lake Lure.)

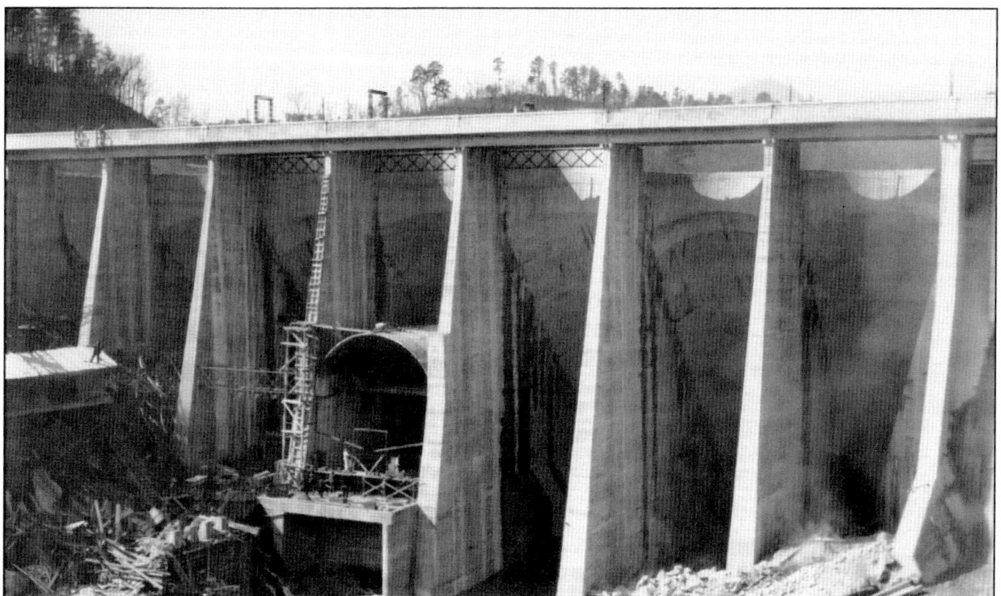

The Lake Lure Dam has been erected, and the power station is well on its way to completion. The finish date for the dam was September 20, 1926. Power was first produced in 1928. Duke Power Company, now Duke Energy, has purchased all the power produced by the power station. (Courtesy of the Town of Lake Lure.)

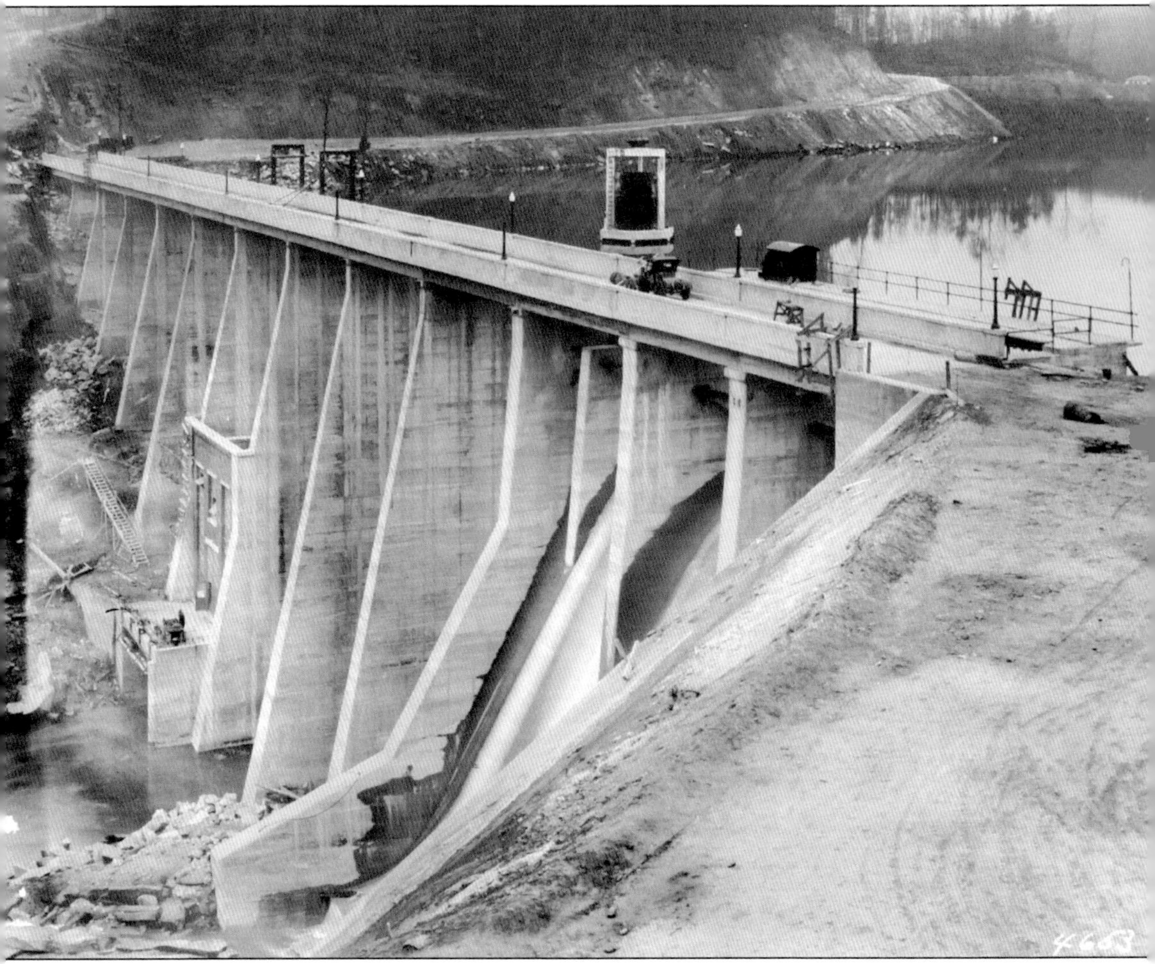

The Lake Lure Dam is complete, and the lake is finally full. The road entering and leaving the dam is, however, still dirt. (Courtesy of the Town of Lake Lure.)

This adventuresome boat was on Lake Lure before the lake had reached full pond. The developers obviously had grand plans, and touring the waters by modern motorboats was only the beginning. (Courtesy of the Greig family.)

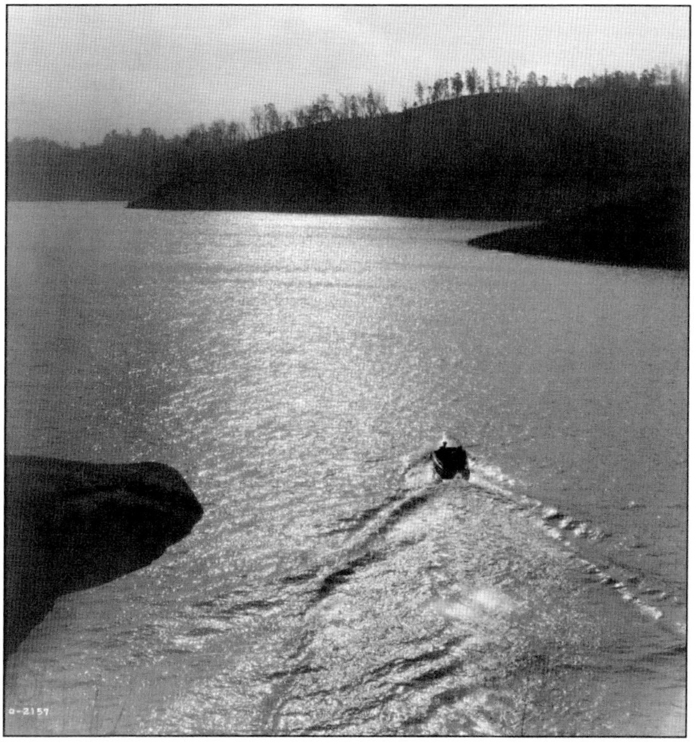

Pictured is another motorboat touring the lake before it is full. Rumbling Bald Mountain in the background looks remarkably the same then as it does now. (Courtesy of the Morse family.)

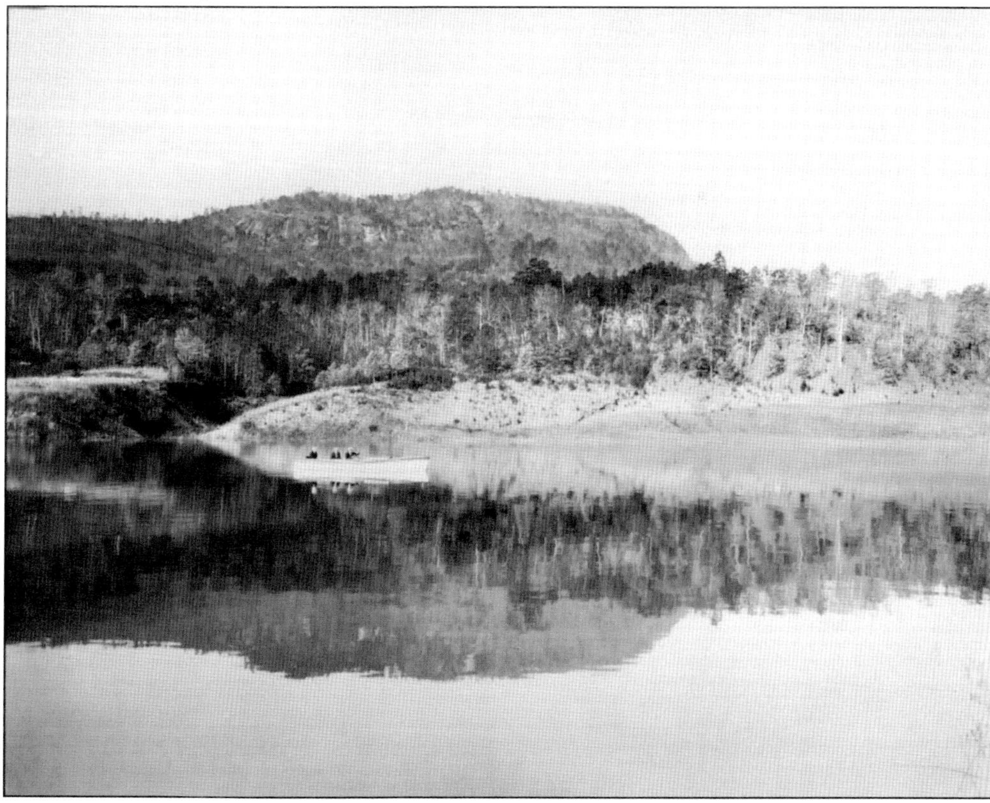

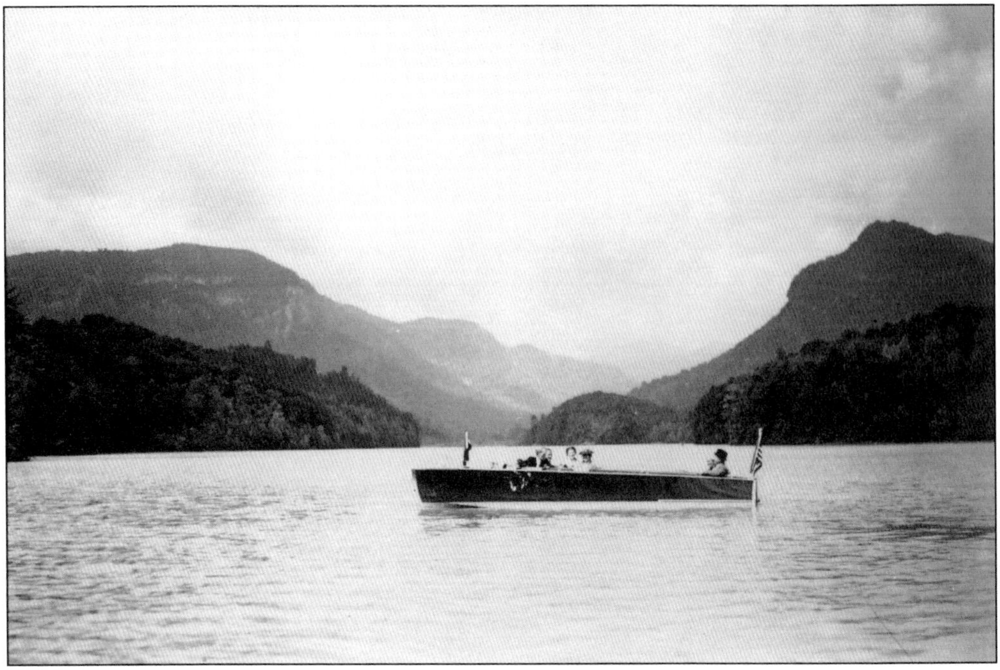

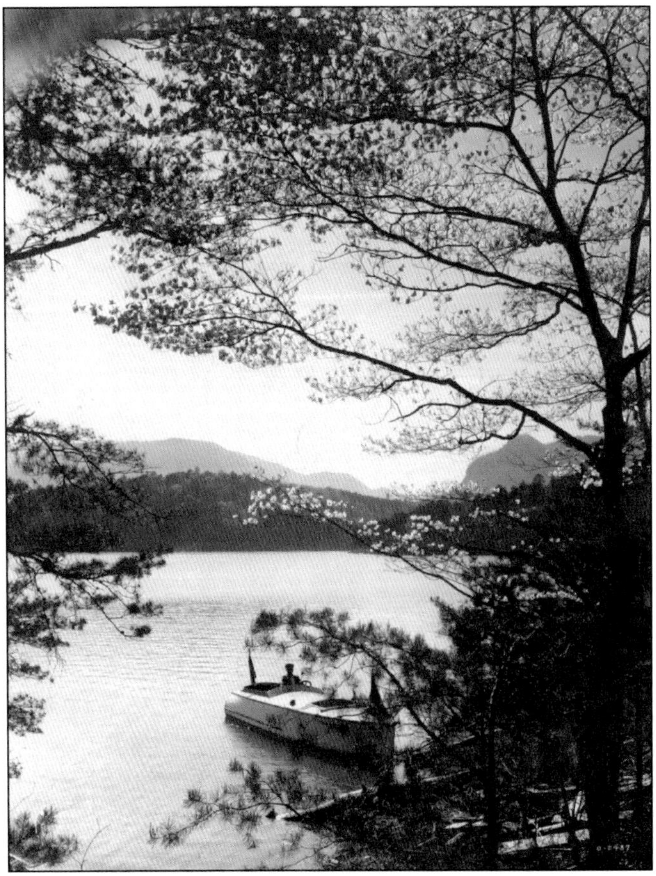

Lake Lure was named by Dr. Lucius Morse's wife, Elizabeth Parkenson "Betty" Morse. Some well-to-do people purchased land and built large homes. (Courtesy of the Morse family.)

Lake Lure is just as fun to cruise now as it was in the 1920s. It is remarkable how the lake looked without homes in every cove. (Courtesy of the Greig family.)

The lake is finally full and ready for boating enthusiasts to enjoy one of the prettiest lakes in the world. All the boats were made of wood and had large enclosures for the engine. (Courtesy the of Morse family.)

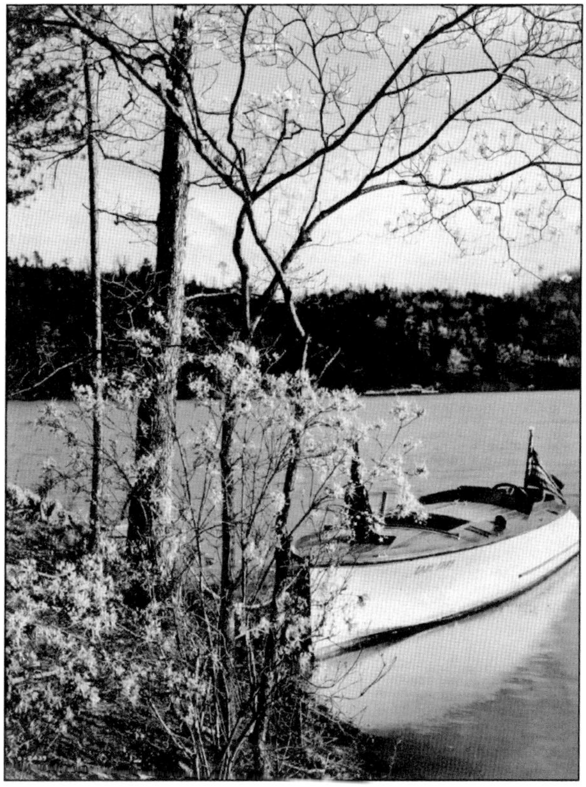

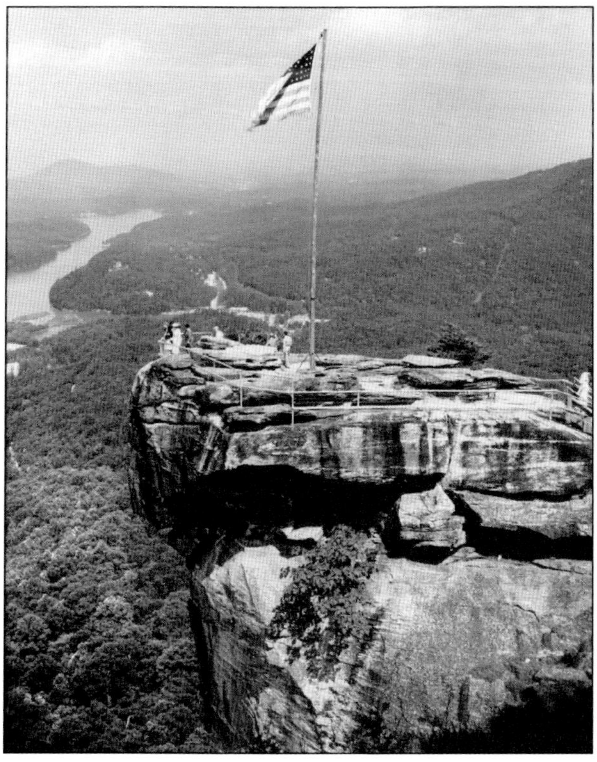

This c. 1928 photograph of Chimney Rock shows the newly created Lake Lure towards the east. (Courtesy of the Morse family.)

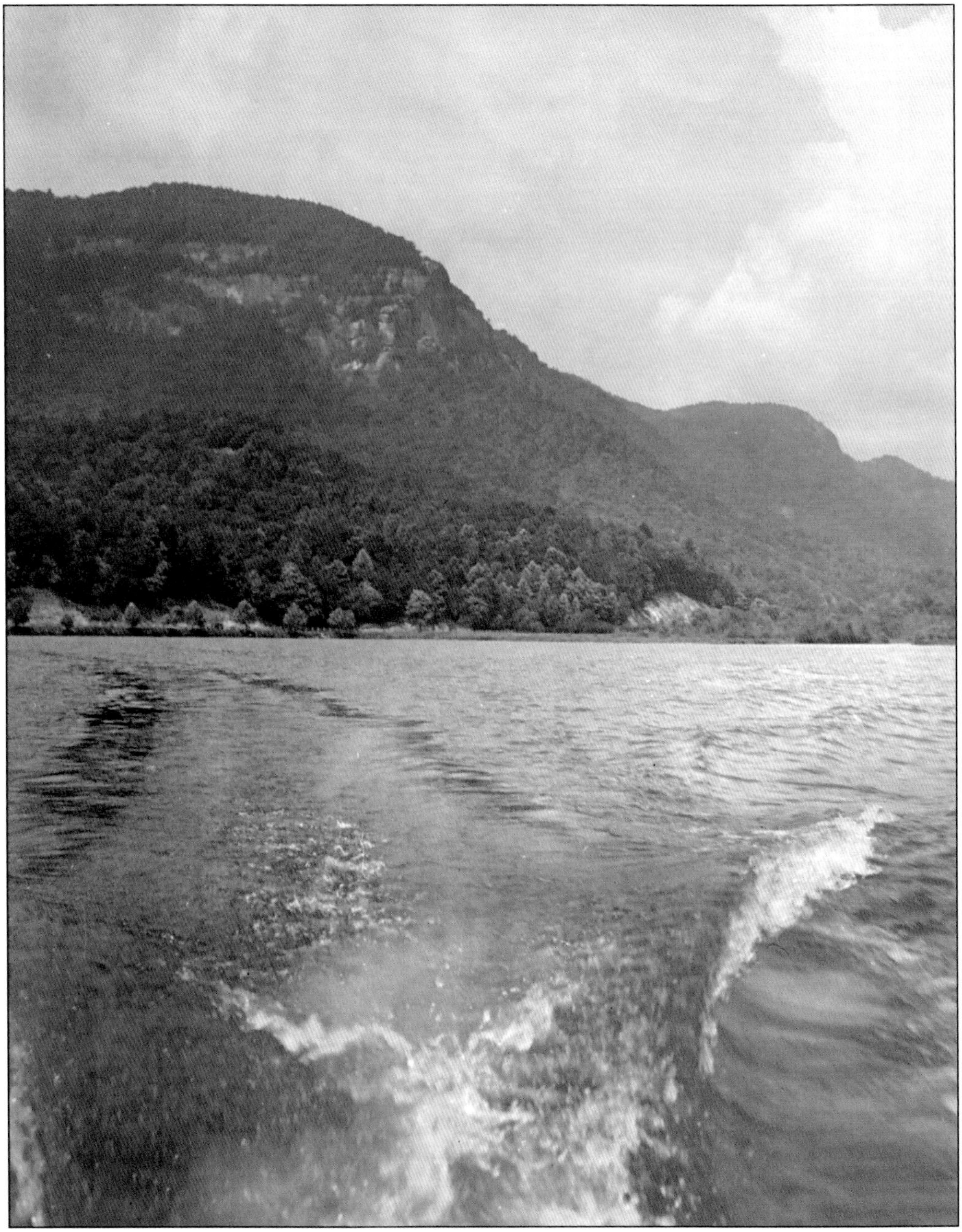

Chimney Rock looks down on beautiful Lake Lure. This area would later be filled in with silt. Enough silt has flowed down from the Rocky Broad River to create the landmass now used for the Lake Lure marina, visitor center, Morse Park, and the town's municipal building. (Photograph by Norman Greig; courtesy of the Greig family.)

The Tryon Bay Bridge finally opened in 1926. NC Highway 20 was relocated, and tourist cars and commercial trucks could now use the new road. Drunkards Flat is under water, but new homes would soon be built. (Courtesy of the Morse family.)

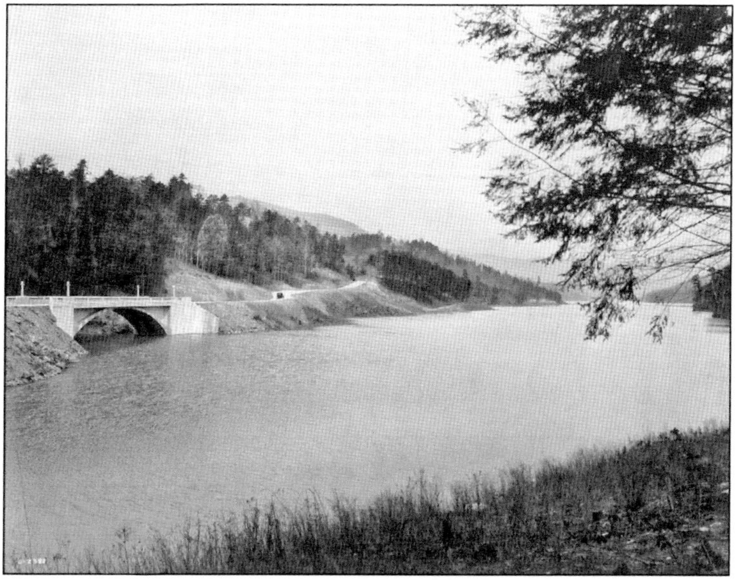

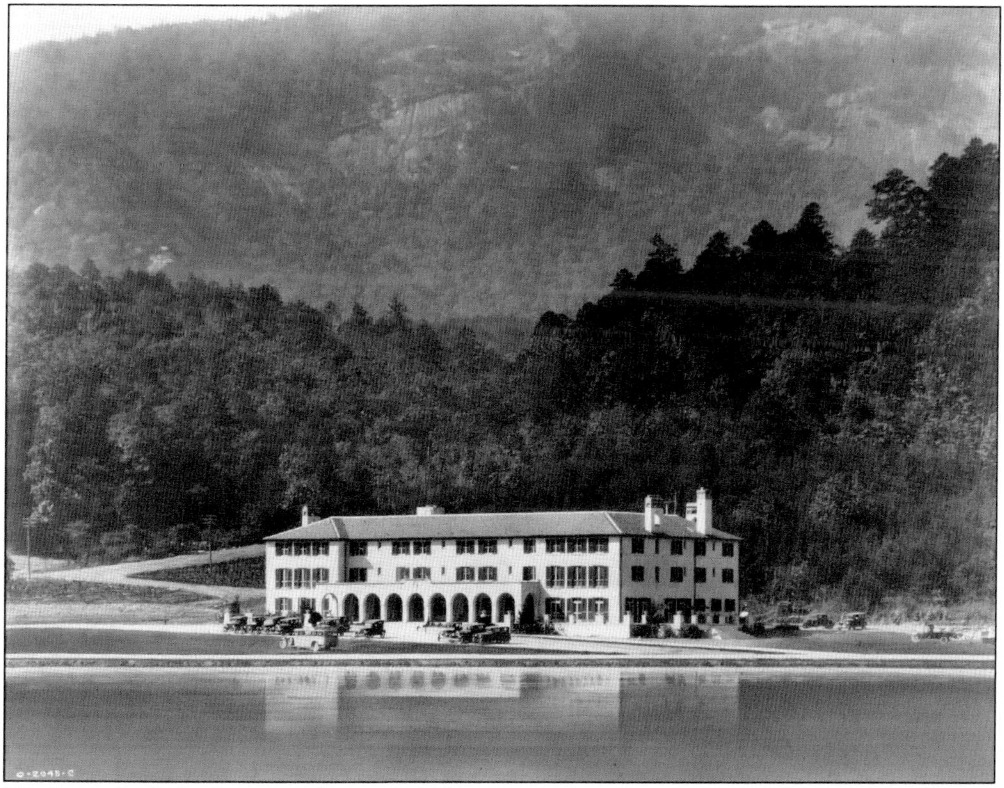

Work on the Lake Lure Inn began in February 1926 and was completed in 1927. Robert R. McGoodwin was the architect, and construction was supervised by M.E. Boyer of Charlotte. The total cost was $400,000. Just like the Lake Lure Administration Building (now called the Arcade Building), the inn has a sprinkler system for fire control and was designed in the Mediterranean architecture style. During World War II, the inn was used by the US Army Air Corps for officer rest and recuperation. (Courtesy of the Greig family.)

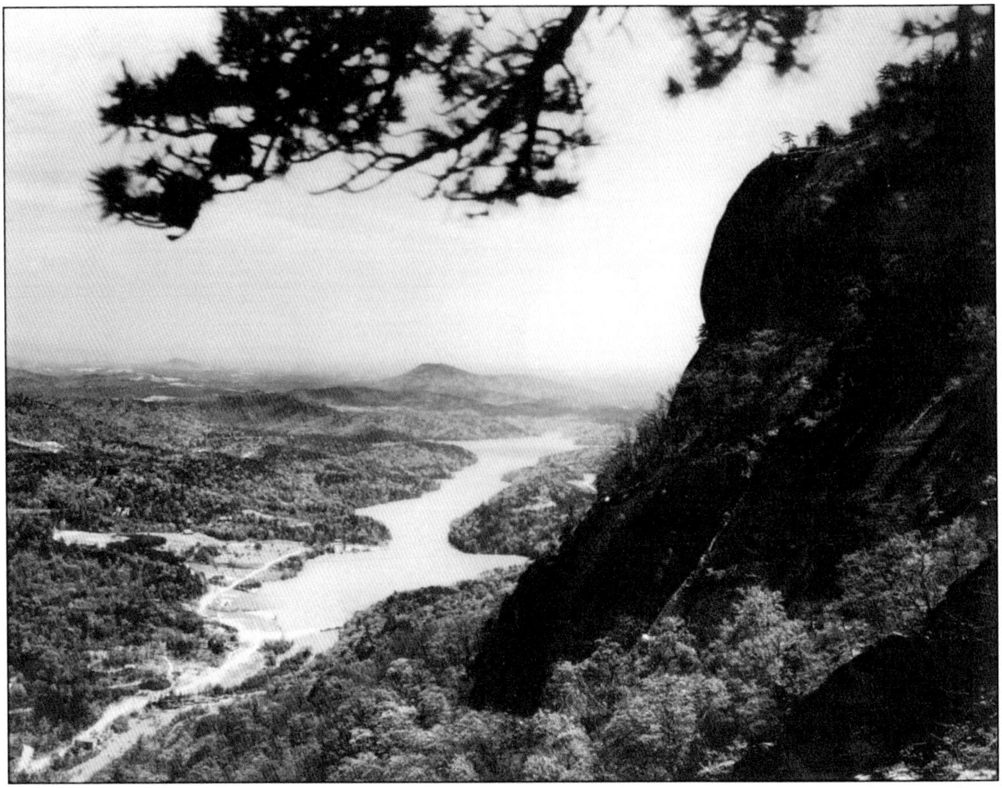

This is one of the earliest photographs taken after the lake was at full pond. With the old stagecoach road and NC Highway 20 under water, the main road had to be moved to higher ground. It is remarkable to think that when Lake Lure was first created, the lake extended more than a hundred yards west of the bridge over the Rocky Broad River. (Courtesy of the Morse family.)

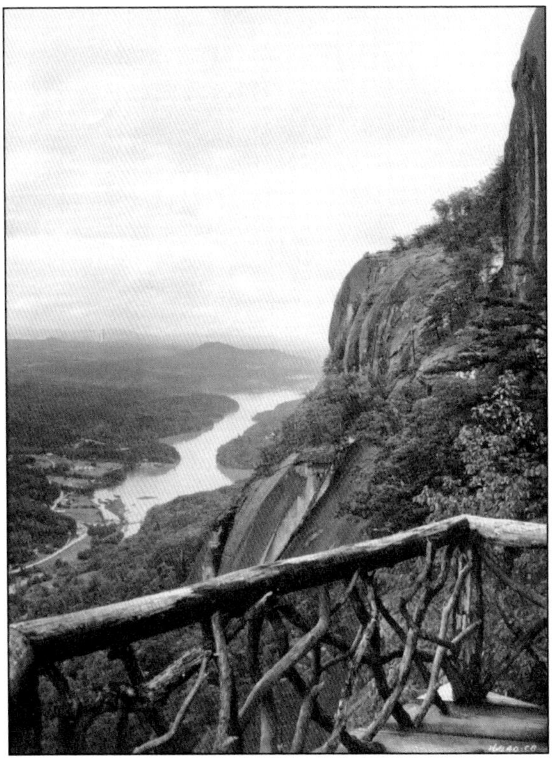

Here is the view of Lake Lure from Inspiration Point at Chimney Rock Park. As noted earlier, silt is building up just below where the Rocky Broad River meets the lake. The developers and, later, the Town of Lake Lure have had ongoing silt removal programs for many decades. (Courtesy of the Morse family.)

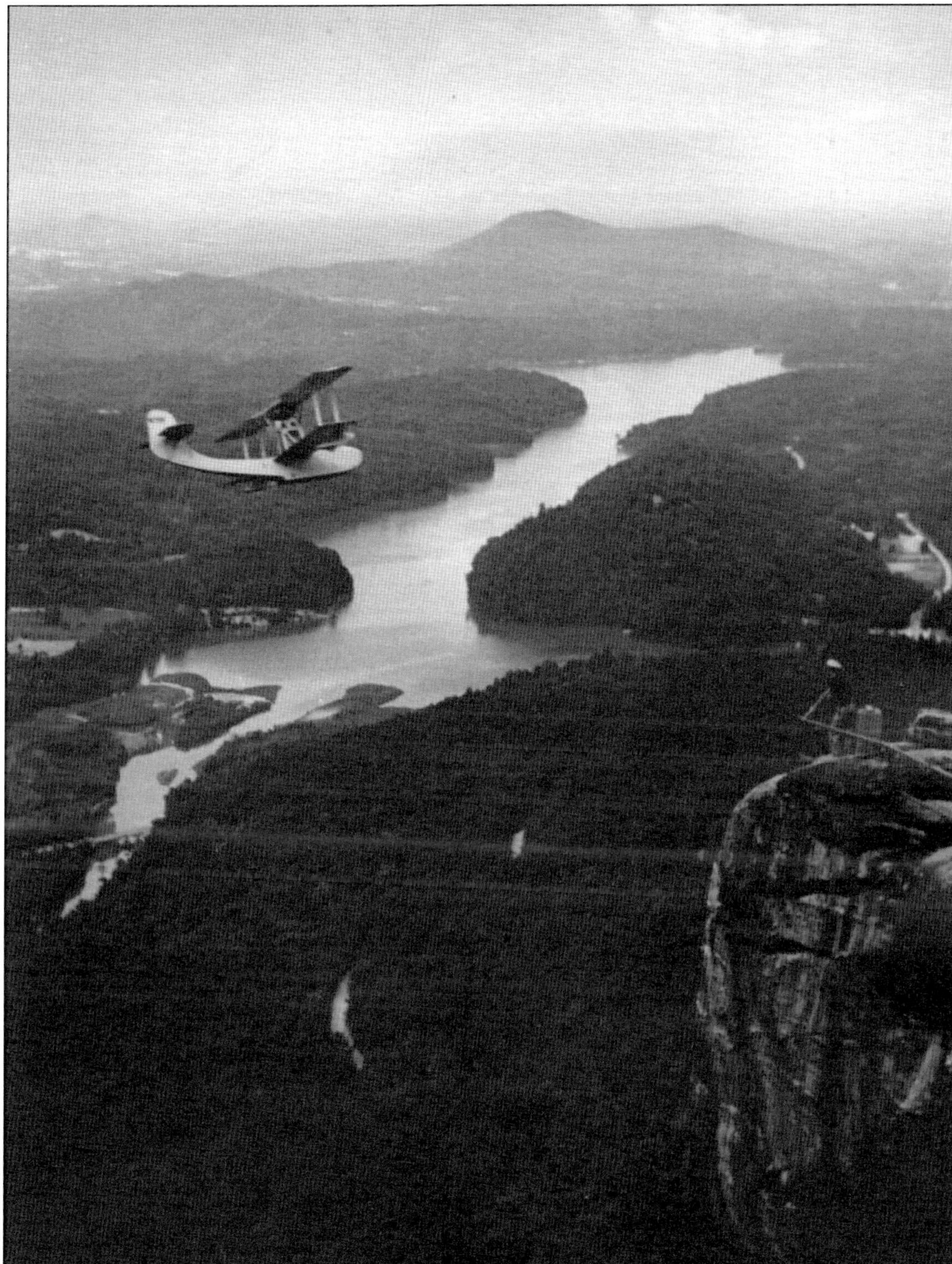
A seaplane takes in the beautiful view of Lake Lure and Chimney Rock. (Courtesy of the Morse family.)

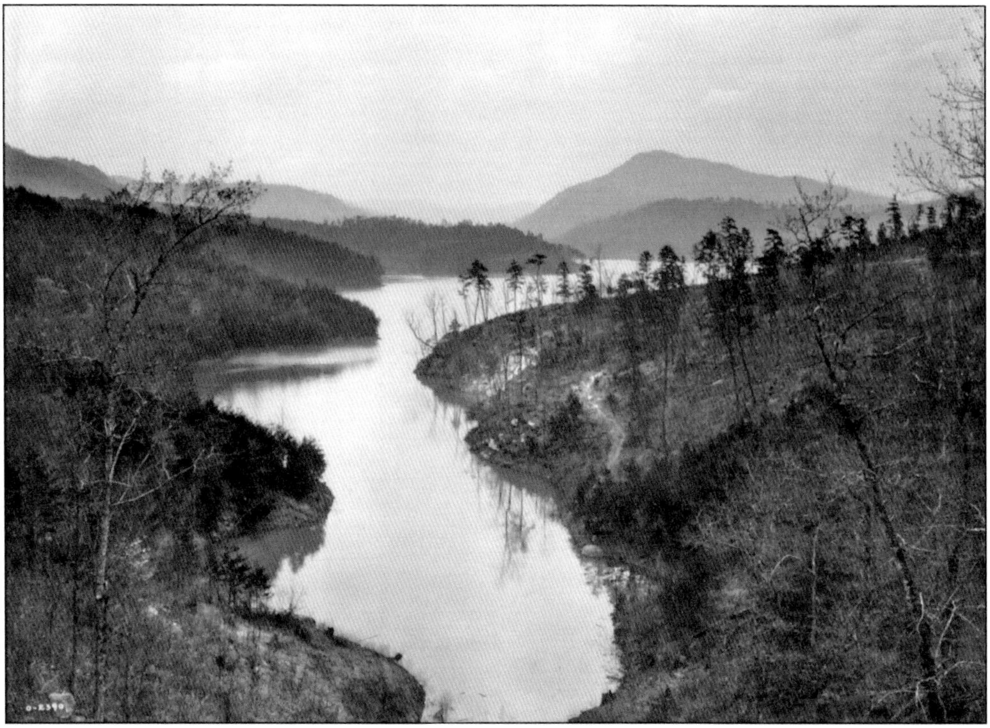

The perimeter of Lake Lure looked much different before homes and boathouses were built on the lake, but the mountains have changed very little. (Both, courtesy of the Morse family.)

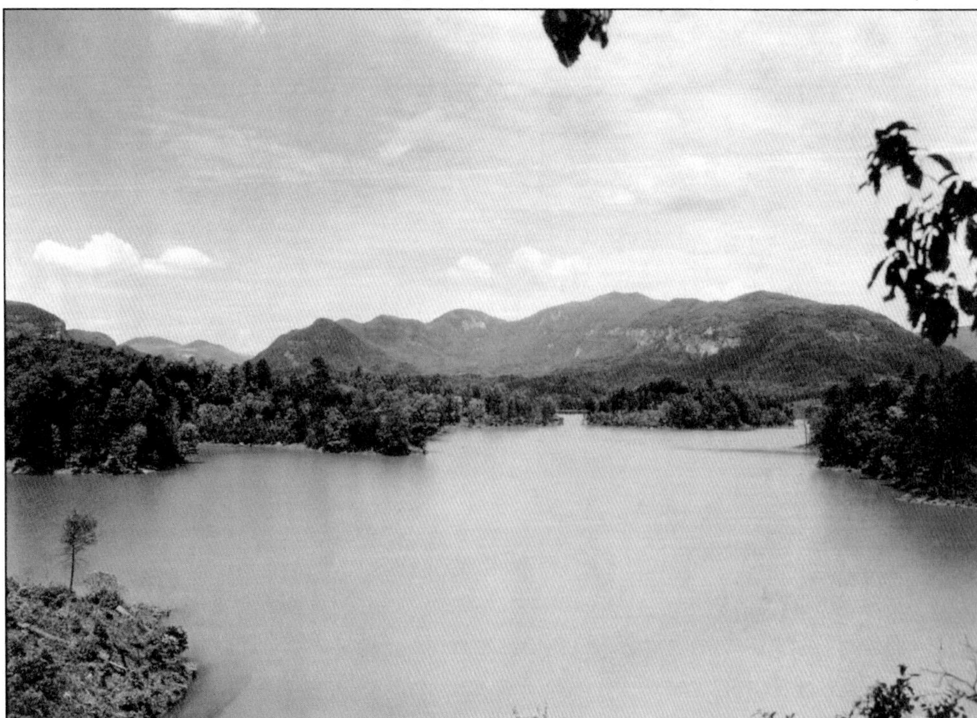

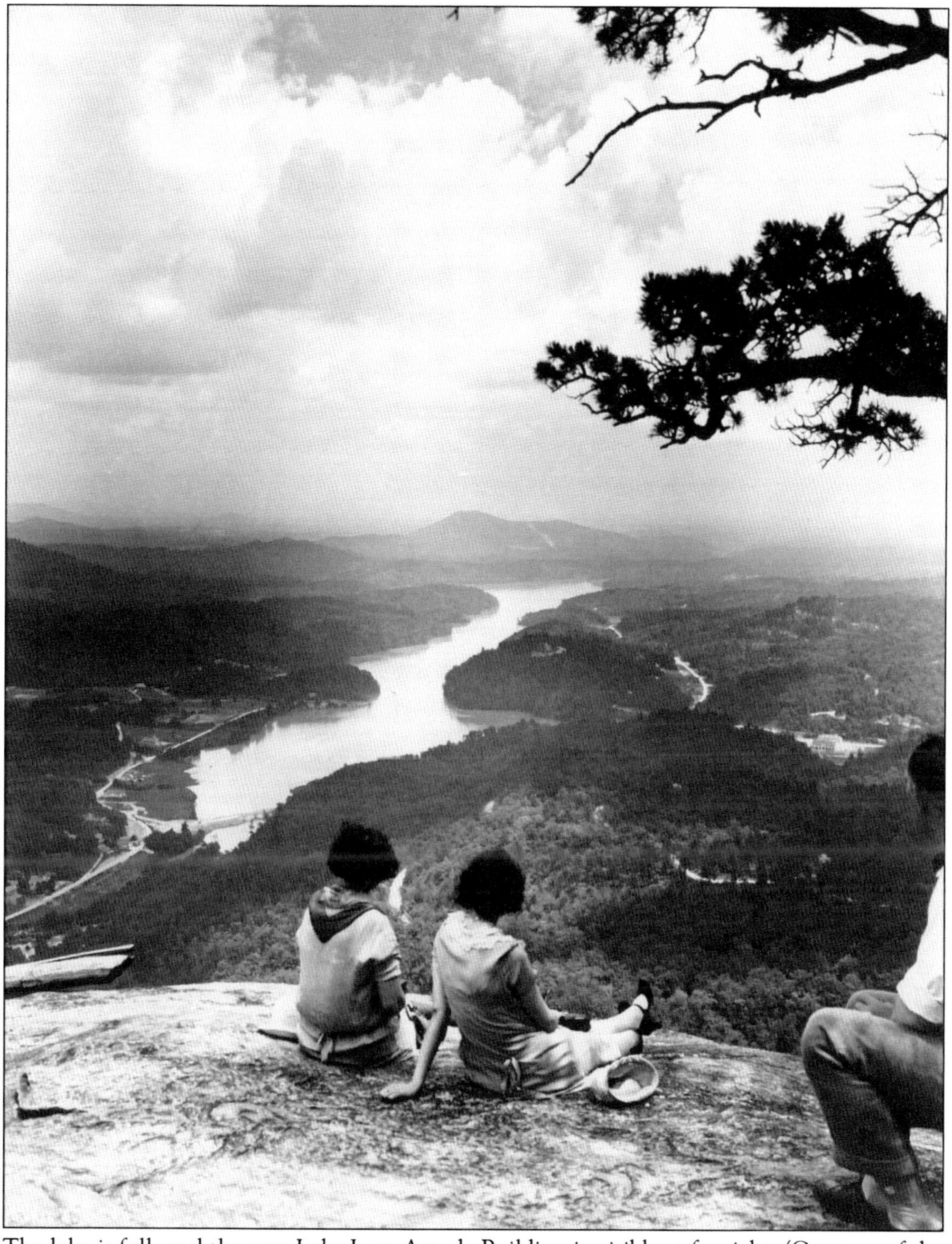

The lake is full, and the new Lake Lure Arcade Building is visible at far right. (Courtesy of the Morse family.)

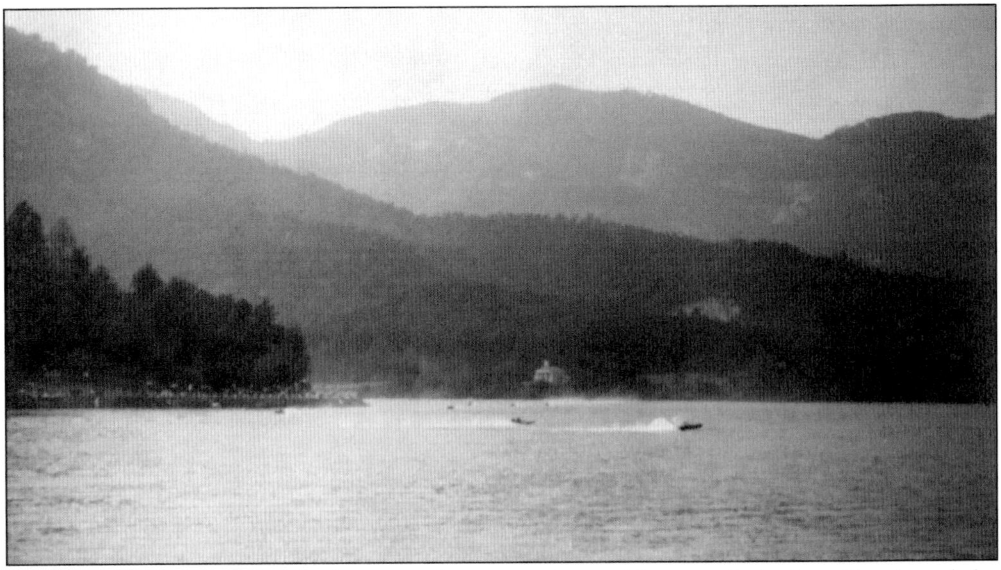

When the lake was first built, there were boat races located between Lake Lure Beach and the Chimney Rock Baptist Church. Accreted soil from the river has since created the land where the Lake Lure Municipal Building and Morse Park are now. (Courtesy of the Washburn family.)

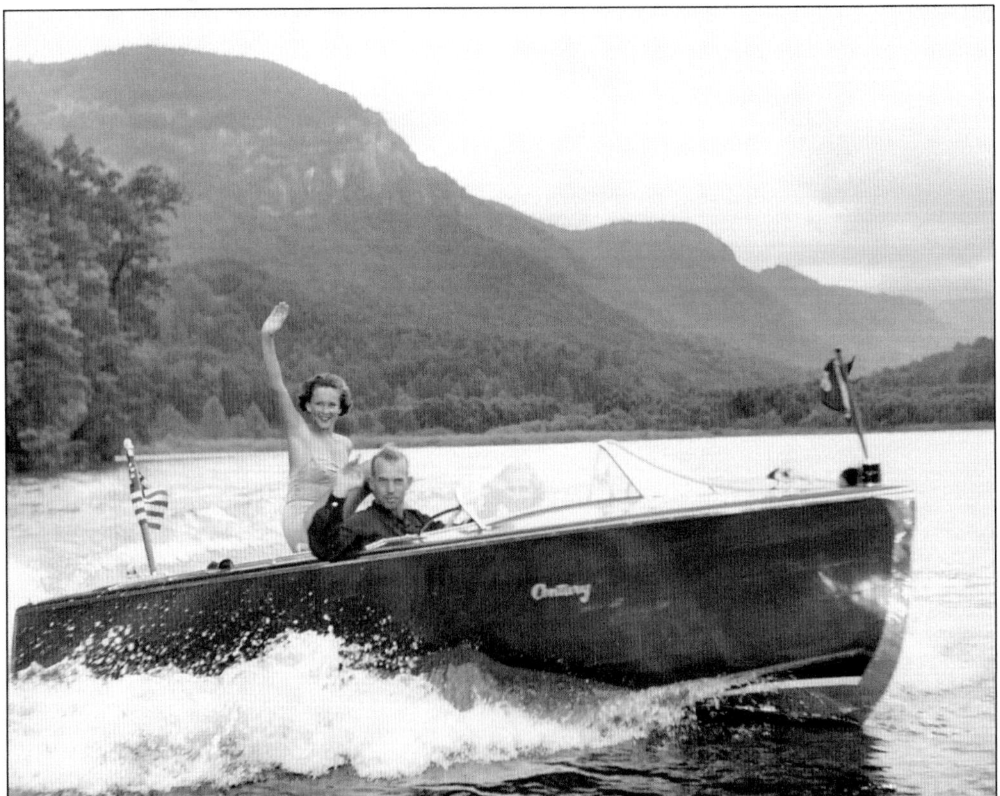

Boaters soon found Lake Lure to be one of the most beautiful lakes in the world. Chimney Rock Mountain is visible in the background. (Courtesy the Town of Lake Lure.)

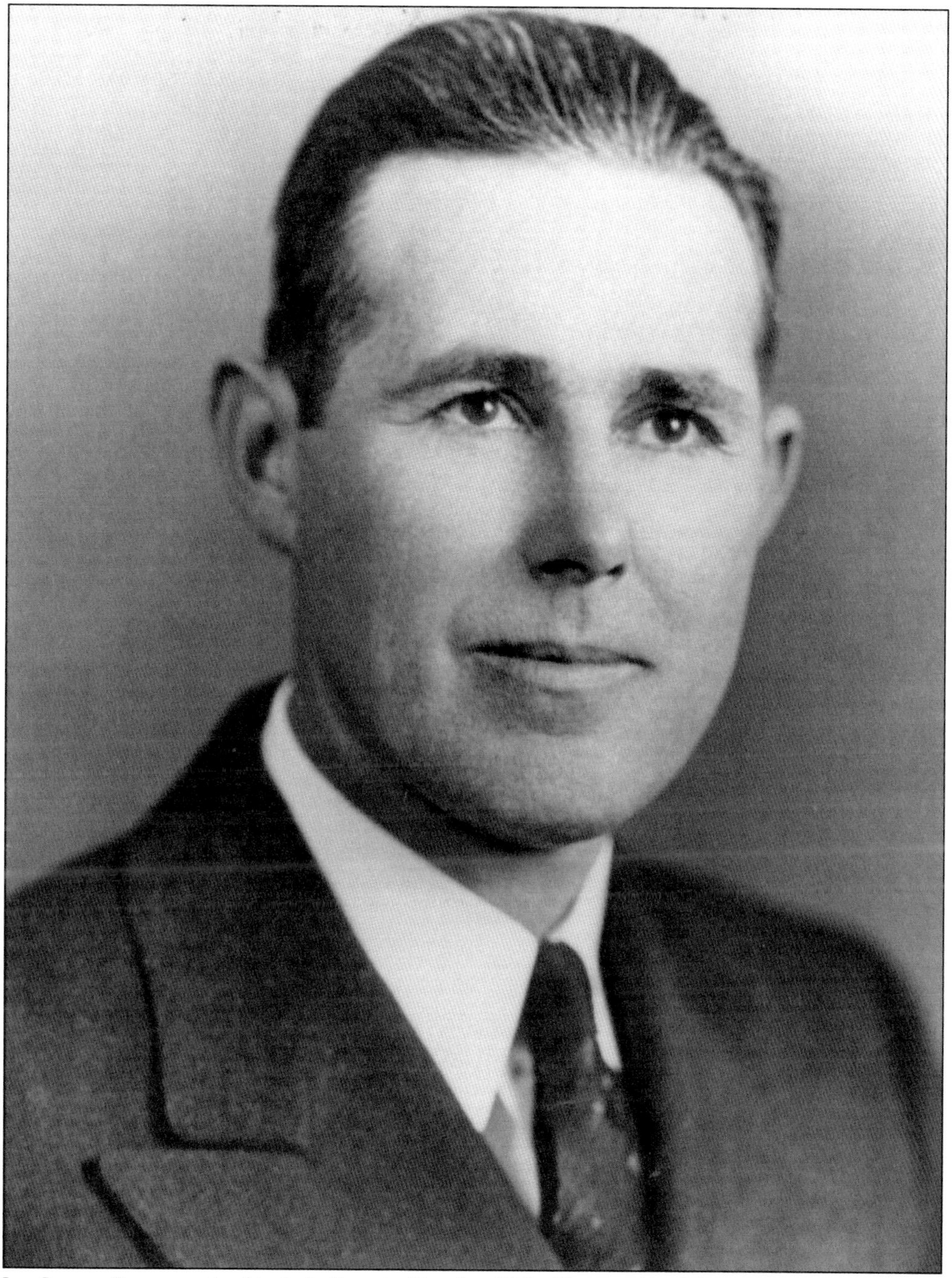

Lee Leeper Powers arrived in Lake Lure in October 1932. Chimney Rock Mountains, Inc., declared bankruptcy during the Great Depression, and its primary lender, USF&G, created the Lureland Realty Company to liquidate the assets with Powers in charge. Powers negotiated to personally purchase most of the property and built a residence at the Bottomless Pools. Along with land sales, Powers was also a very successful building contractor. (Courtesy of the Morse family.)

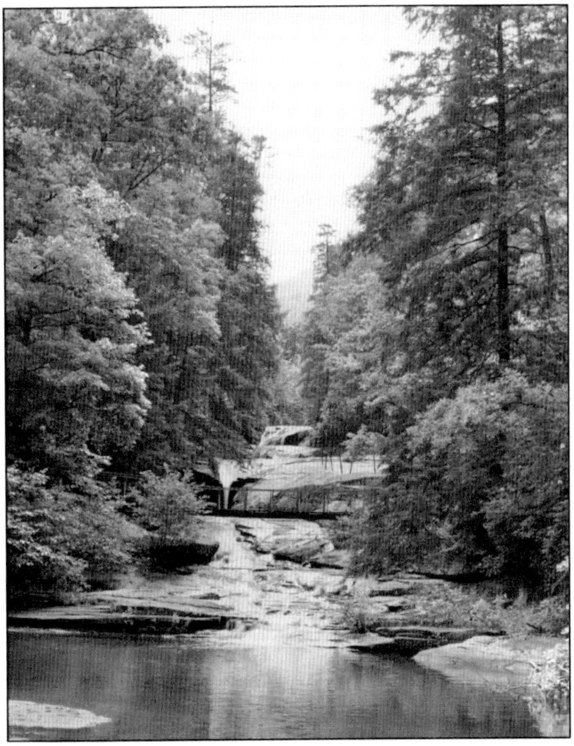

Bottomless Pools was a natural wonder. Powers constructed a pedestrian bridge across Pool Creek to allow tourists a better view of the Bottomless Pools. (Both, photograph by Norman Greig; courtesy of the Greig family.)

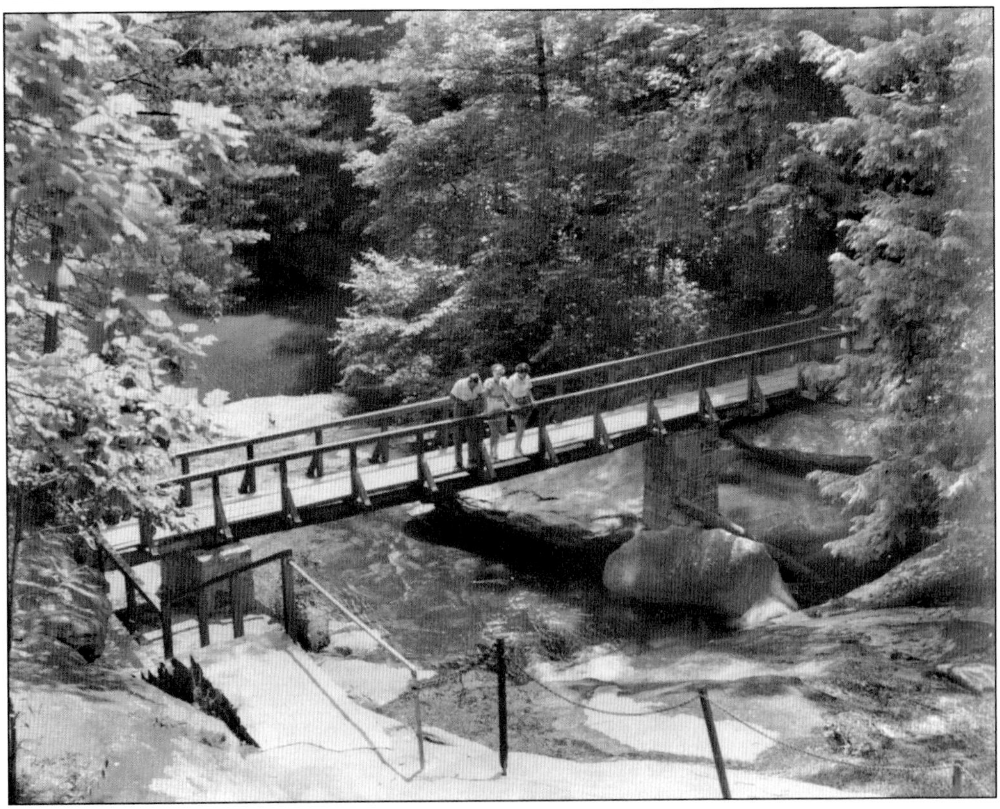

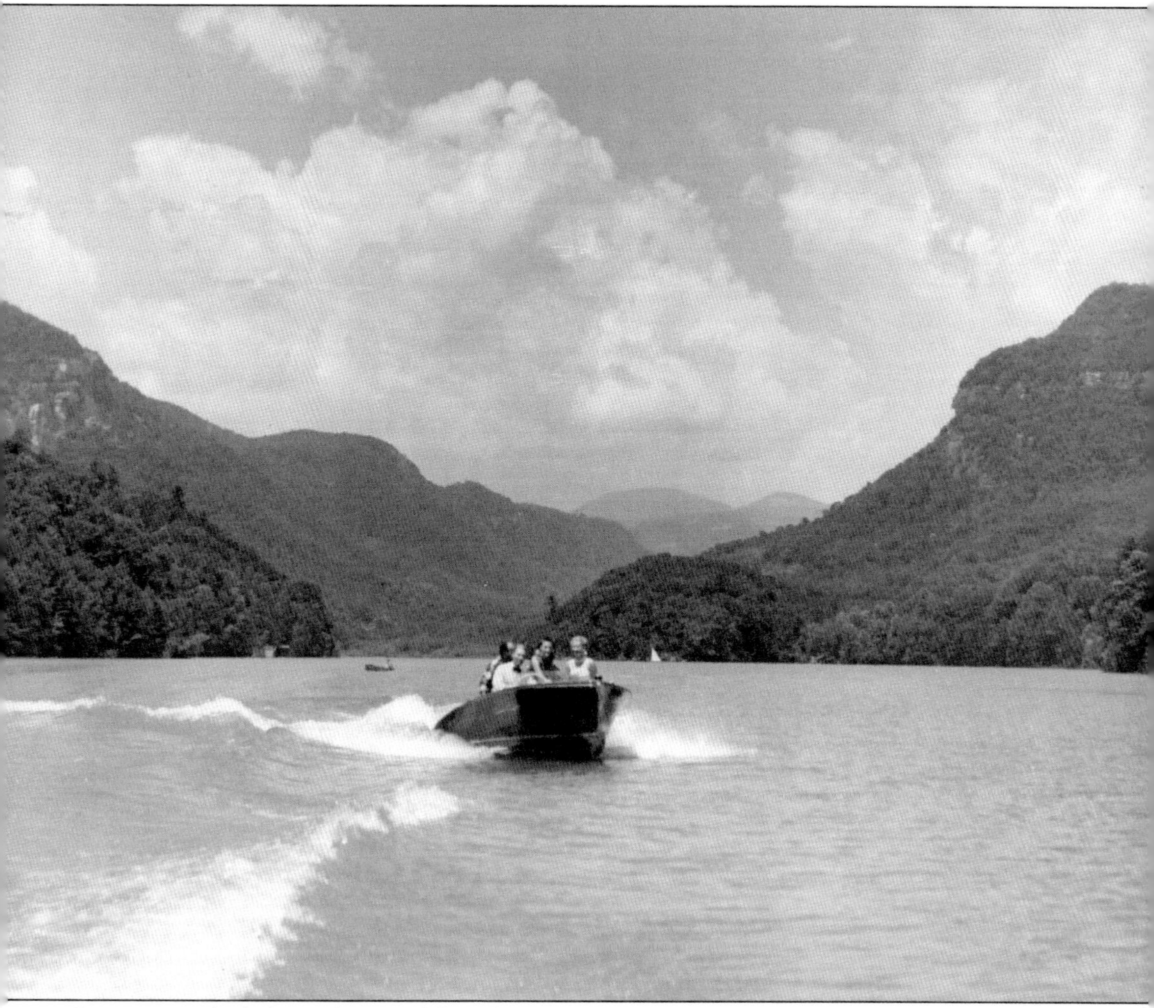

Powers is at the helm with several friends as they enjoy Lake Lure. As seen in the background, Lake Lure is also fun for sailboats and canoes. (Courtesy the Town of Lake Lure.)

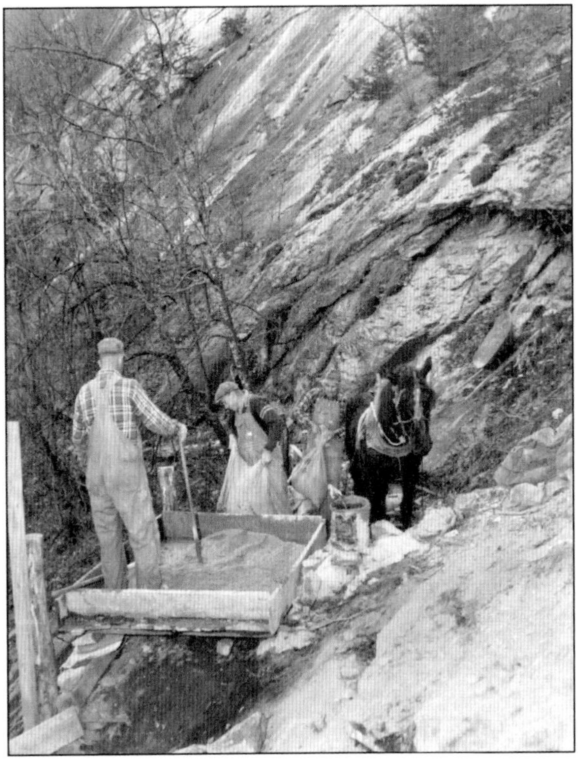

Workers prepare to blast a hole for an elevator at Chimney Rock Park. Work started in 1946, and after 18 months and with the help of eight tons of dynamite, a 198-foot tunnel into the mountain and a 258-foot elevator shaft were completed in 1949. (Both, photograph by Norman Greig; courtesy of the Greig family.)

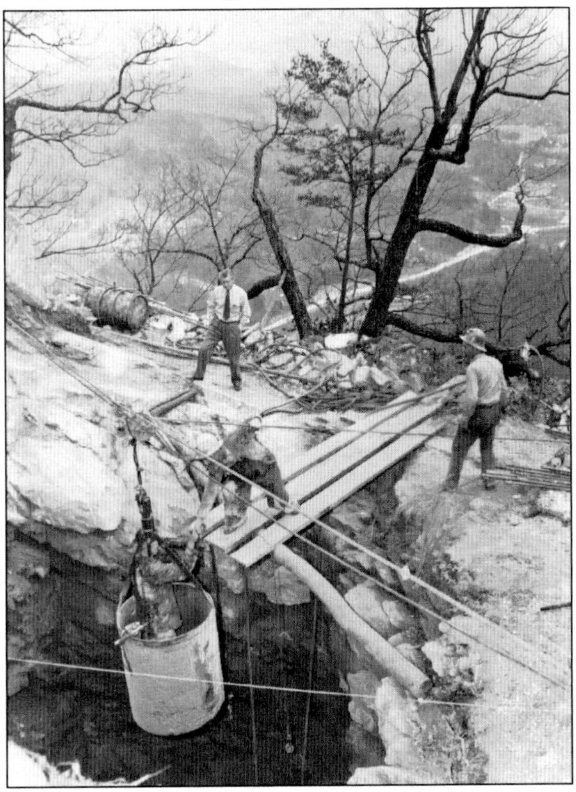

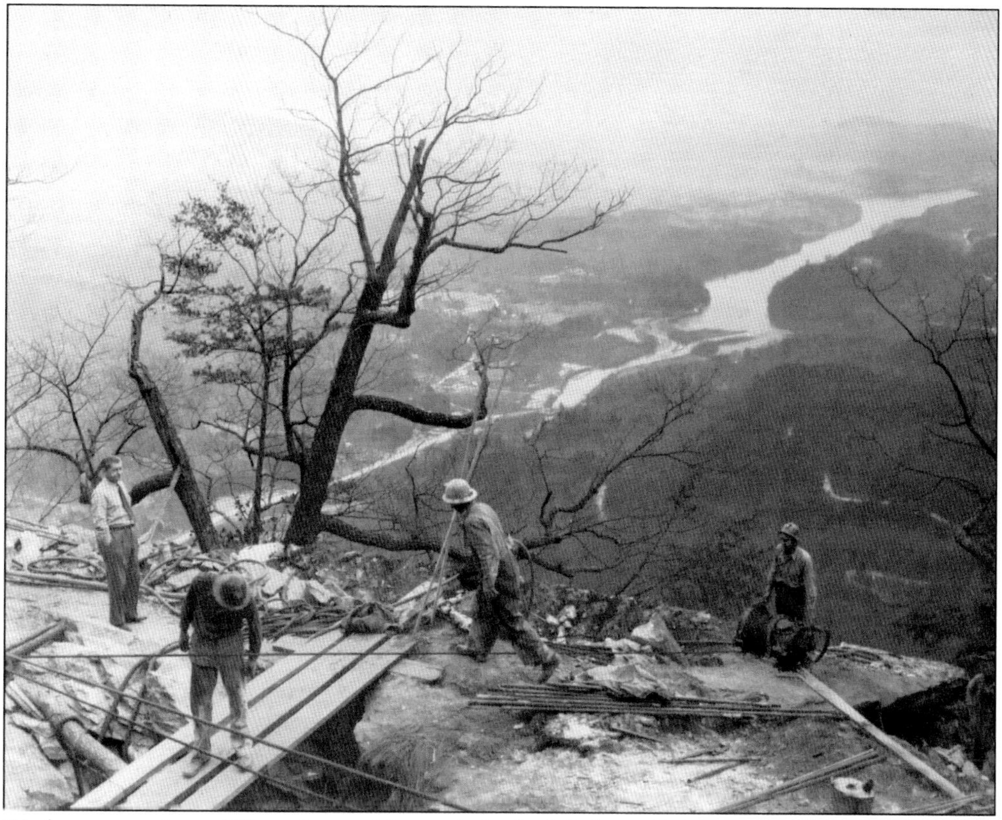

Workers atop a sheer cliff continue to blast rock for the 248-foot-tall elevator shaft and prepare for the Sky Lounge and elevator. (Both, photograph by Norman Greig; courtesy of the Greig family.)

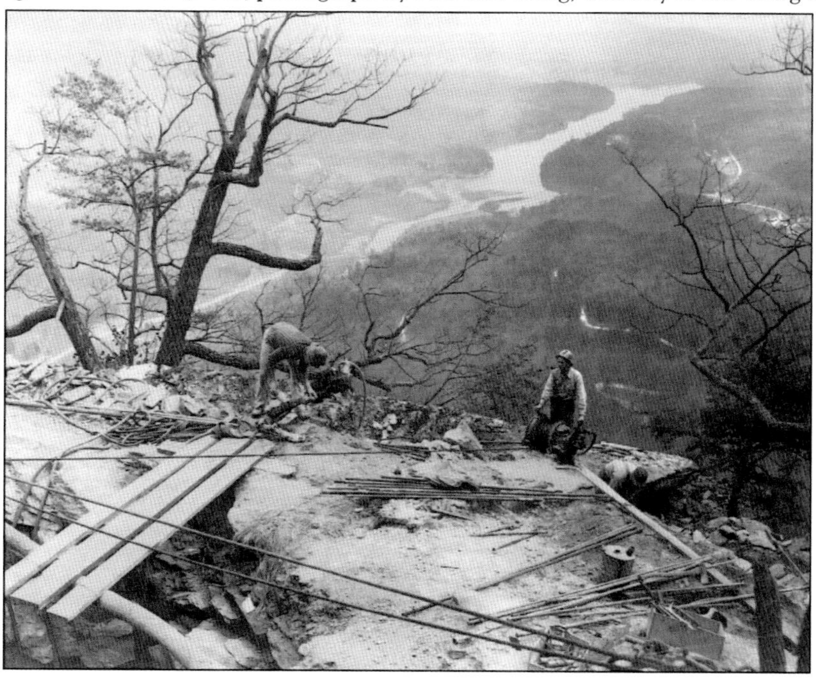

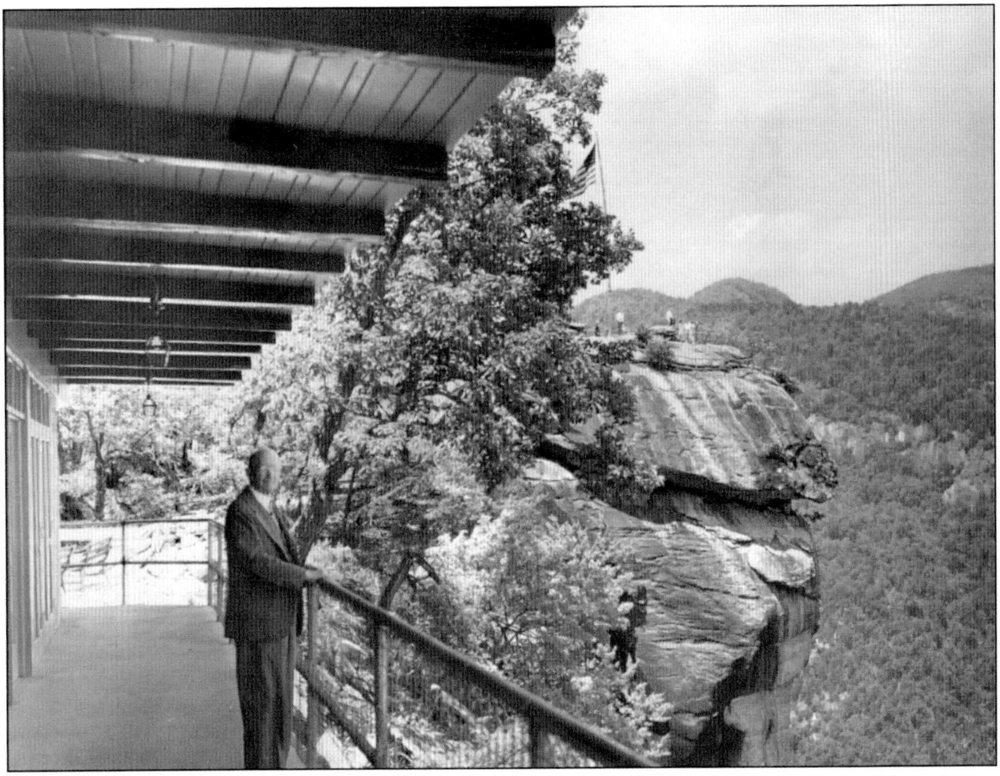

The original Sky Lounge was truly an engineering work of art. On a clear day, one could see Kings Mountain. The Sky Lounge included both a gift shop and a small restaurant. (Both, photograph by Norman Greig; courtesy of the Greig family.)

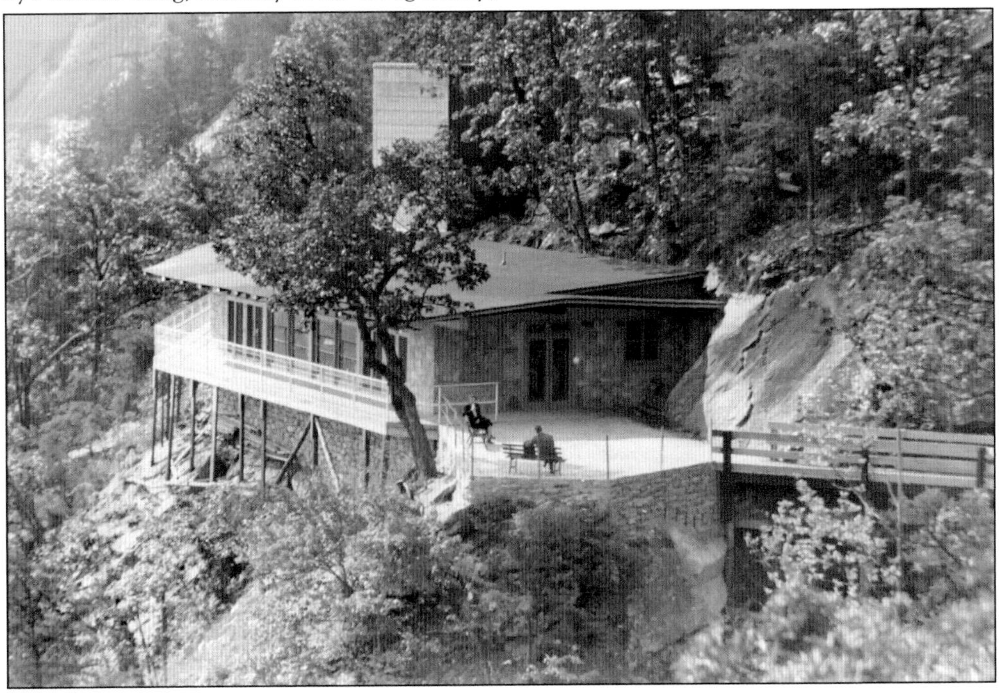

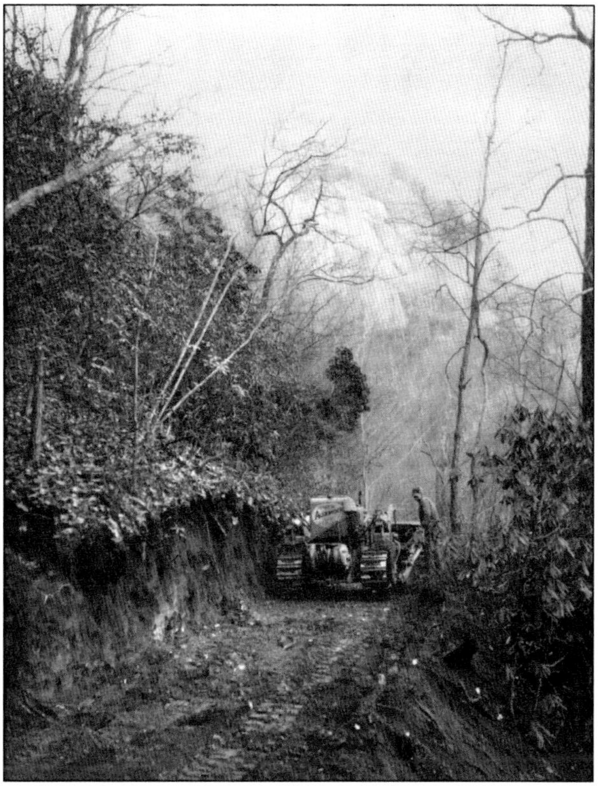

With the road to the upper parking lot and the elevator completed, the next large project was to build a road to the base of Hickory Nut Falls. Mules and steam engines were now replaced with diesel dozers. The Perry M. Alexander Company of Asheville was the grading contractor and is still in the grading business today. (Both, photograph by Norman Greig; courtesy of the Greig family.)

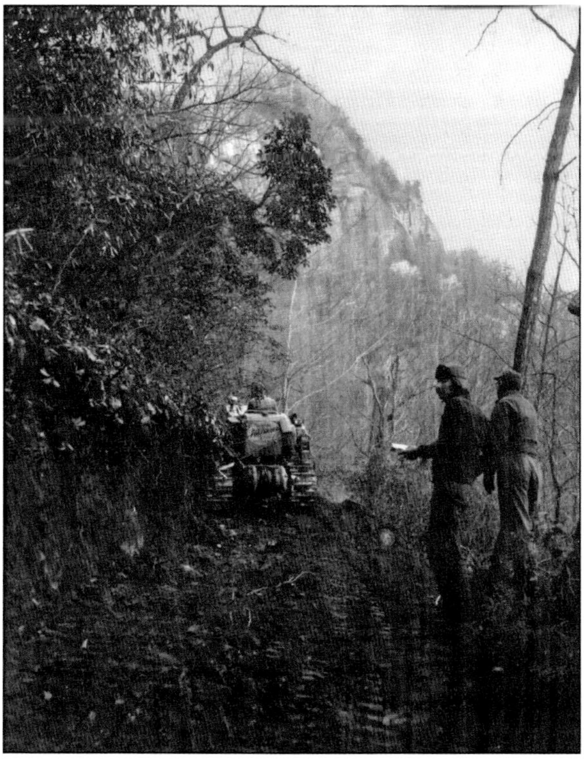

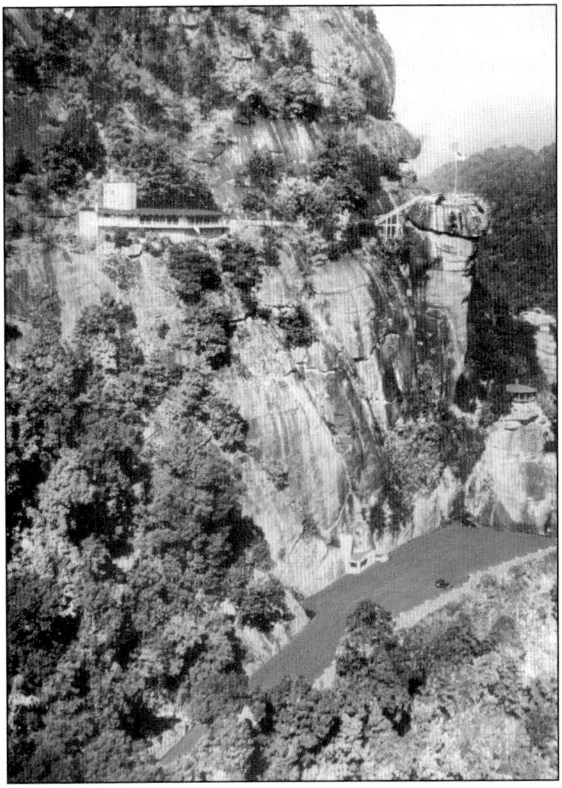

This aerial view of Chimney Rock was captured just after the elevator's completion in 1948. (Photograph by Norman Greig; courtesy of the Greig family.)

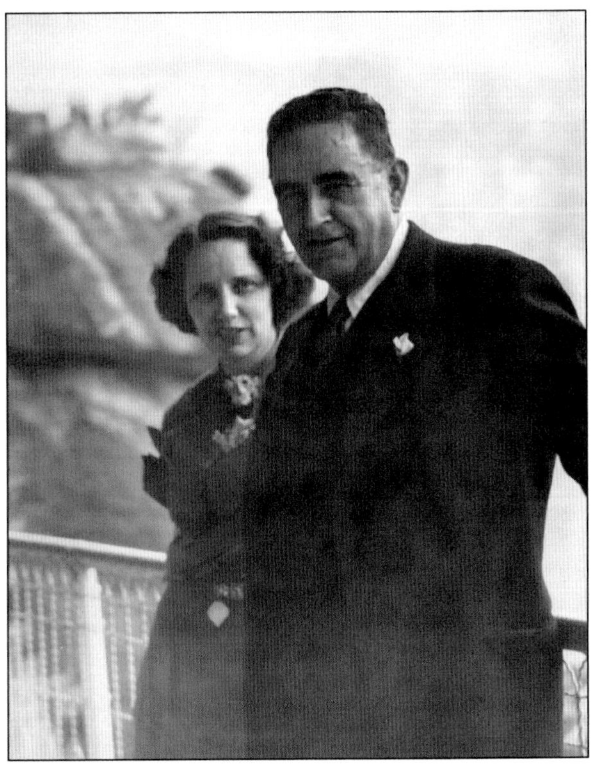

Soon after the elevator was completed, North Carolina governor Kerr Scott visited Chimney Rock Park. Kerr is seen here with Elizabeth Greig. (Courtesy of the Morse family.)

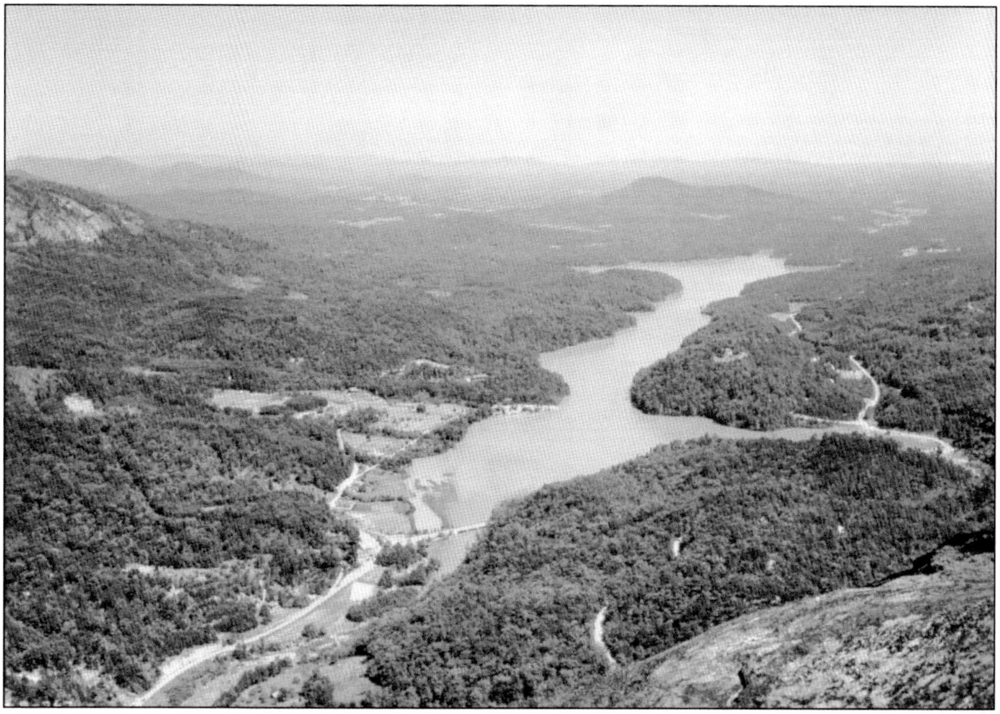

The c. 1930 photograph above shows a sandbar starting to form just past the Rocky Broad River bridge. The view below of Lake Lure from Chimney Rock Mountain shows how sediment from the Rocky Broad River filled in more than a dozen acres that use to be part of the lake. The Town of Lake Lure has dredged more than a half million cubic yards of silt from the lake to date. (Both, courtesy of the Morse family.)

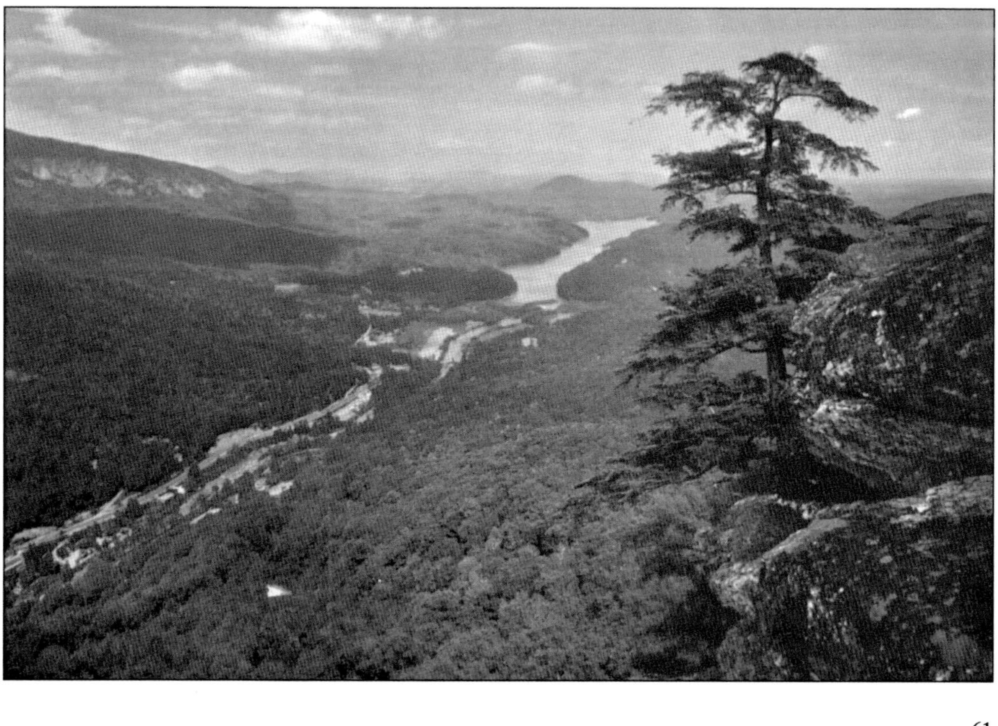

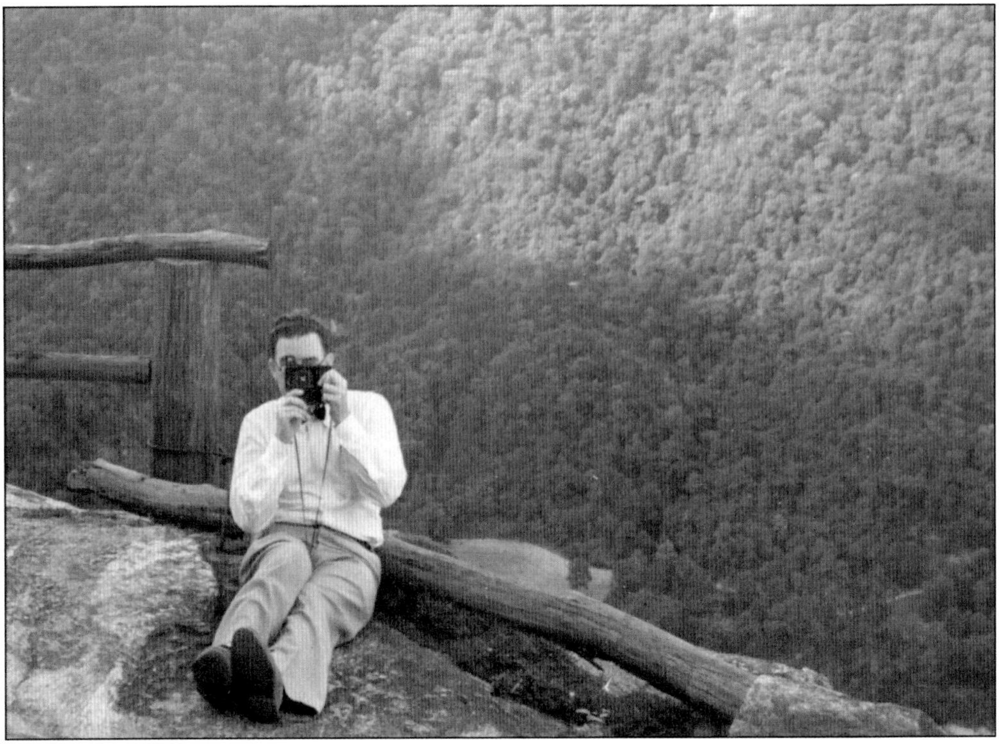

The best promoter of Lake Lure and Chimney Rock was, of course, Dr. Lucius Morse. When he retired, Norman Greig took over the management of Chimney Rock Park. He was the manager from 1933 to 1970. Greig loved to promote the park to the rest of the world. Whenever there was a venue that allowed any sort of promotion, Grieg was there. He was also a well-known photographer. (Courtesy of the Greig family.)

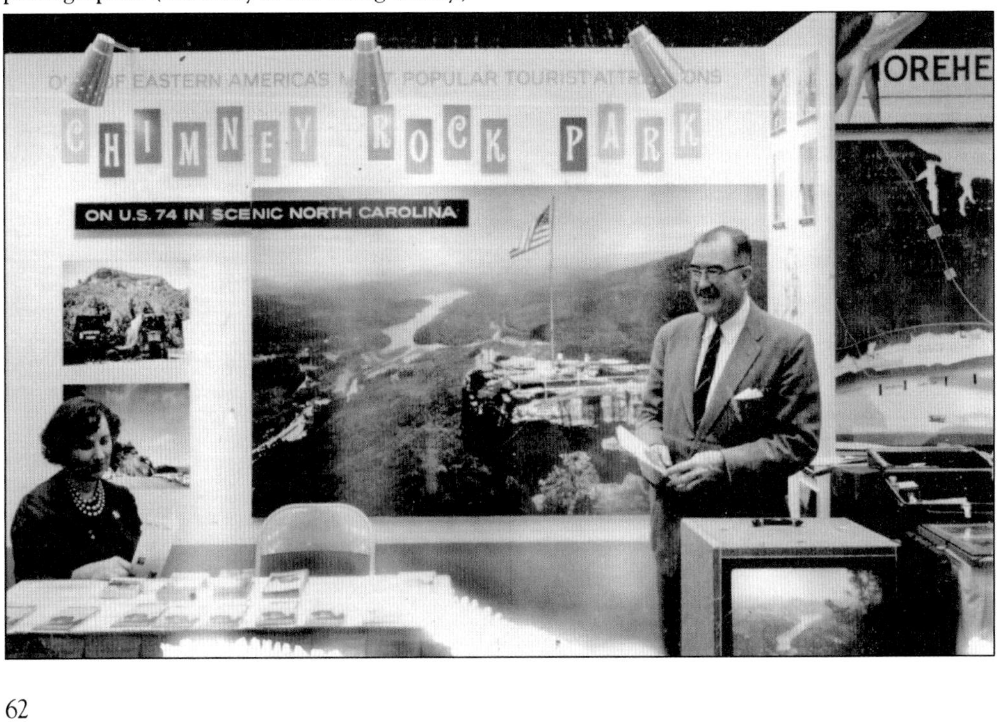

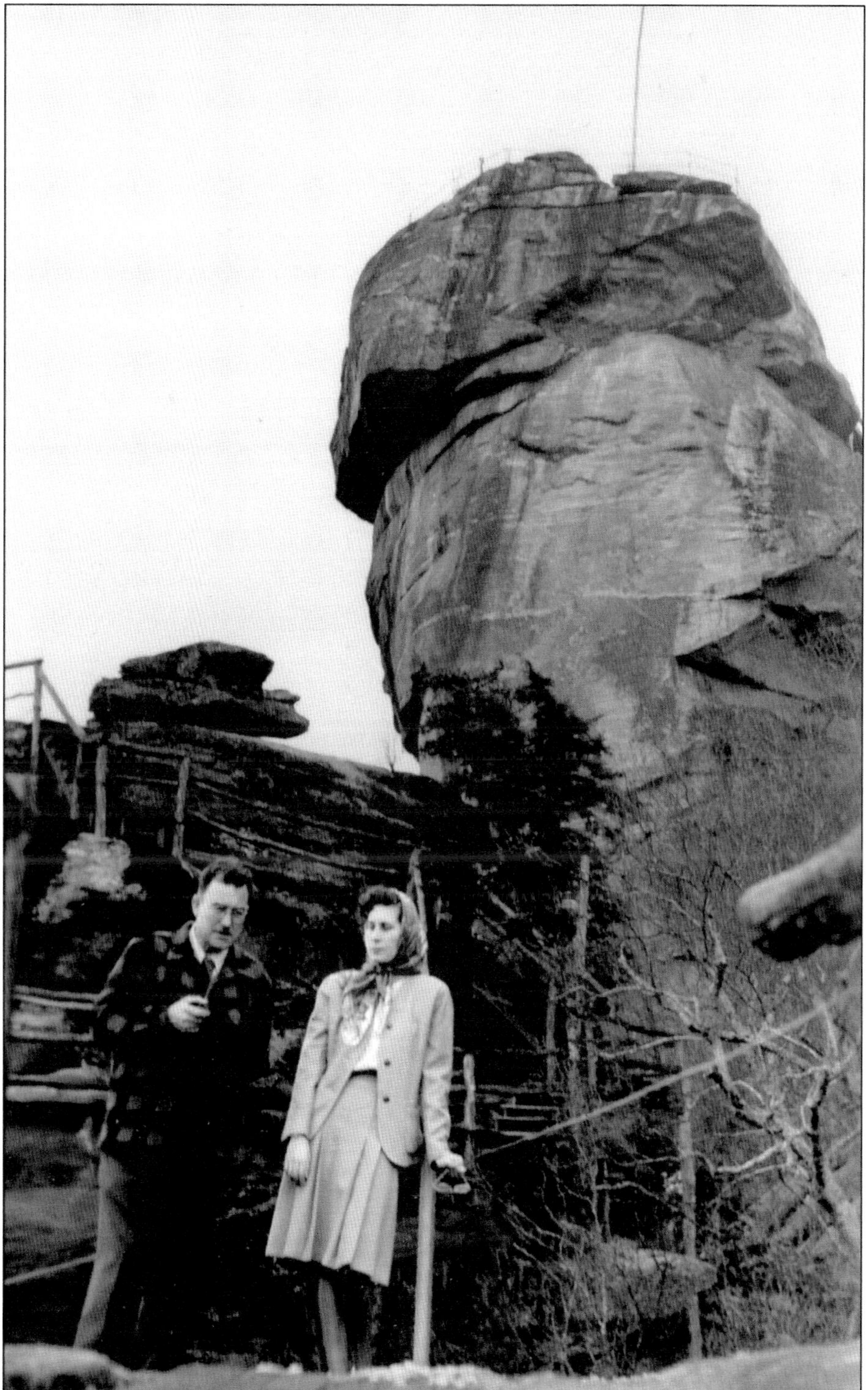

Norman and Elizabeth Greig are pictured below Chimney Rock. Elizabeth was Lucius Morse's daughter. (Photograph by Norman Greig; courtesy of the Greig family.)

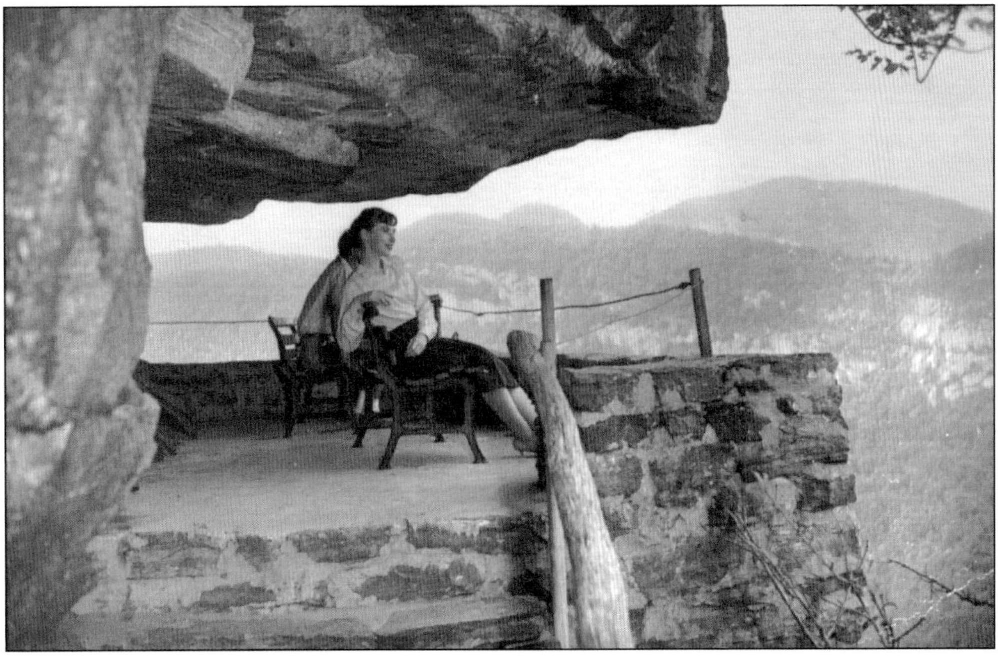

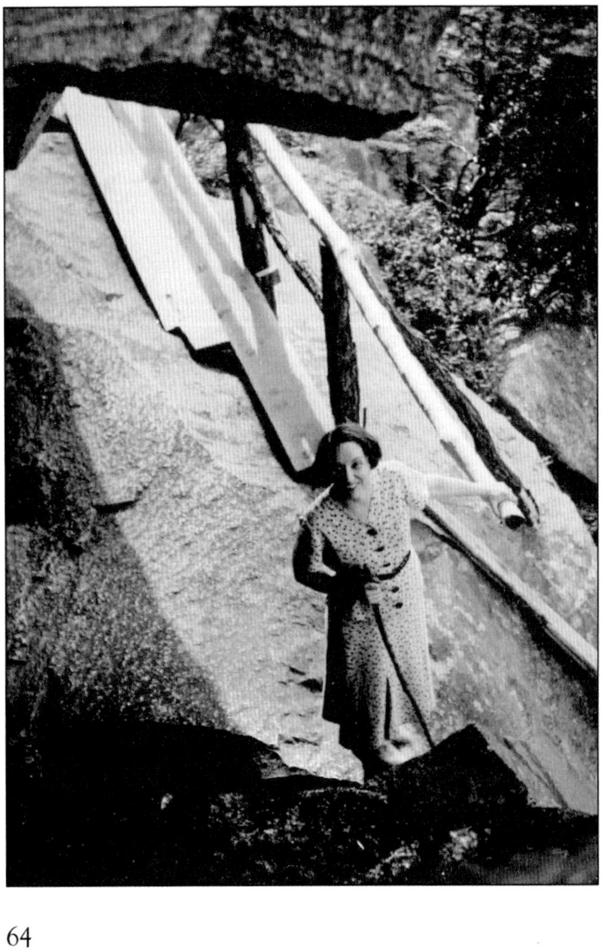

In the photograph above, Elizabeth Greig enjoys the view from the Opera Box. At left, she strolls on the newly reconstructed trails from the parking lot to Chimney Rock. (Both, photograph by Norman Greig; courtesy of the Greig family.)

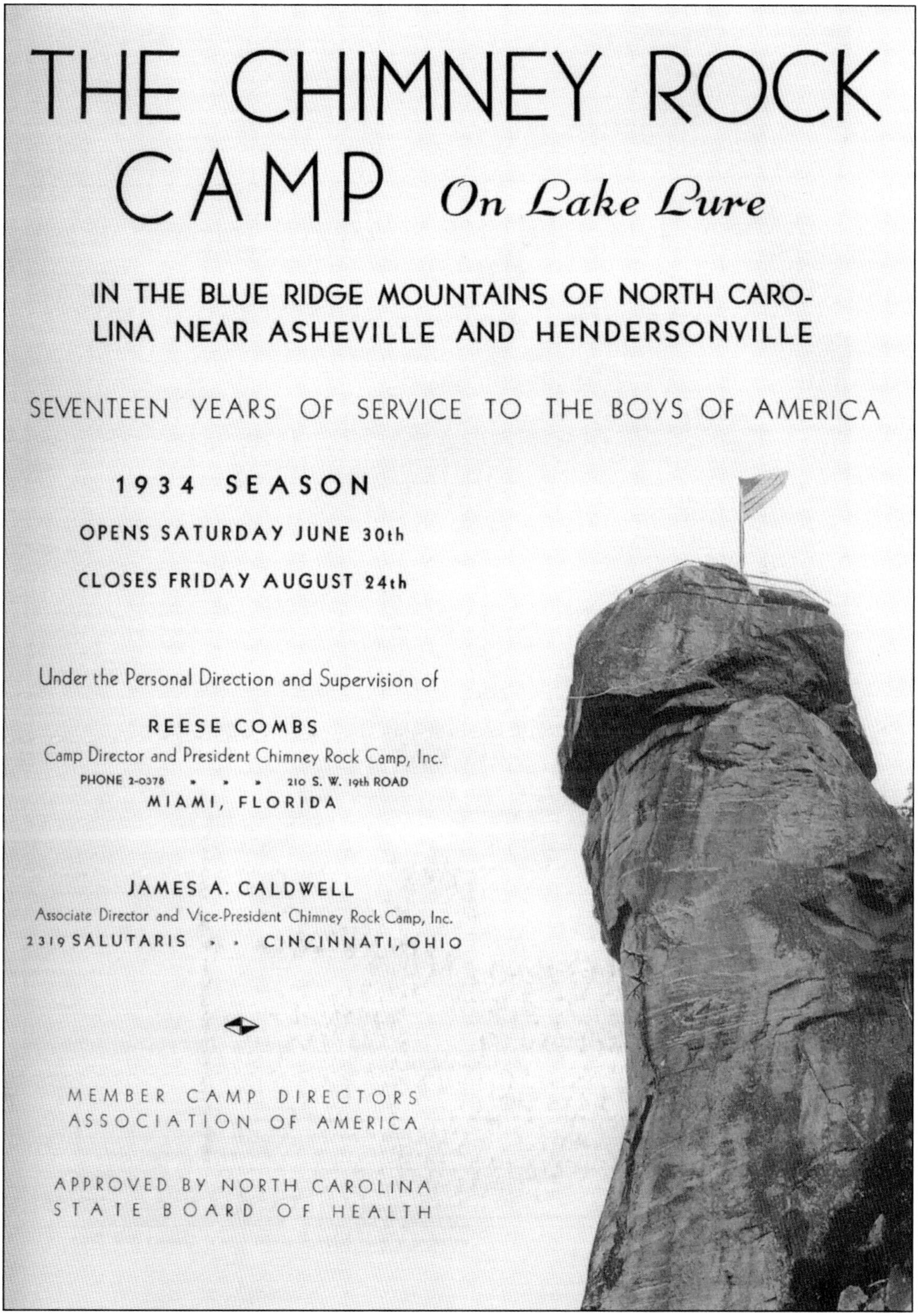

There have been many camps in what is now the town of Lake Lure. The first was Camp Chimney Rock for Boys (later know as Camp Chimney Rock for Boys and Girls). It was organized by Reese Combs of Florida in 1917. (Author's collection.)

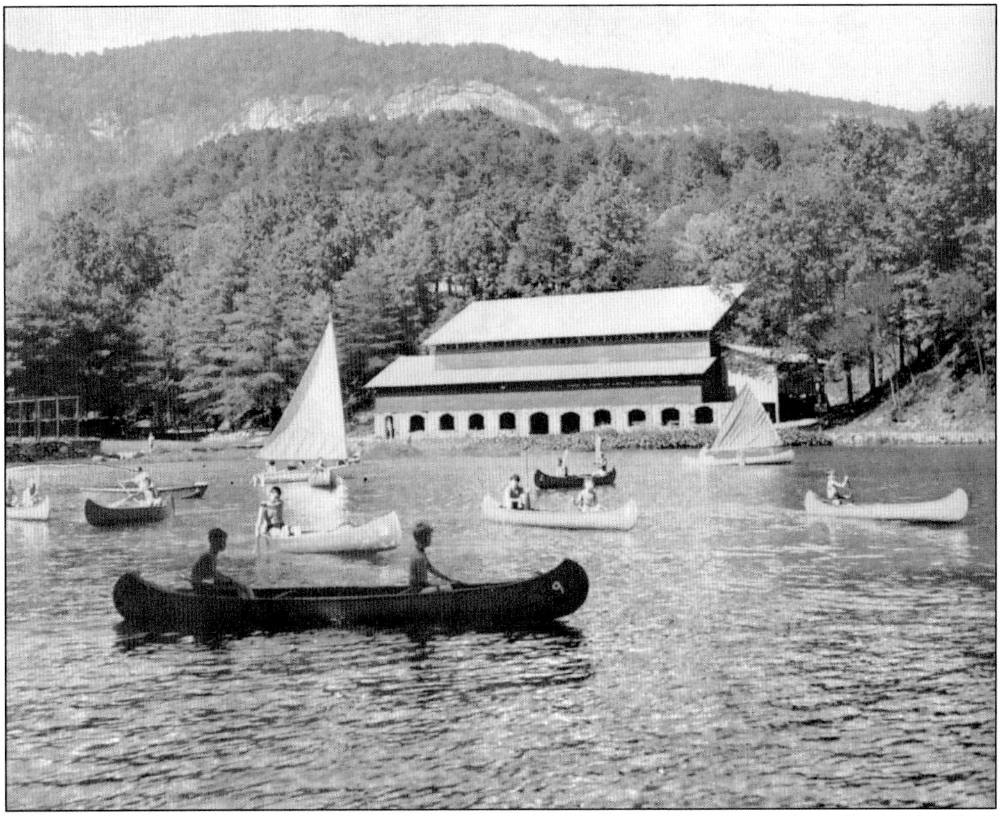

Camp Chimney Rock for Boys was one of the premier camps in North Carolina. In 1934, it had 44 employees (not including junior counselors). The camp was later famous as the film location for the movie *Dirty Dancing*. (Author's collection.)

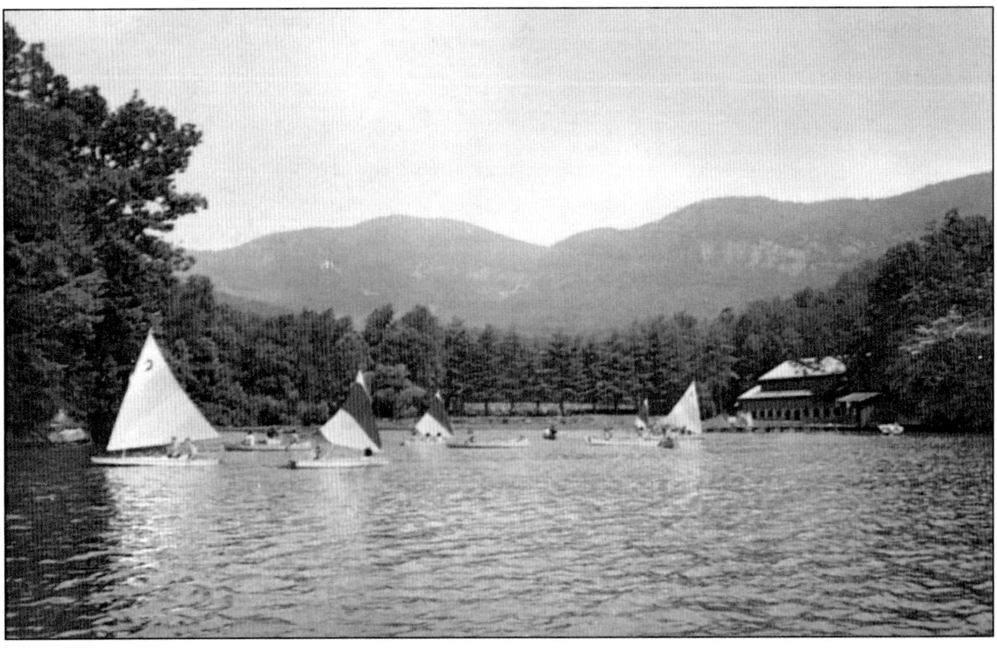

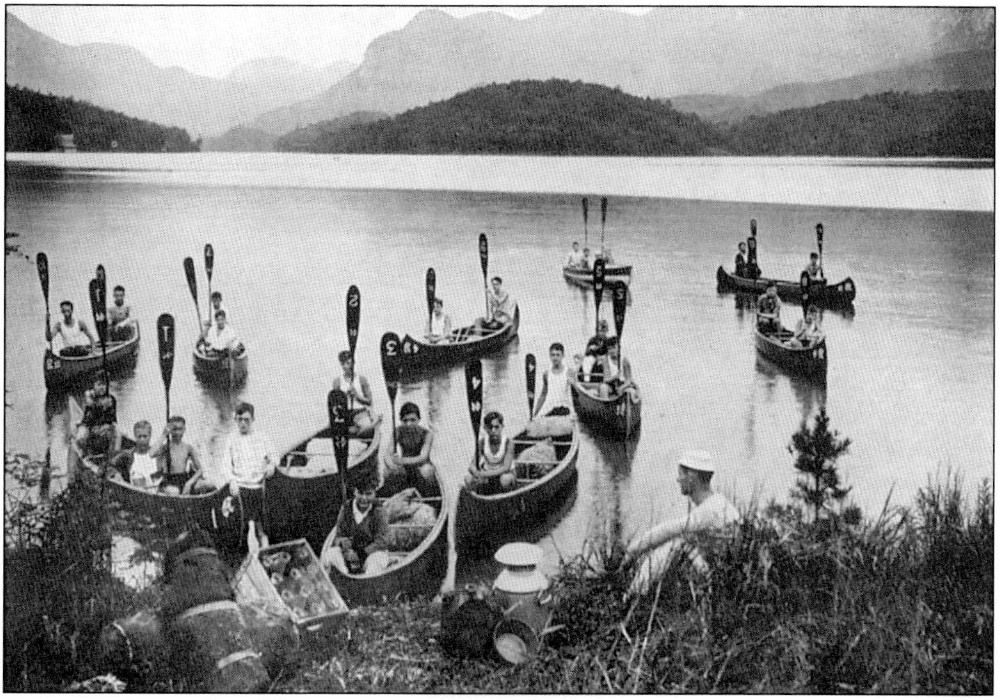

Water sports were plentiful at Camp Chimney Rock for Boys. All the camp structures have since been removed, and the area is now a residential development known as Firefly Cove. (Both, author's collection.)

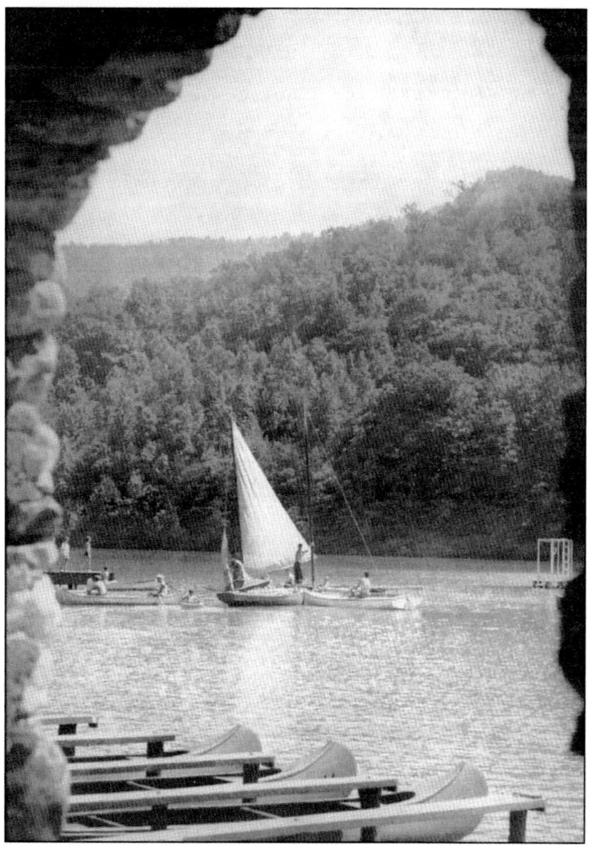

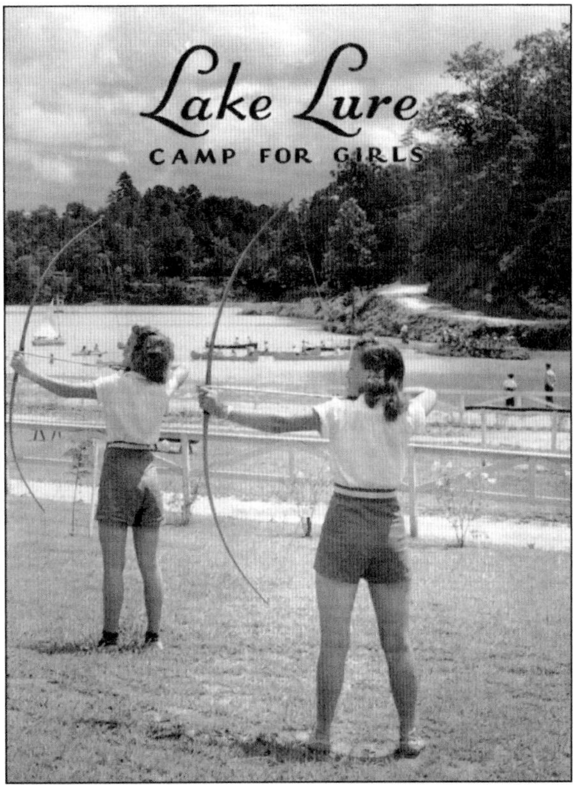

The Lake Lure Camp for Girls was later a Girl Scout camp called Camp Occoneechee. It was located behind the current Ingles Grocery Store off NC Highway 9. (Author's collection.)

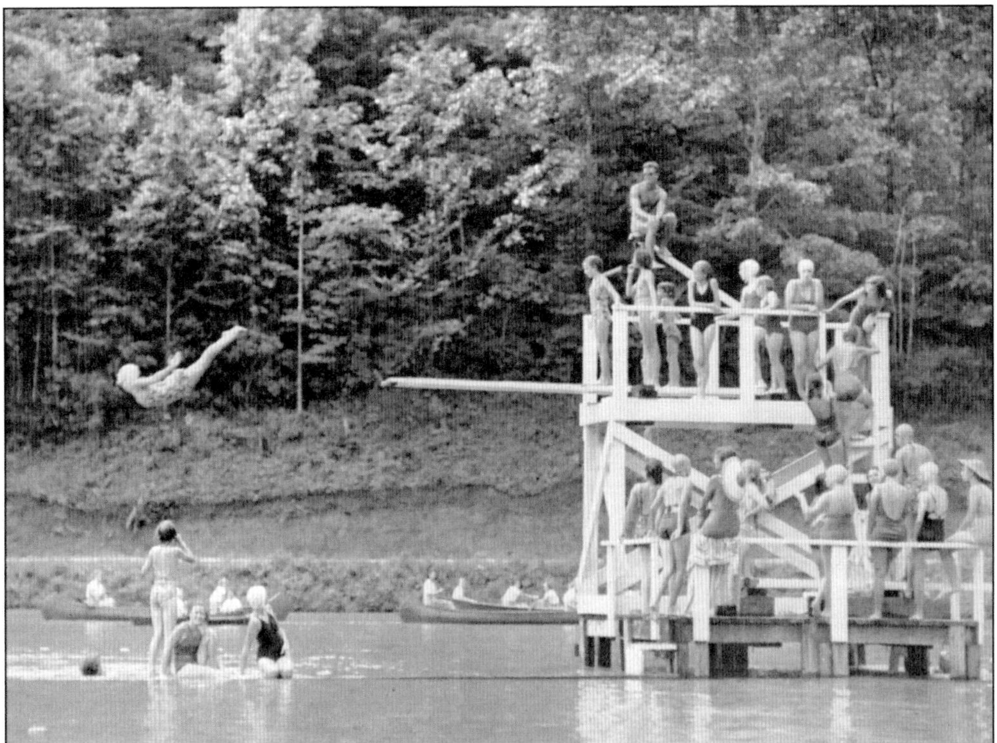

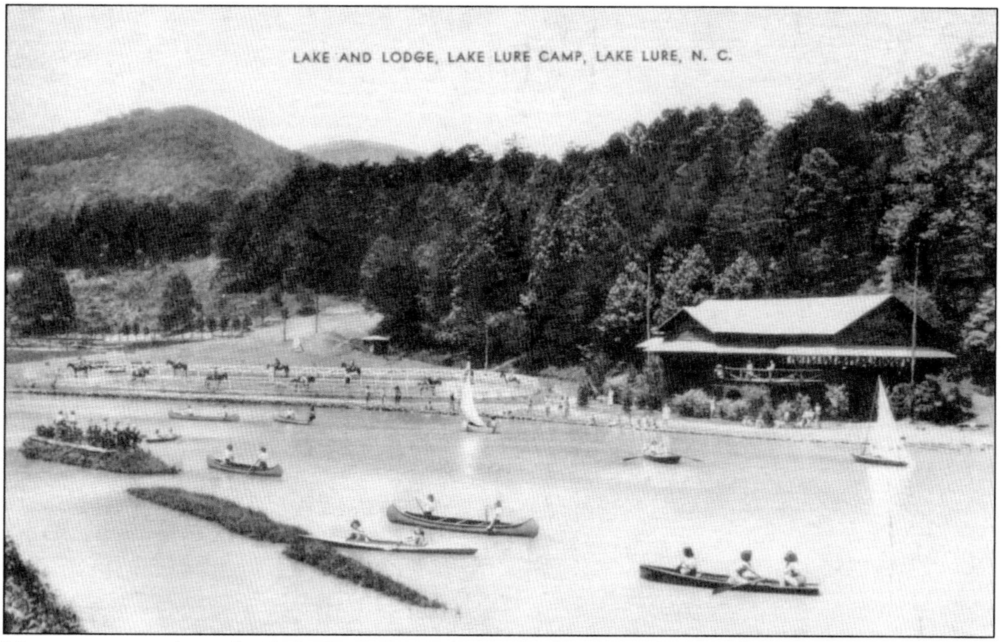

Here are scenes from the Lake Lure Camp for Girls. (Both, author's collection.)

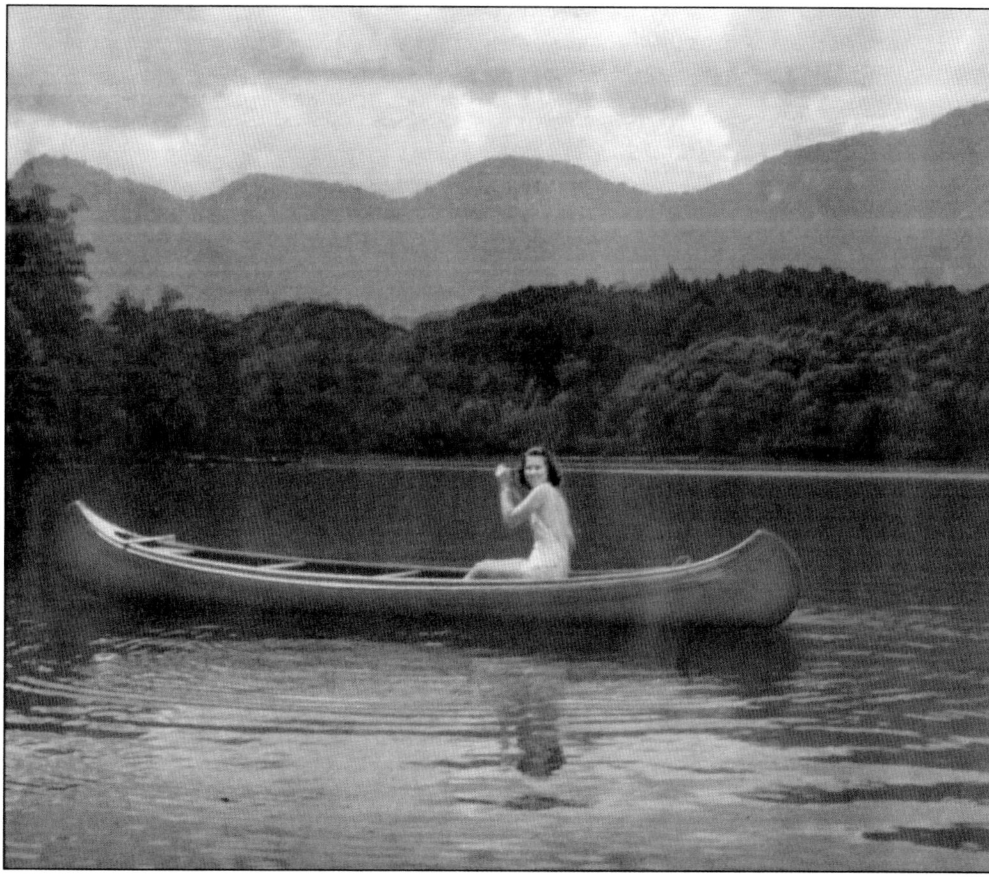

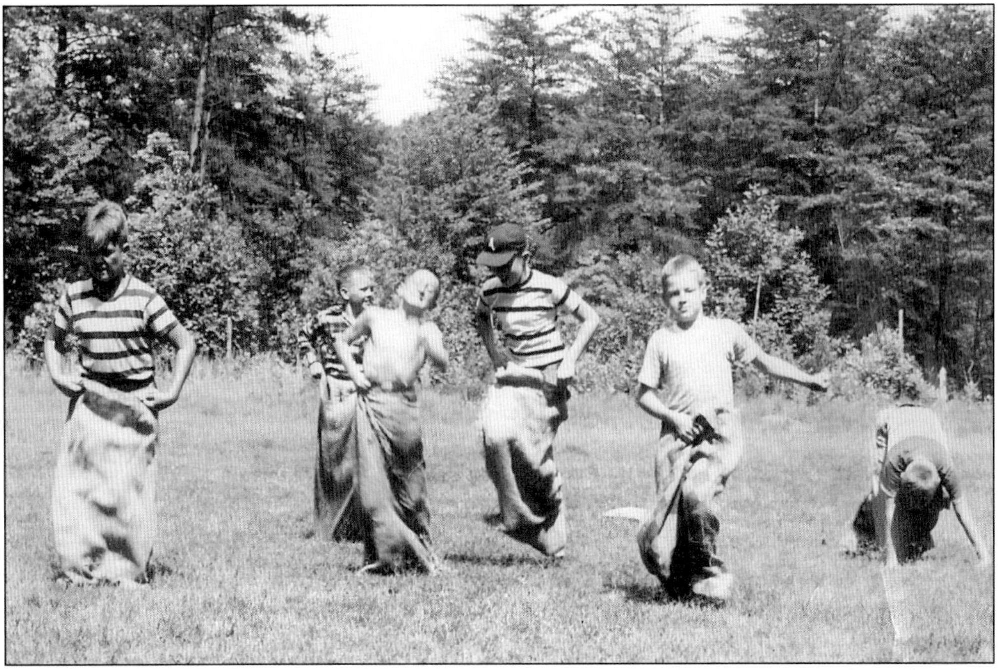

Upon returning from the World War II in Europe, Col. Alfred Garr presented an idea for a summer camp to the members of Garr Memorial Church in Charlotte, North Carolina. The church supported the idea, and Colonel Garr purchased 33 acres on Lake Lure for $6,500. In 1948, Camp Lurecrest opened with 75 boys. The following year, the program was expanded to include both boys and girls. Over the next several decades, the camp grew to encompass more than 60 acres. (Both, courtesy of Camp Lurecrest.)

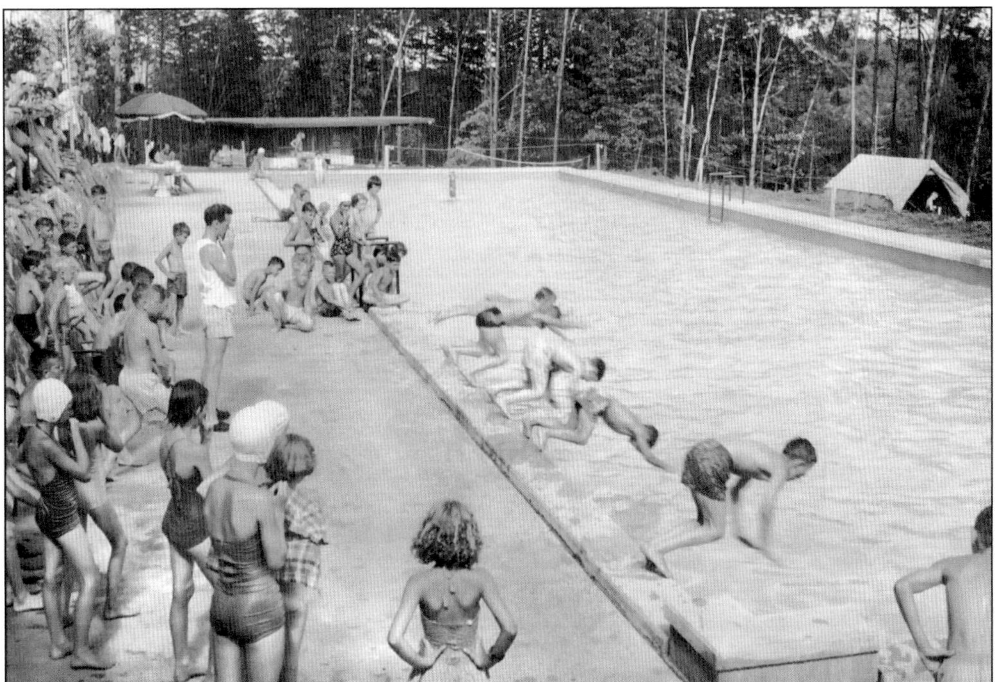

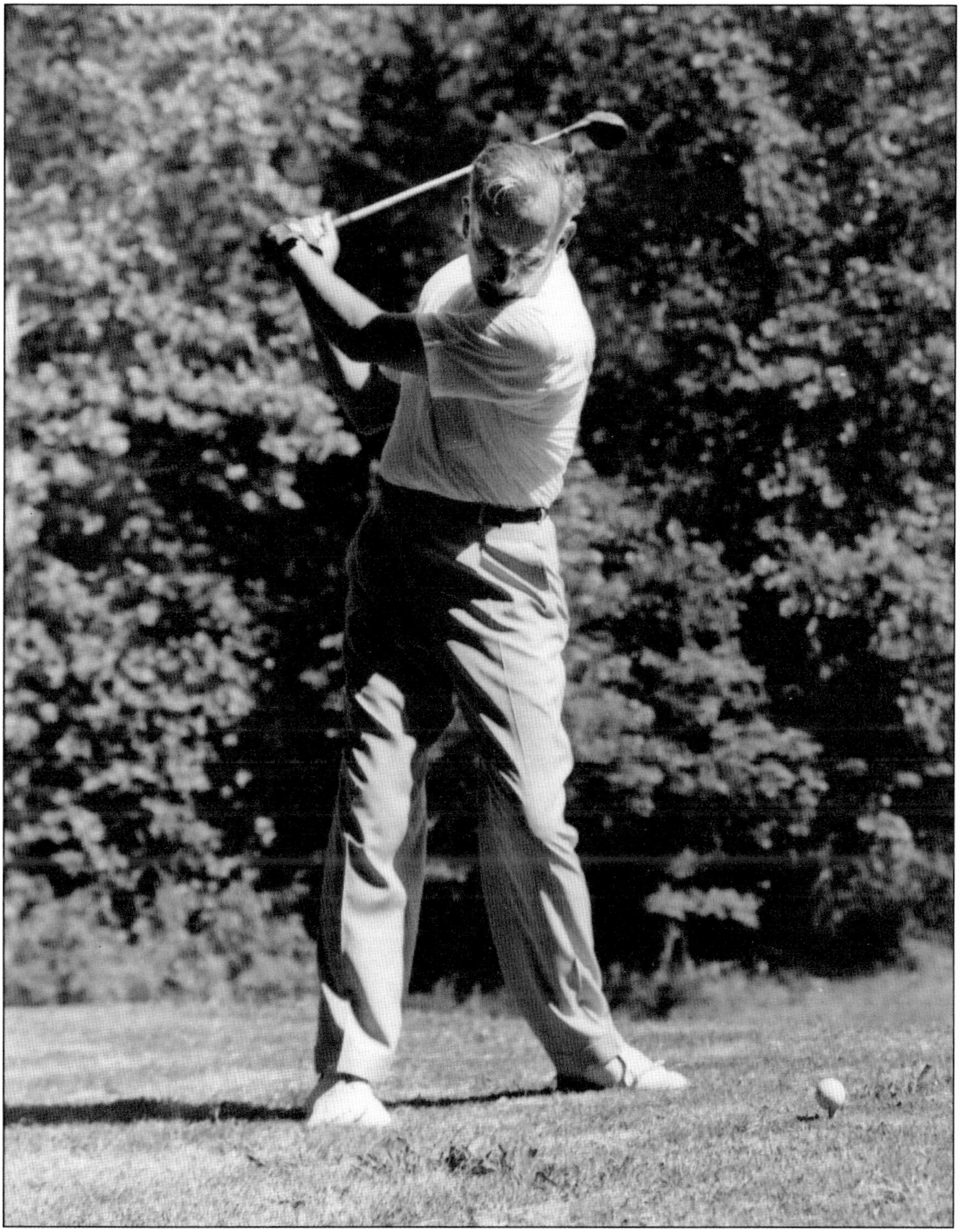

The Lake Lure Municipal Golf Course may have been designed by renowned early golf course designer Donald Ross. It has been documented that the course was designed by the firm of Van Kliek & Stiles of Boston, which also supervised the construction. Wayne Stiles was a contemporary of Donald Ross and had close relationship with Walter Hagen. The golf course was constructed around 1930. (Photograph by Norman Greig; courtesy of the Greig family.)

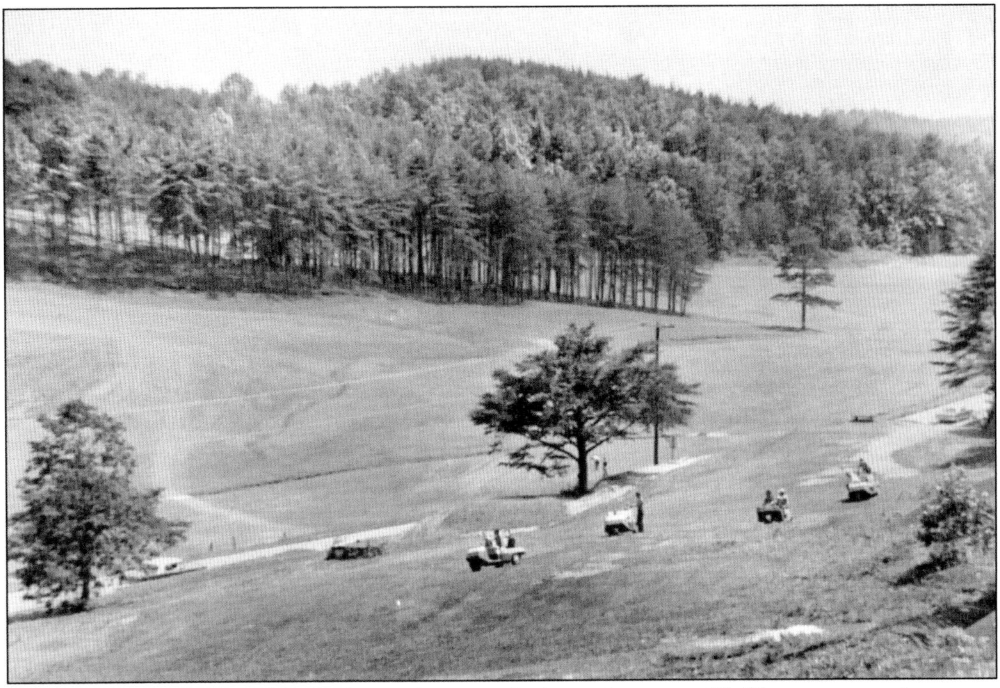

The Lake Lure Municipal Golf Course has nine holes and is a par 35. The course underwent a major renovation during early 2010 to return it to its original design and playing condition. The photograph below shows Walter Hagen (left) looking over the construction of the golf course with an unidentified man. (Above, photograph by Norman Greig, courtesy of Greig family; below, courtesy of the Morse family.)

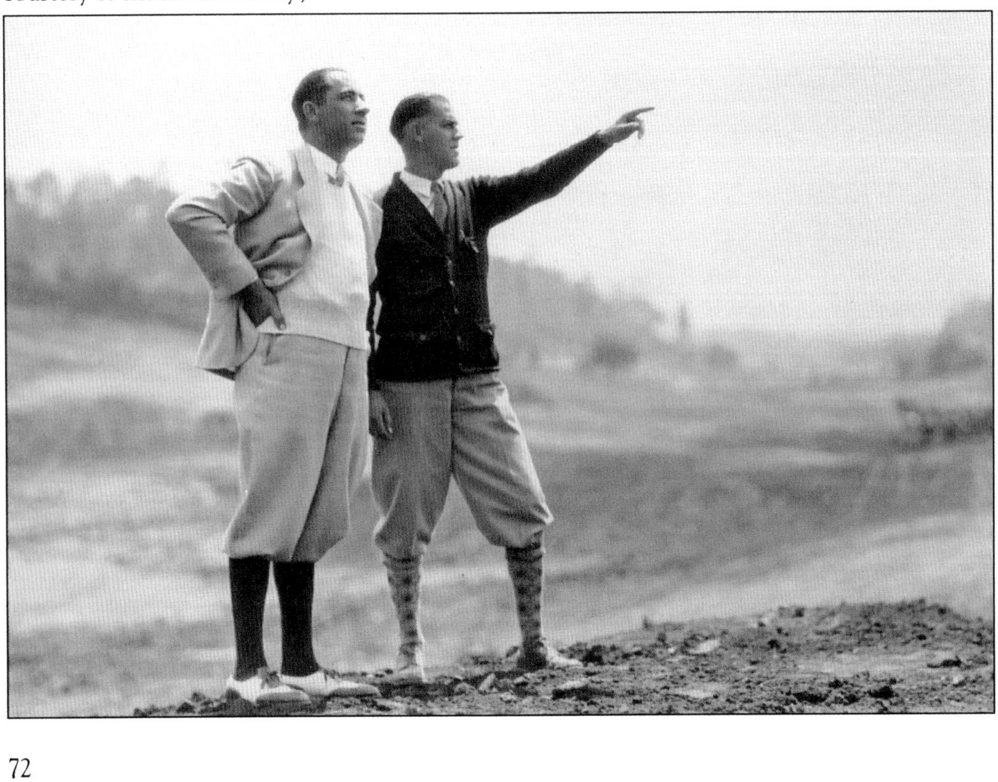

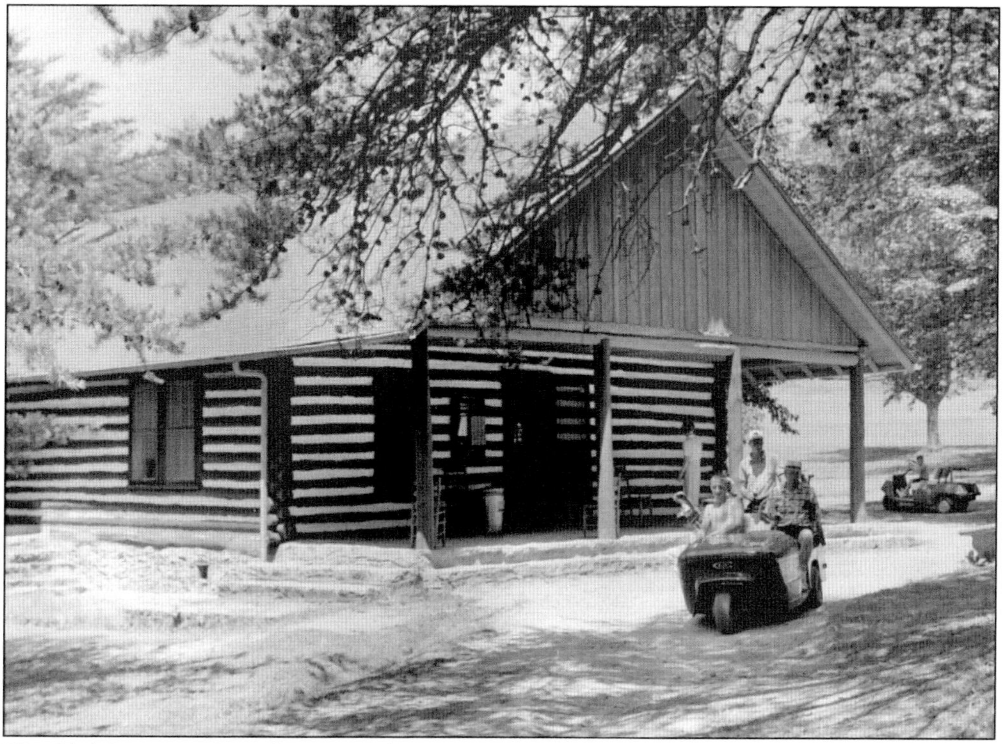

The Club House at the Lake Lure Golf Course was built by Civilian Conservation Corps (CCC) workers during the Great Depression. It is still in use today and houses a pro shop and snack bar The challenging Lake Lure Golf Course is still a beautiful mountain course. (Above, photograph by Norman Greig, courtesy of Greig family; below, author's collection.)

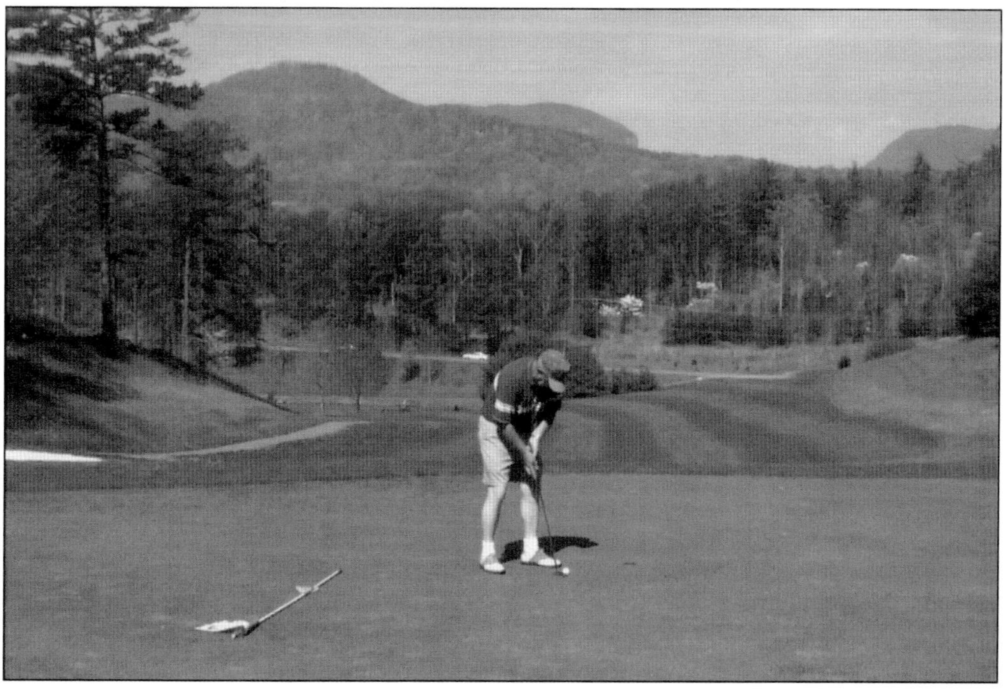

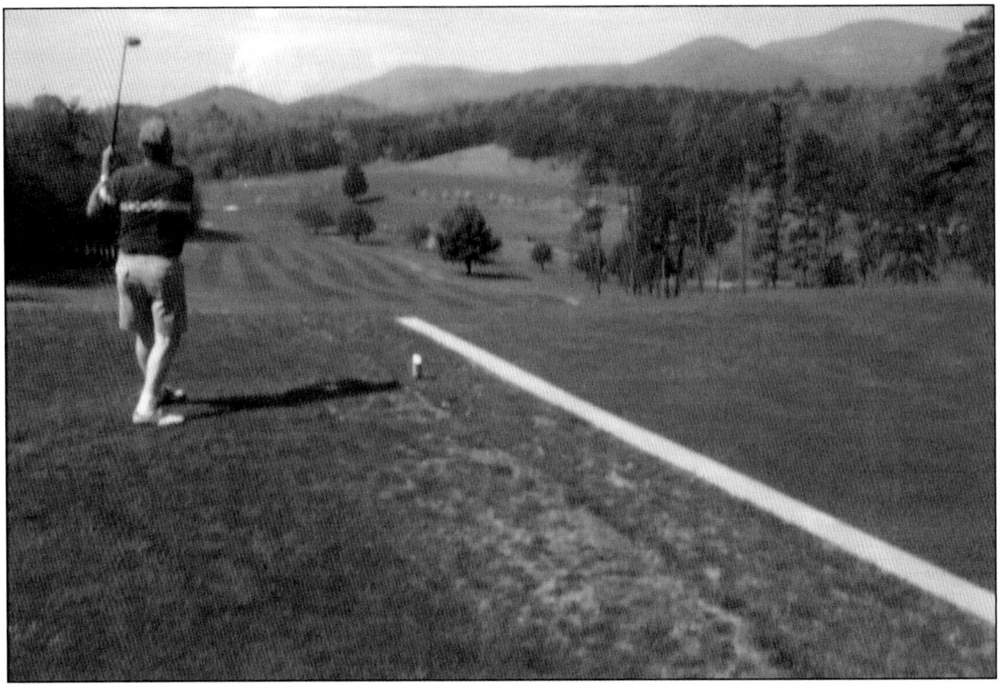

The mountain scenery surrounding the Lake Lure Golf Course is equaled by none. One may walk the course, but it is not for the faint of heart. (Author's collection.)

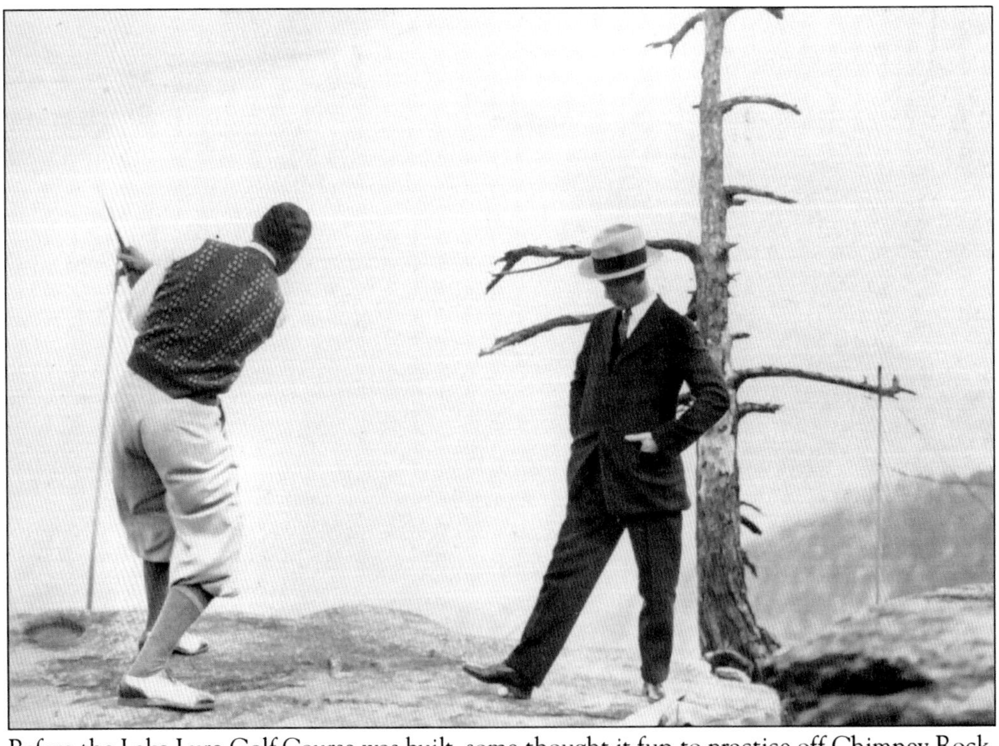

Before the Lake Lure Golf Course was built, some thought it fun to practice off Chimney Rock. (Courtesy of the Morse family.)

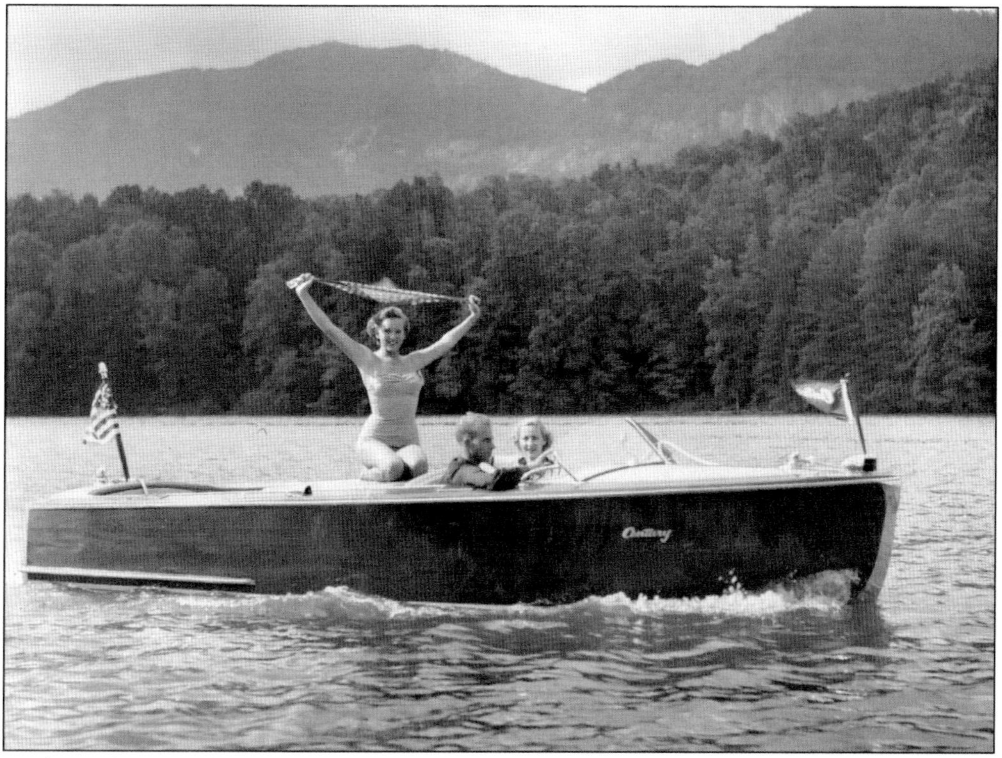

In the early years, beautiful wooden-hulled boats were the norm. (Both, courtesy Town of Lake Lure.)

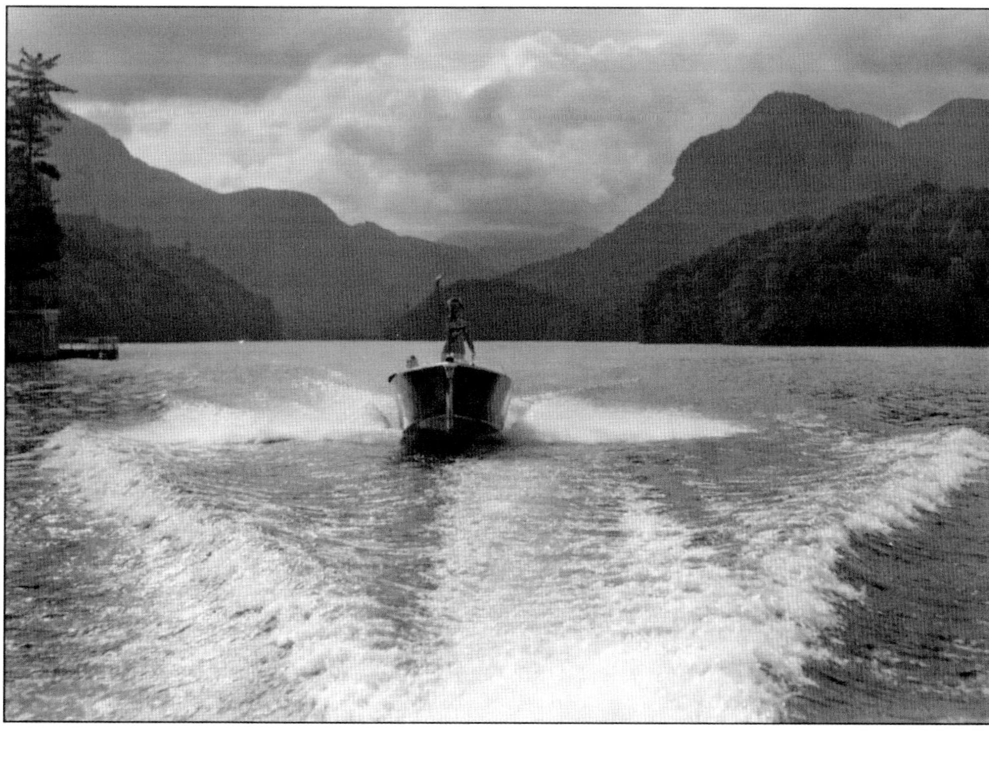

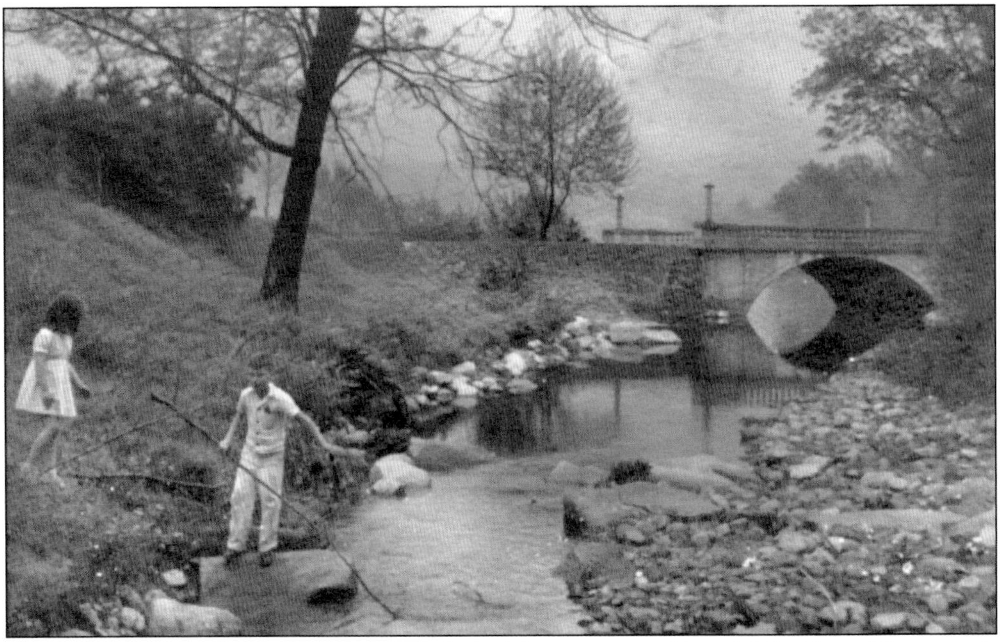

Children play in Pool Creek near the Lake Lure Administration (Arcade) Building. (Photograph by Norman Greig; courtesy of the Greig family.)

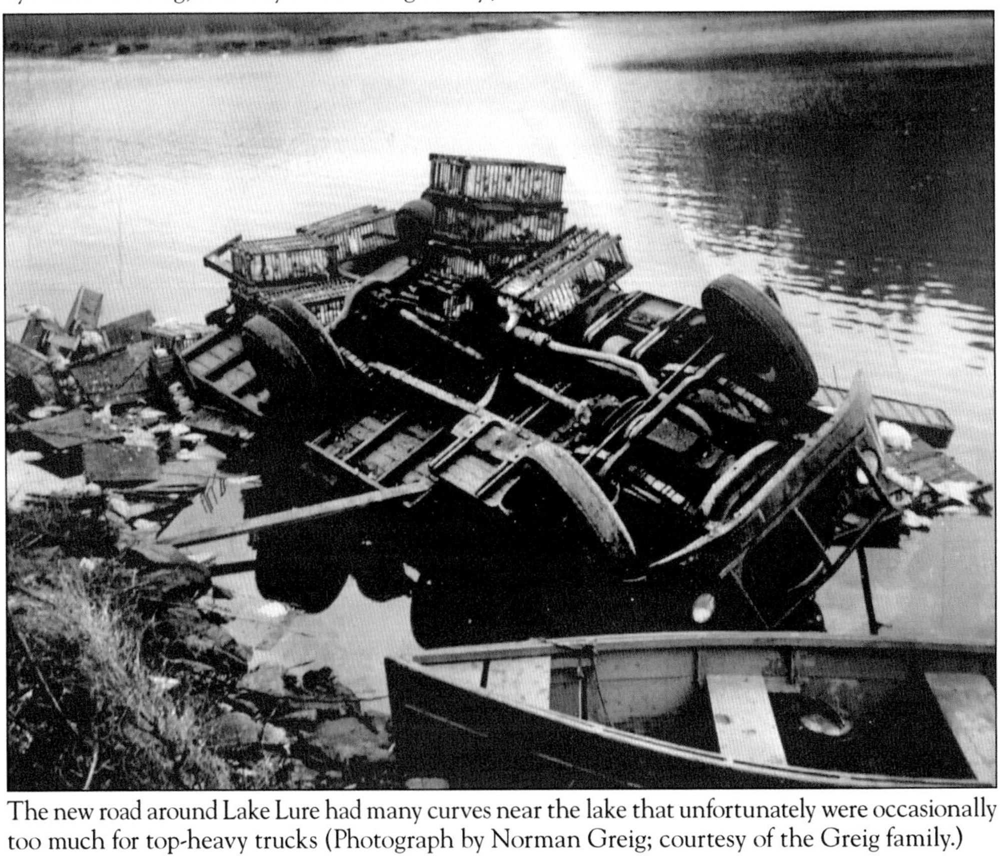

The new road around Lake Lure had many curves near the lake that unfortunately were occasionally too much for top-heavy trucks (Photograph by Norman Greig; courtesy of the Greig family.)

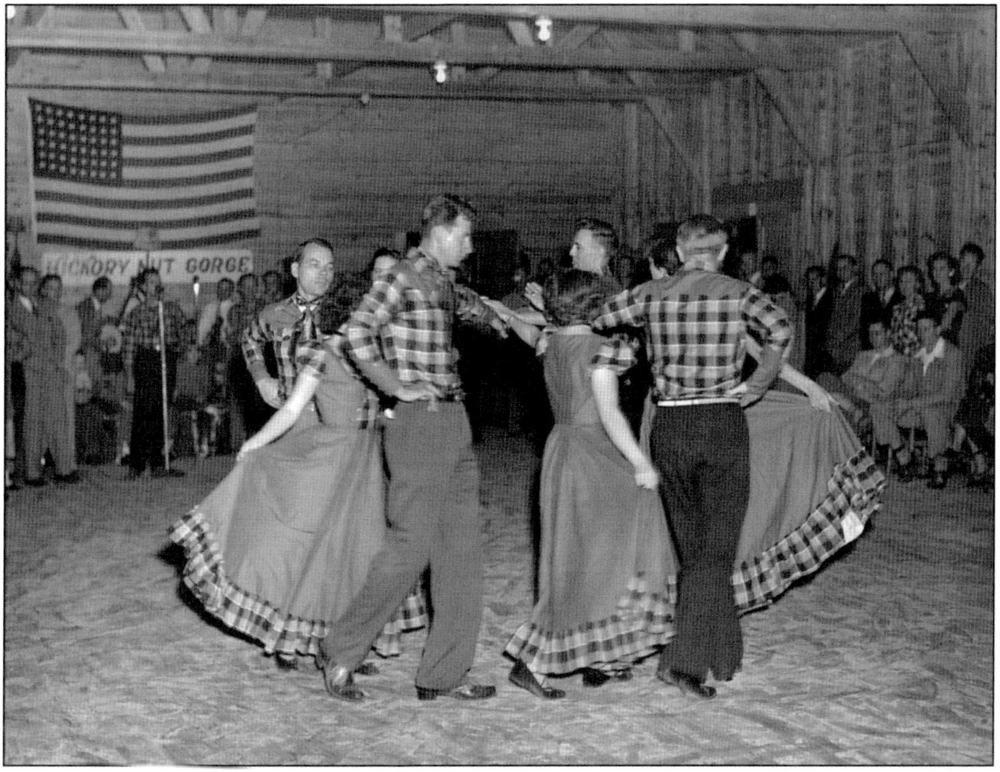

The Red Barn was constructed behind the Lake Lure Inn. Soon after World War II, the Hickory Nut Gorge Civic Club hosted local events with live music, an opportunity for locals and tourists to dance. The Red Barn has been renovated and is now called the Roosevelt Hall of the Lake Lure Inn. (Both, photograph by Norman Greig; courtesy of the Greig family.)

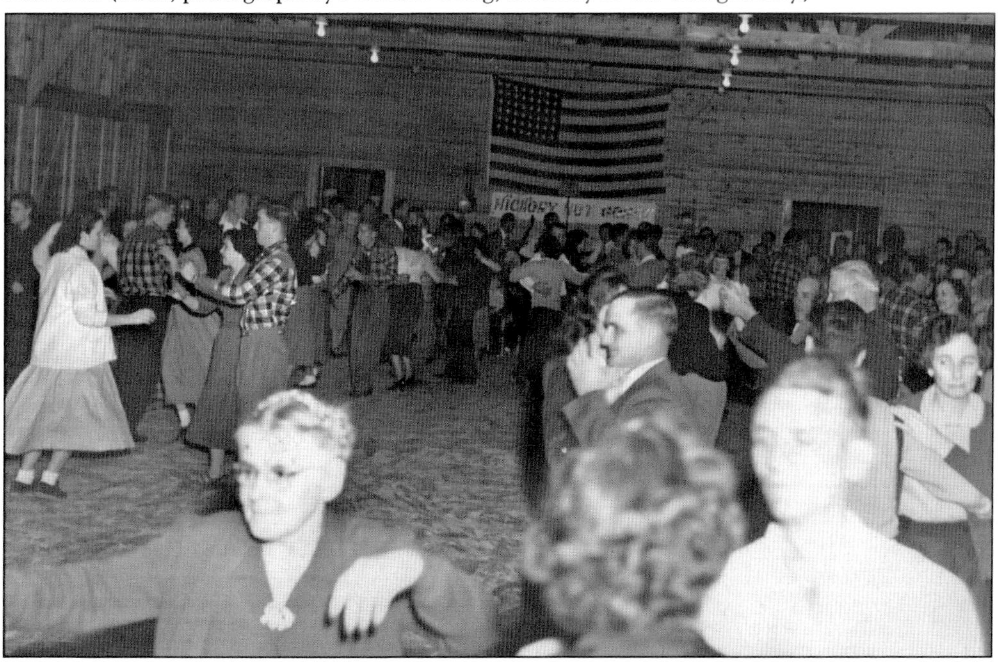

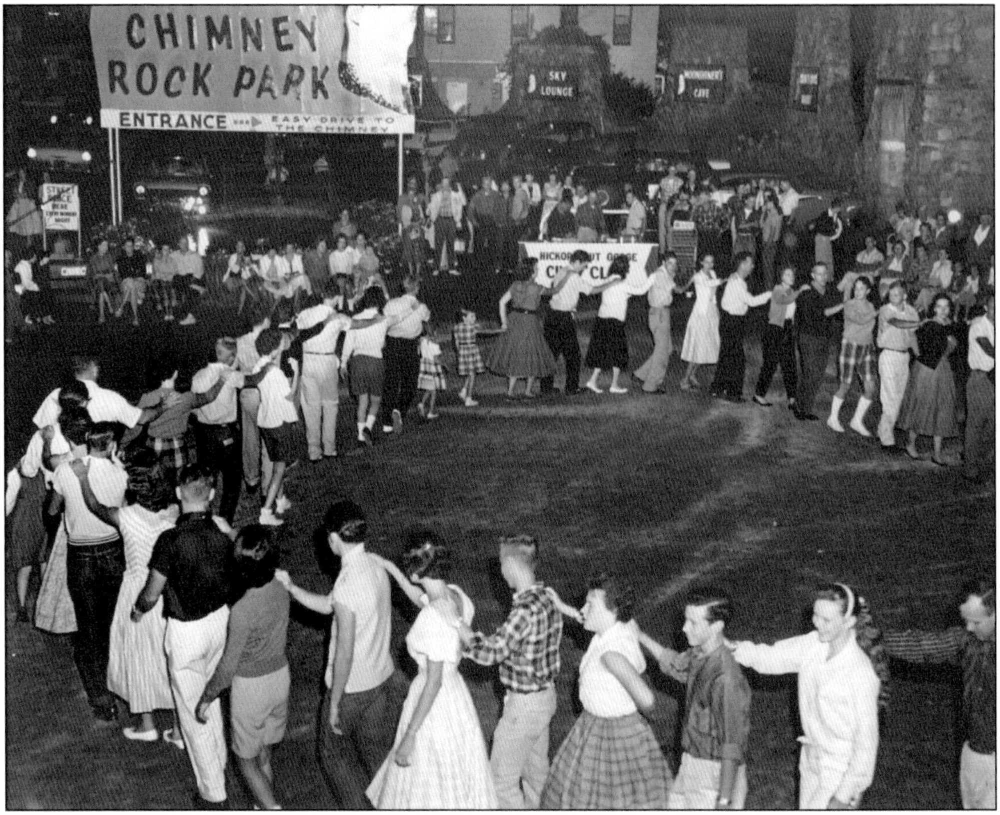

Hickory Nut Gorge Civic Club street dances were also held for a brief period at the entrance to Chimney Rock Park. The club, later known as the Lake Lure Community Club, sponsored Monday night dances from 1948 to the 1980s. (Courtesy of the Morse family.)

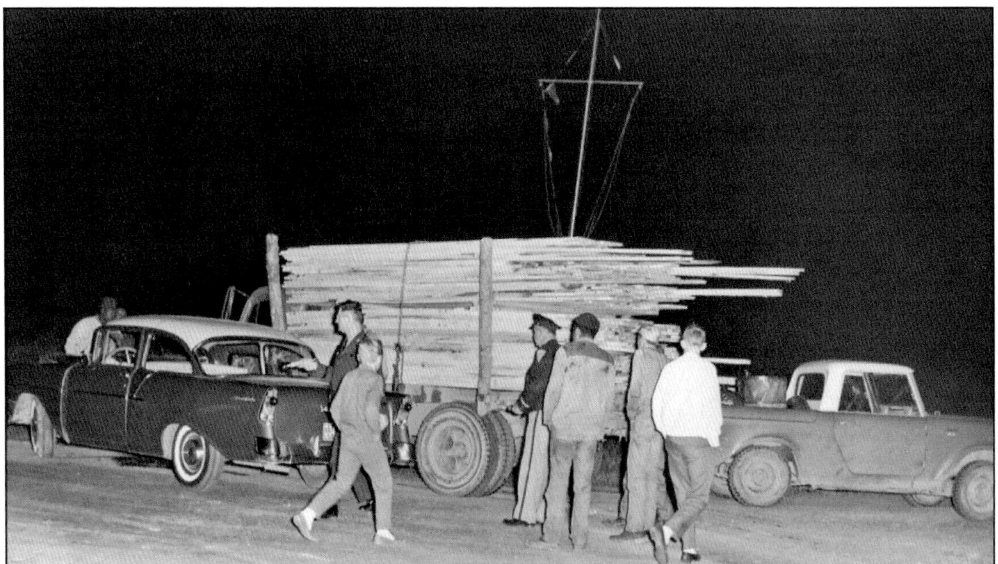

A 1955 Chevrolet was accidently hit by a loaded logging truck. Chief Walter Lee Pye is at the scene. (Photograph by Norman Greig; courtesy of the Greig family.)

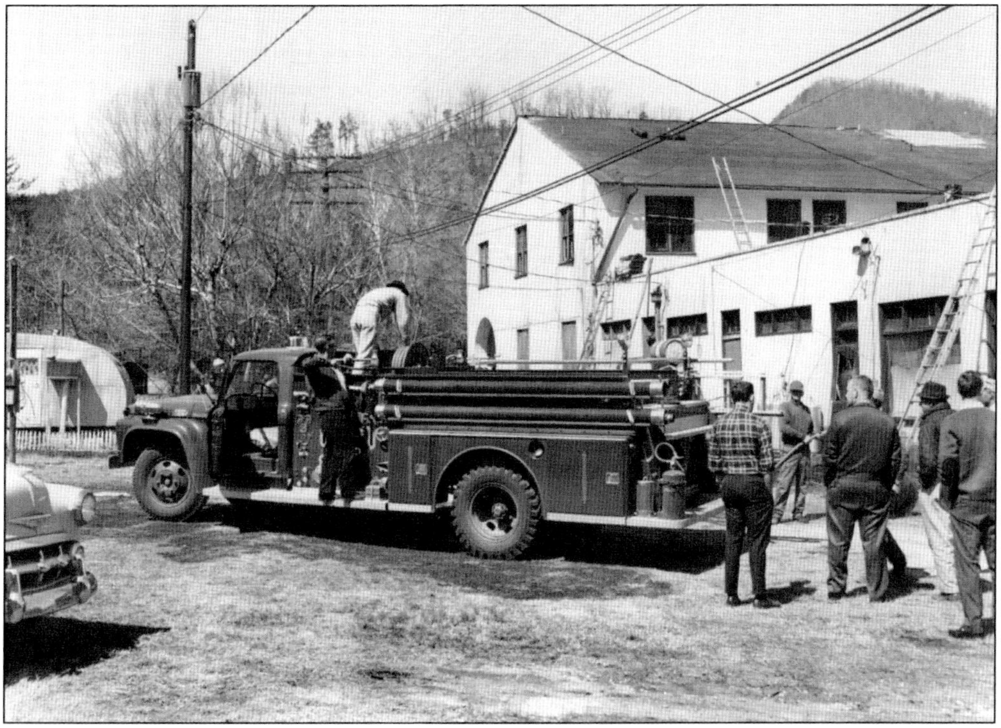

This fire truck is behind the Lake Lure Arcade Building. Note the camper trailer with a picket fence next to the power pole. (Photograph by Norman Greig; courtesy of the Greig family.)

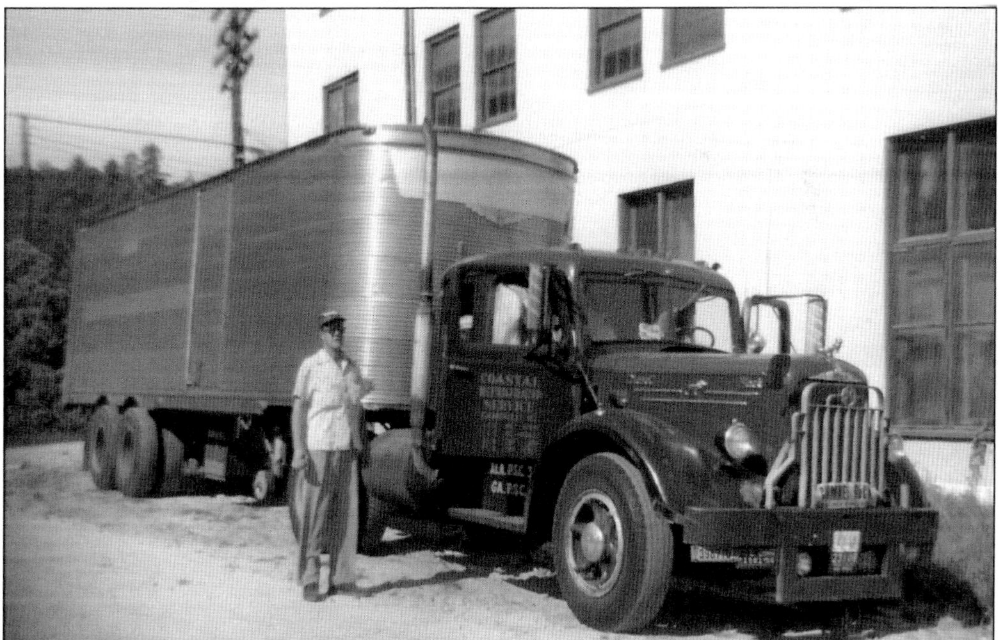

Francis "Proc" Proctor stands alongside his prized Mack truck behind the Lake Lure Arcade Building. Believe it or not, before Interstate Highways 26 and 40 were completed, US Highway 74 was the primary truck route between Charlotte and Asheville. (Author's collection.)

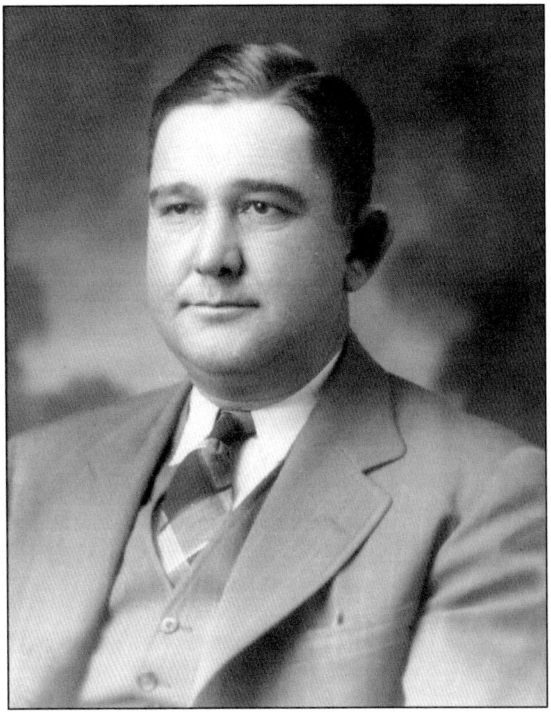

Jim Washburn was a lifelong resident of Rutherford County. In 1946, he and his wife, Alice (nicknamed "Tootsie"), bought the old Logan House. They soon built more cabins and created Pine Gables Cabins. (Author's collection.)

Jim and Tootsie Washburn lounge on the porch at the Old Logan House. Judge Logan was Tootsie's great-grandfather. (Author's collection.)

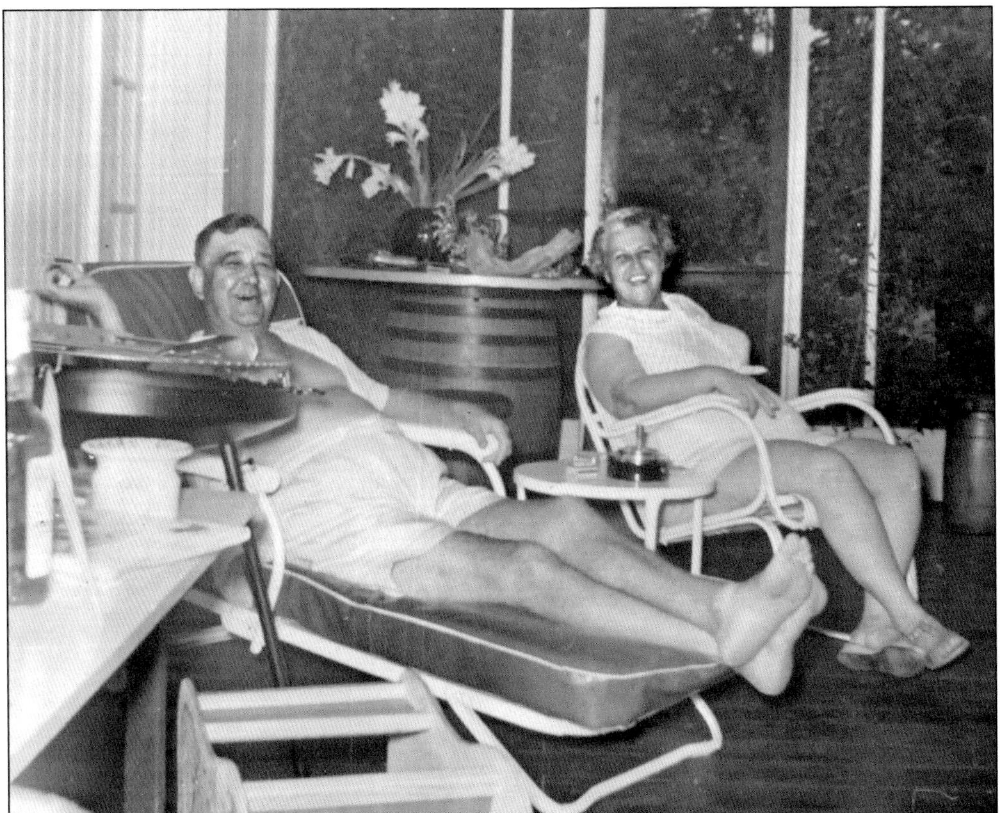

Three

1965 TO PRESENT

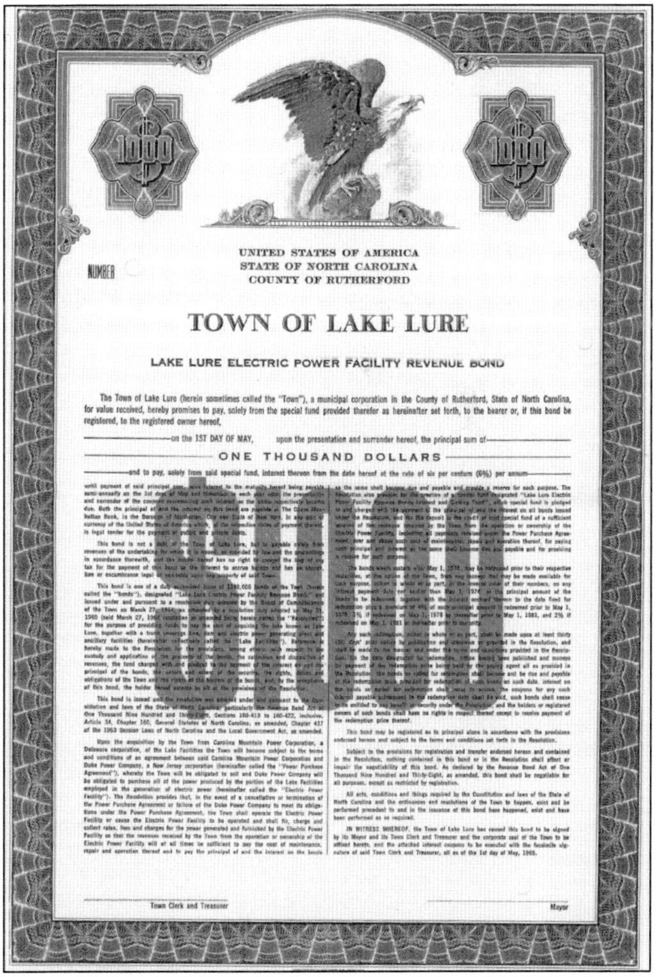

NUMBER

UNITED STATES OF AMERICA
STATE OF NORTH CAROLINA
COUNTY OF RUTHERFORD

TOWN OF LAKE LURE

LAKE LURE ELECTRIC POWER FACILITY REVENUE BOND

The Town of Lake Lure (herein sometimes called the "Town"), a municipal corporation in the County of Rutherford, State of North Carolina, for value received, hereby promises to pay, solely from the special fund provided therefor as hereinafter set forth, to the bearer or, if this bond be registered, to the registered owner hereof,

on the 1ST DAY OF MAY, upon the presentation and surrender hereof, the principal sum of

ONE THOUSAND DOLLARS

and to pay, solely from said special fund, interest thereon from the date hereof at the rate of six per centum (6%) per annum

Town Clerk and Treasurer

Mayor

In 1963, the North Carolina General Assembly authorized the Town of Lake Lure to issue revenue bonds for the purpose of acquiring Lake Lure. The Town of Lake Lure immediately started negotiating with the Carolina Mountains Power Corporation, and the purchase of Lake Lure was finalized on July 26, 1965. (Author's collection.)

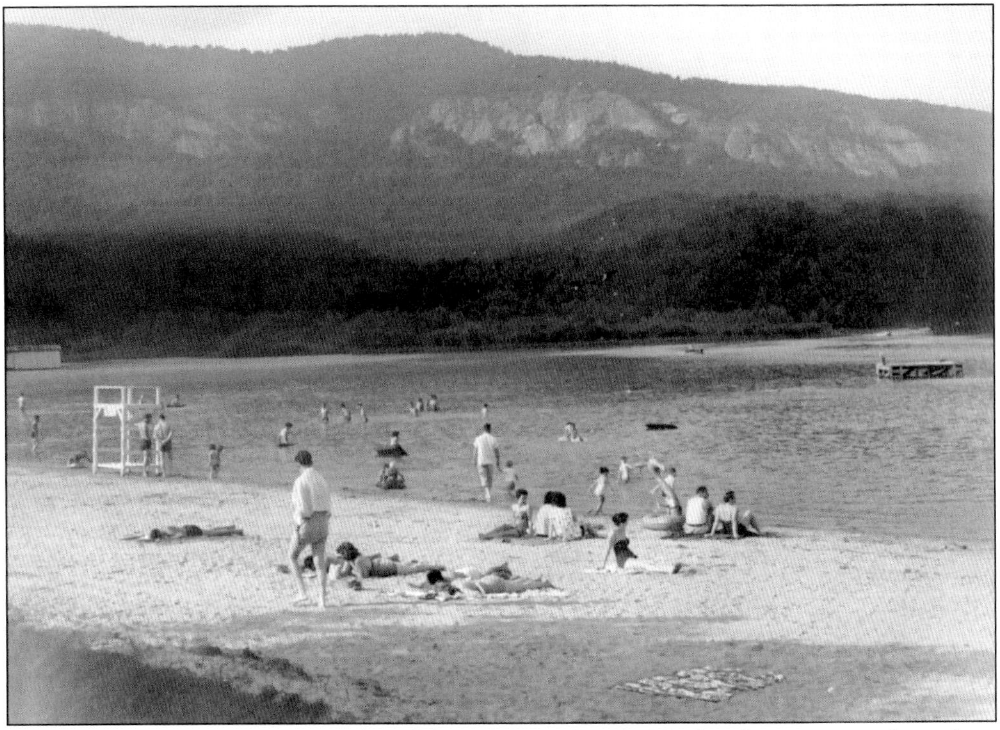

Along with the lake, the town purchased the Lake Lure Beach. The beach area covers about three acres and has over 100 yards of clean, sandy beach. From the very first day, the Lake Lure Beach has been a wonderful place to swim and sunbathe. Except for the town gazebo at Morse Park across the bay, the Lake Lure Beach looks very much the same as it did many decades ago. The photograph above was taken in the 1950s, and the image below was captured in 2000. (Above, photograph by Norman Greig, courtesy of Greig family; below, author's collection.)

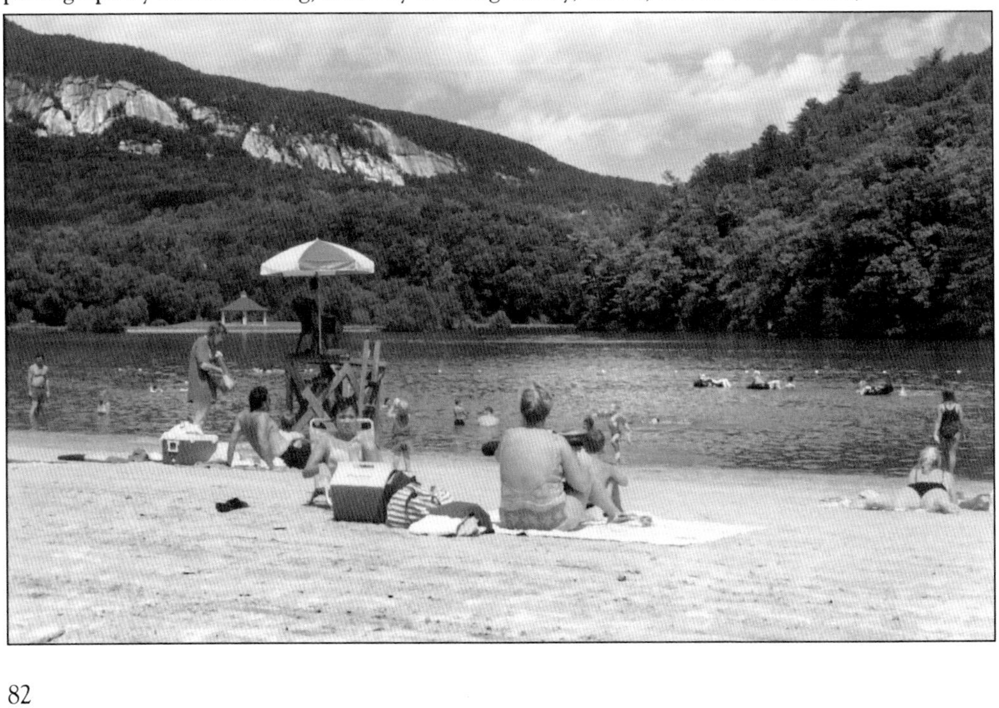

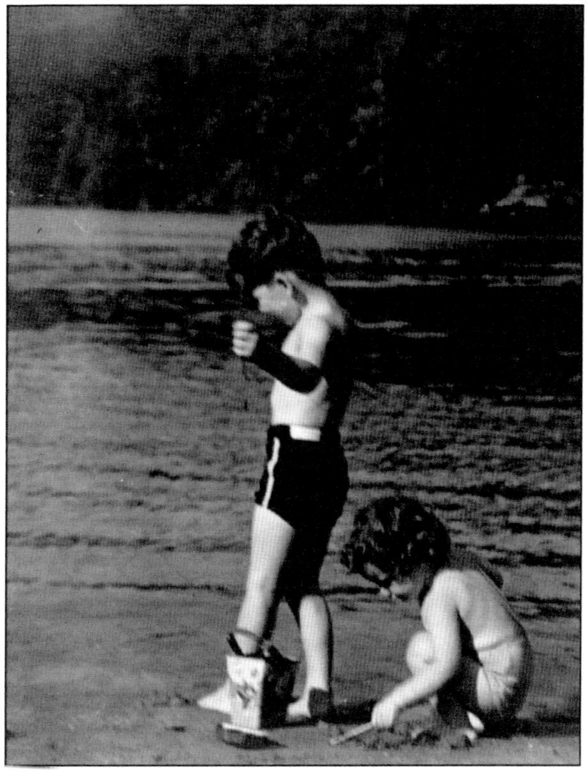

The beach by the lake, perhaps one of Lake Lure's best-known landmarks, is used by both visitors and locals. At first, the Lake Lure Beach was open to anyone and had no fence. The town soon found that lifeguards were needed, so they sold tickets to pay for the expenses. Sonny and Alisa Greig are in the photograph at right. (Both, photograph by Norman Greig, courtesy of the Greig family.)

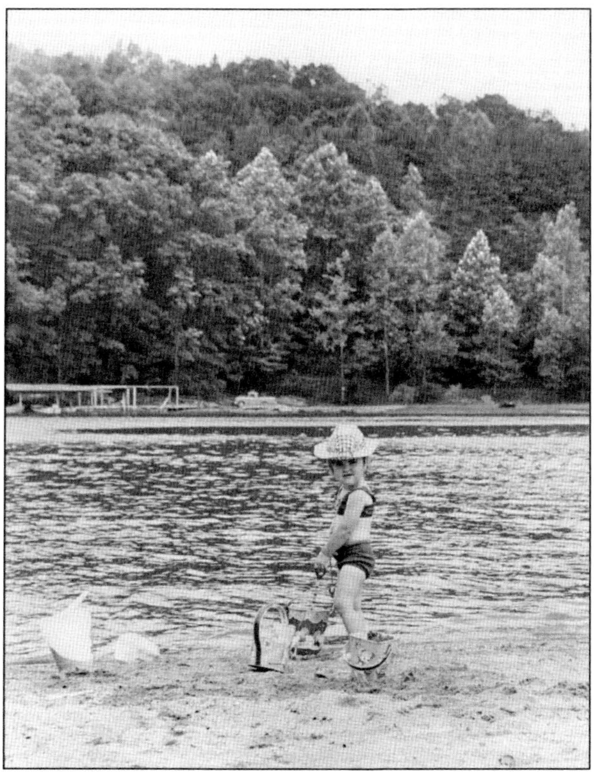

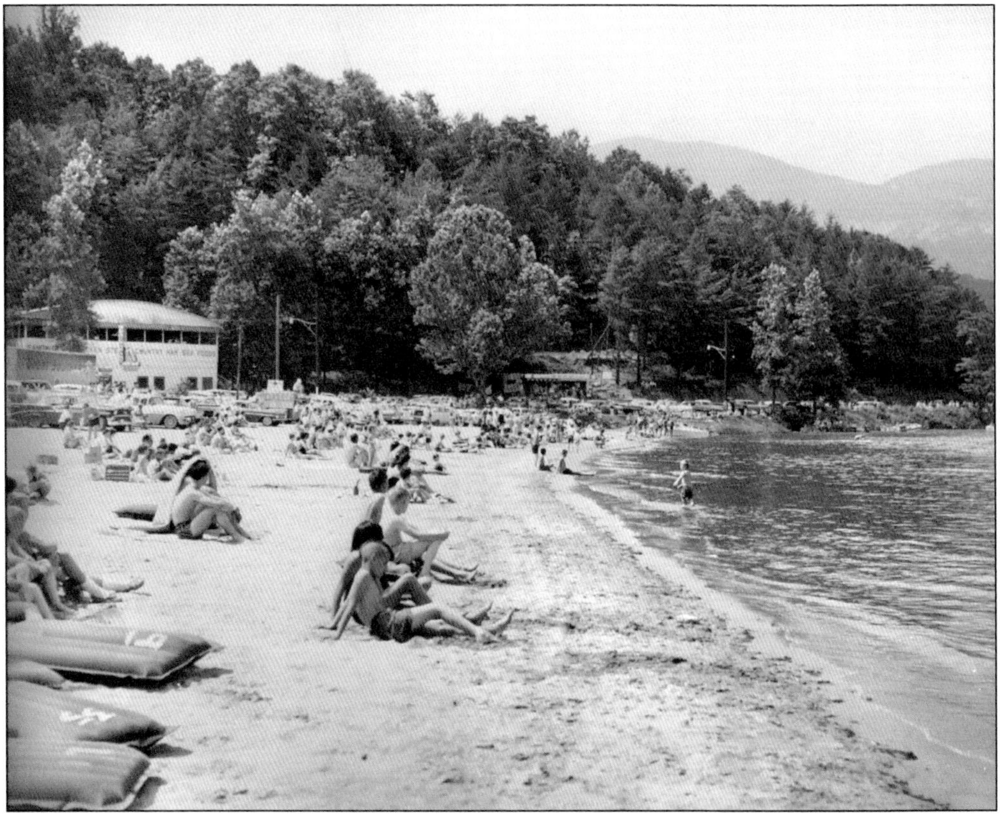

Along with the Lake Lure Inn, several restaurants opened near the beach. Above, the El Tango restaurant and music hall and John's Restaurant can be seen across the road. The building in the middle of the photograph below, the Lake Lure Movie Theater, is visible behind the trees. (Both, photograph by Norman Greig, courtesy of the Greig family.)

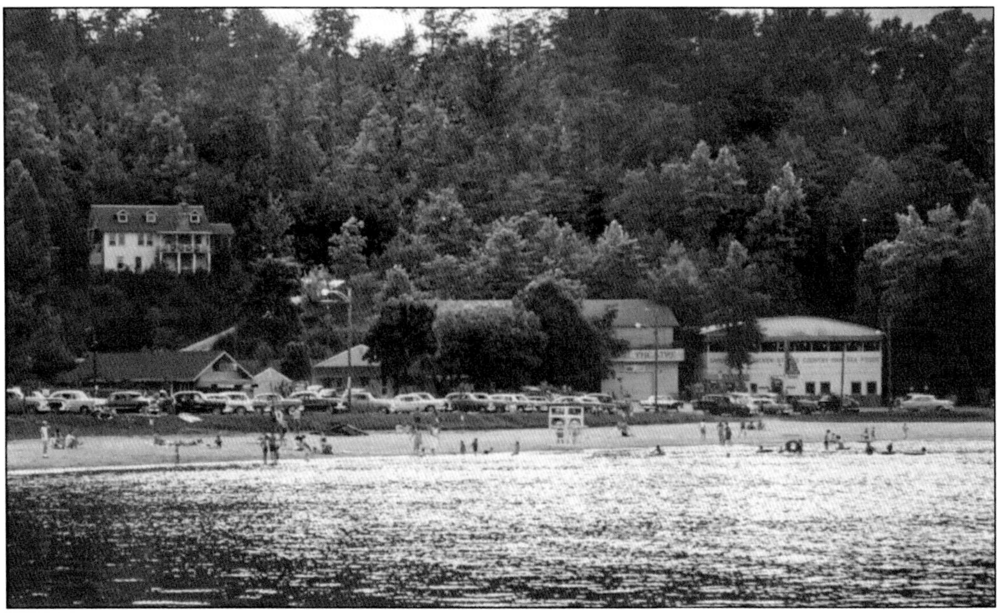

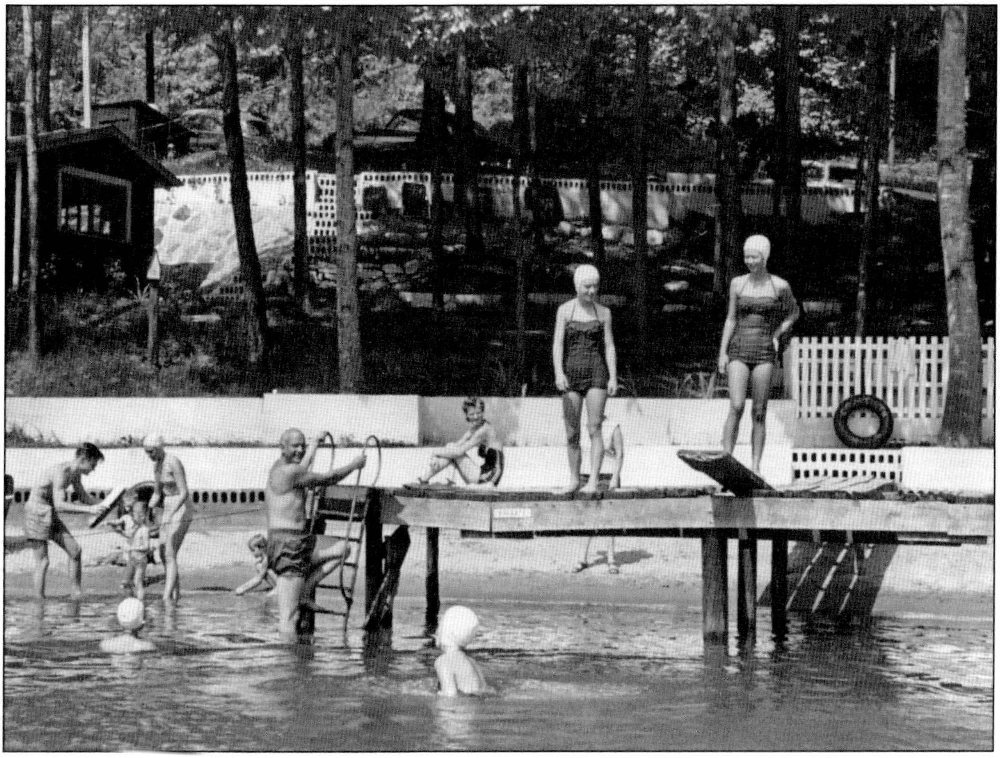

After the town purchased Lake Lure, it soon allowed lakefront owners to build boat docks and boathouses. The former owner had restricted boathouses, and the lakefront properties were now worth much more with lake access. (Both, photograph by Norman Greig; courtesy of the Greig family.)

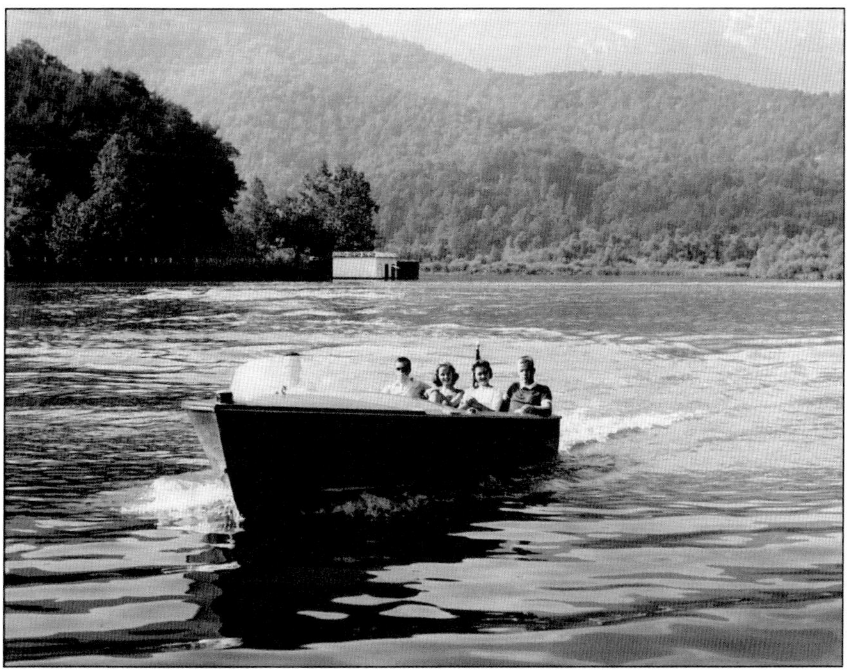

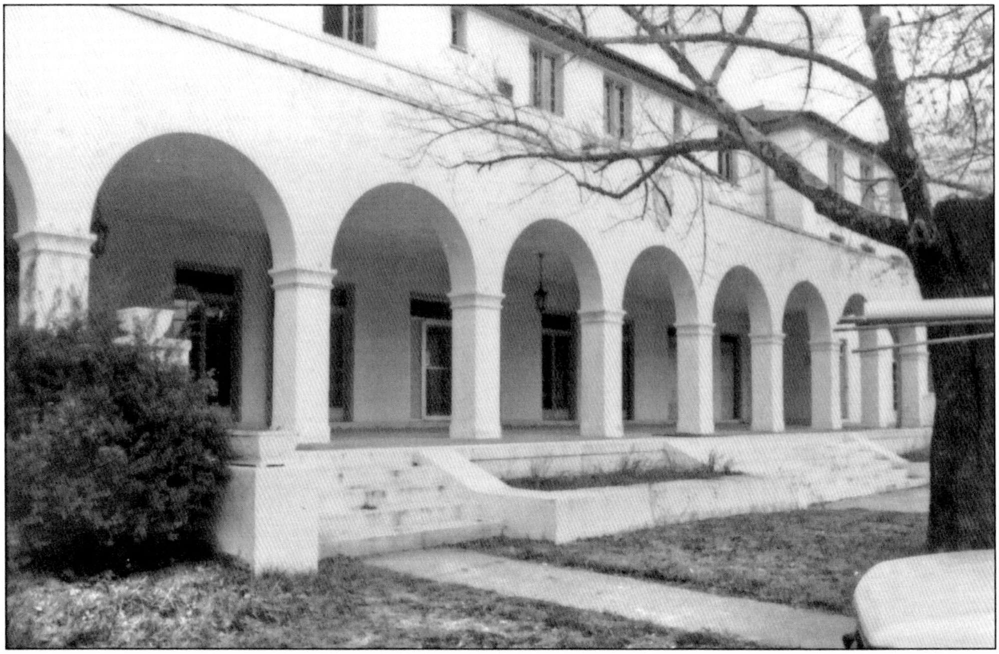

In the early 1960s, the Lake Lure Inn was abandoned for a short period of time and, at one point, was even given to the Boy Scouts of America for a tax write-off. It is fortunately now back to its original splendor. Renovations to the Lake Lure Inn transformed the neglected treasure back to its prime. (Both, photograph by Norman Greig; courtesy of the Greig family.)

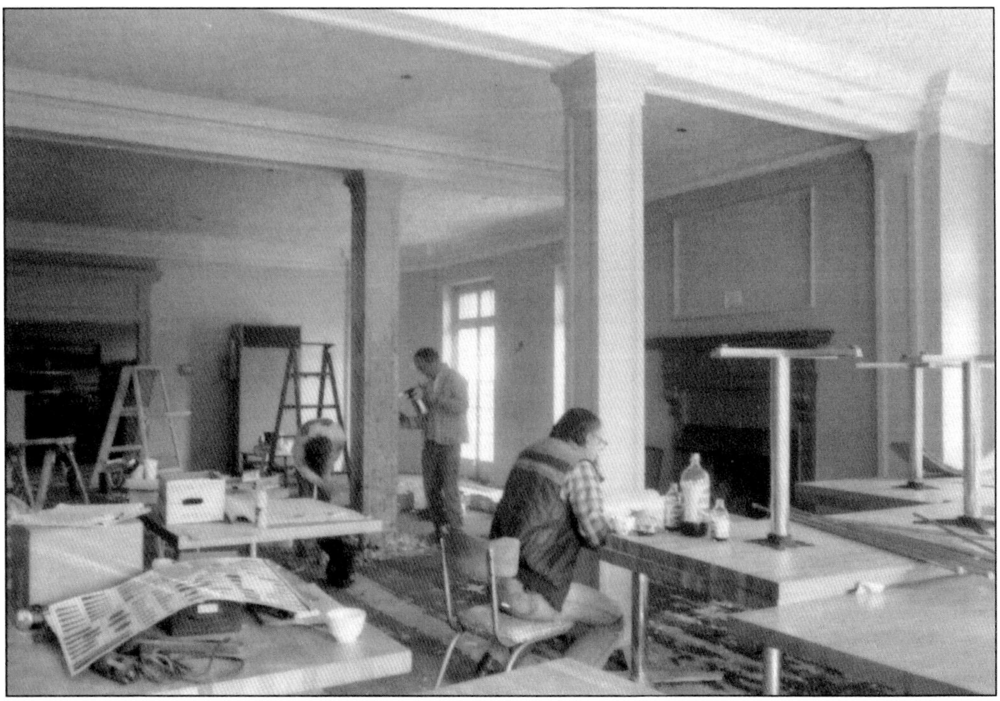

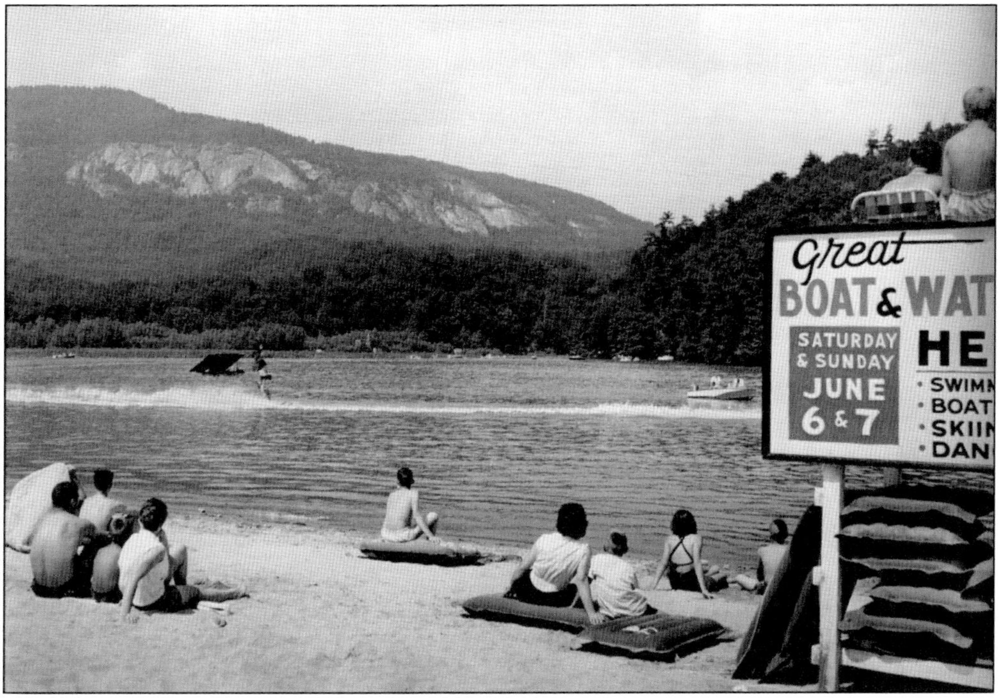

The Lake Lure Ski Club, founded in 1963, is one of the region's oldest ski clubs. The first president was Richard Kimberly. The early ski shows took place at the Lake Lure Beach cove. The cove is now too shallow for skiing. (Both, photograph by Norman Greig; courtesy of the Greig family.)

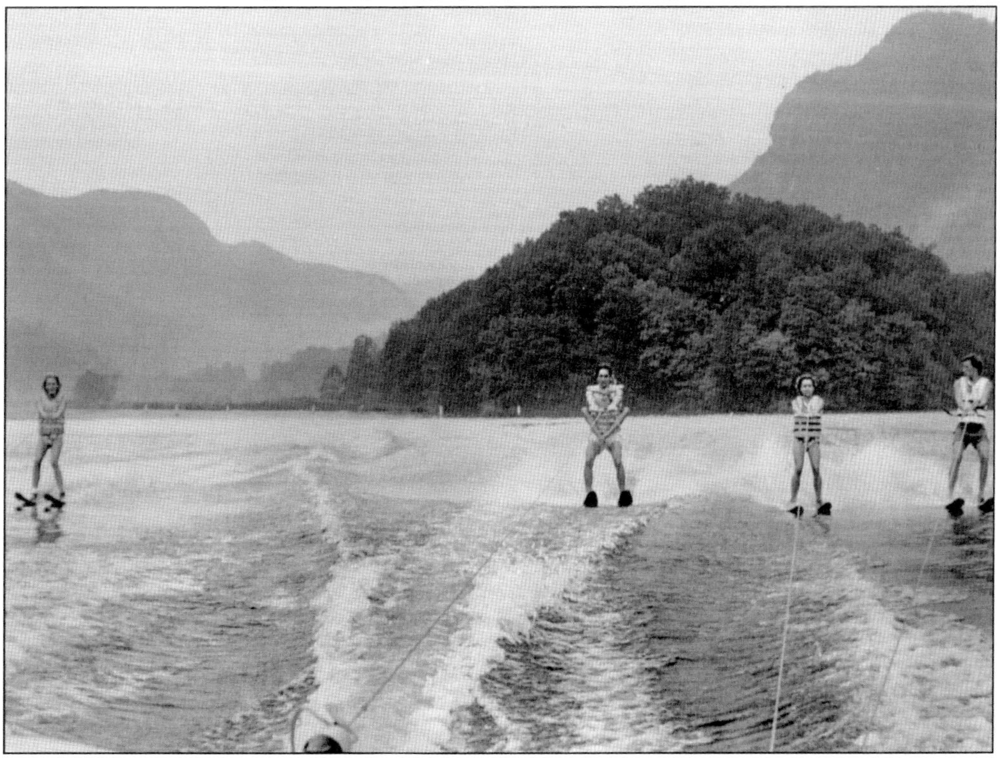

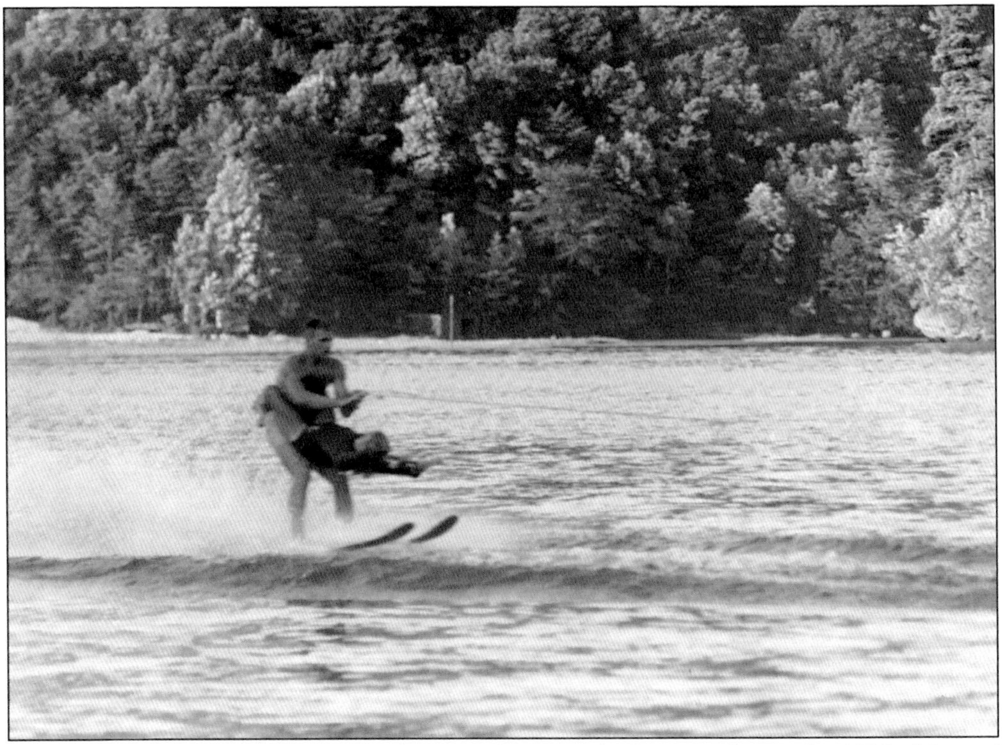

The ski club activities diminished in the 1970s but came back strong during the 1980s. Many of the original founding members returned with their children. The ski club again reformed in 2006. The ski club has had members from age three to over 70. The above photograph shows George Bond and Barbara Taylor (now Bond) participating in one of the early ski shows. The photograph below shows, from left to right, Barbara Taylor, two unidentified skiers, Mary Lou Lipinski, and Robin Burch. (Both, photograph by Norman Greig; courtesy of the Greig family.)

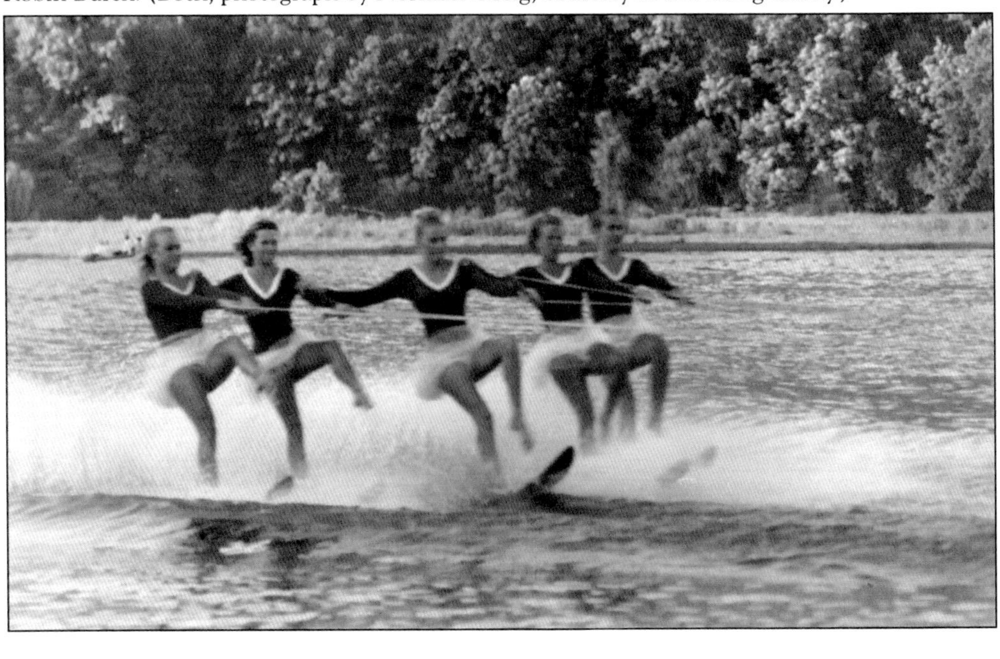

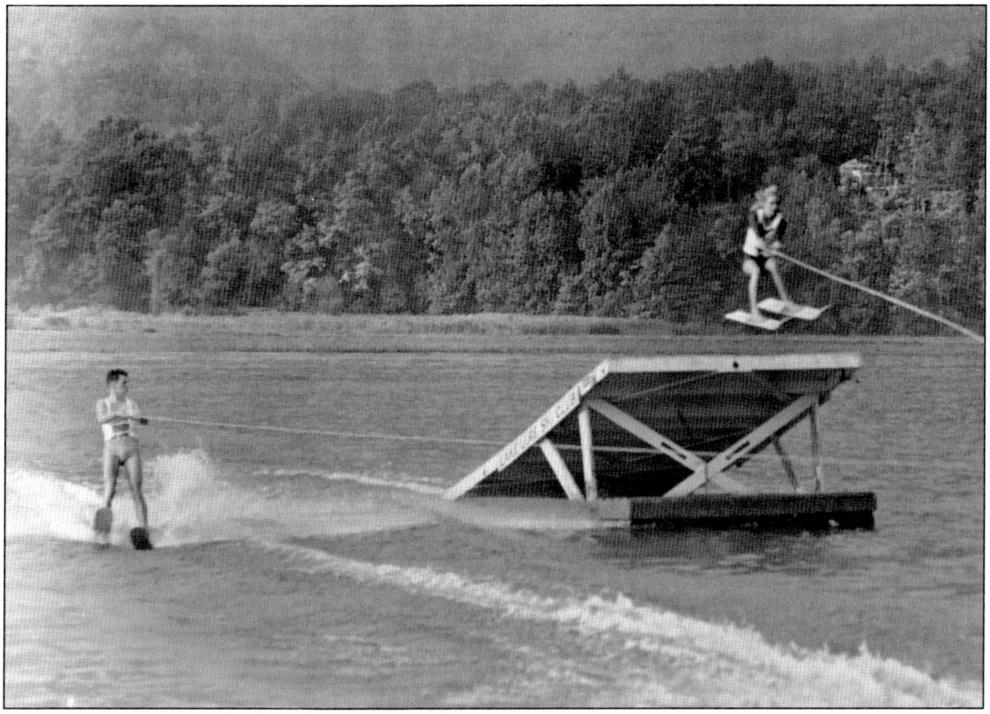

The Lake Lure Ski Club constructed its own ski ramp for local shows. In the 1960s, ski ramps were a novelty previously seen only at large resorts for the most part. Above, Martin Nesbit, later a North Carolina senator, is pictured on the left, and Ina Gottlieb, above and below, skis off the ramp. (Both, photograph by Norman Greig; courtesy of the Greig family.)

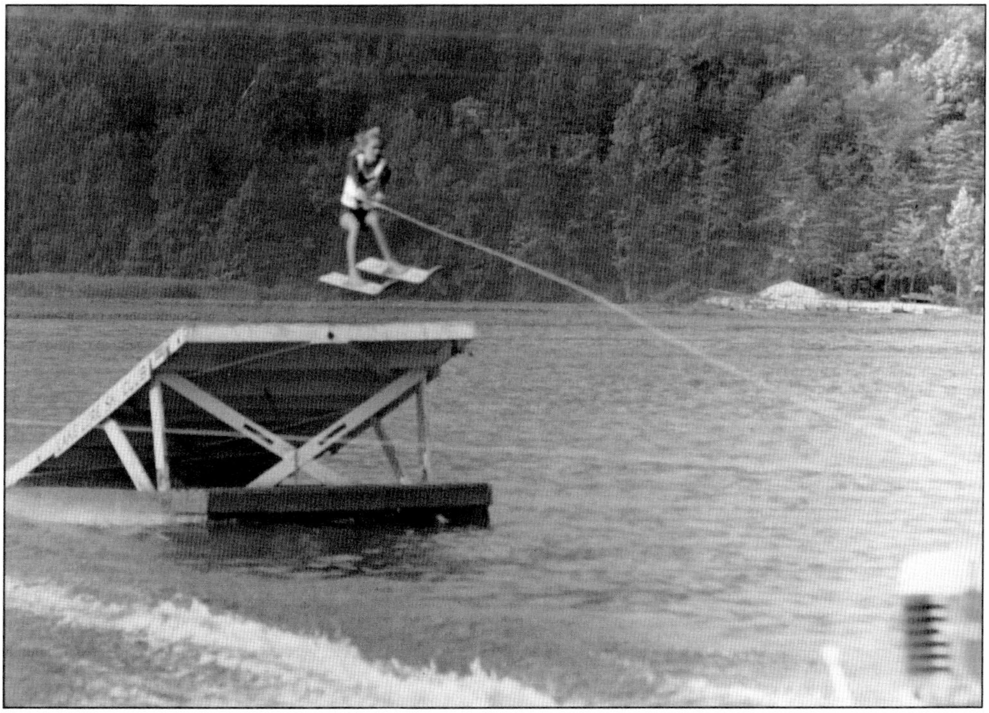

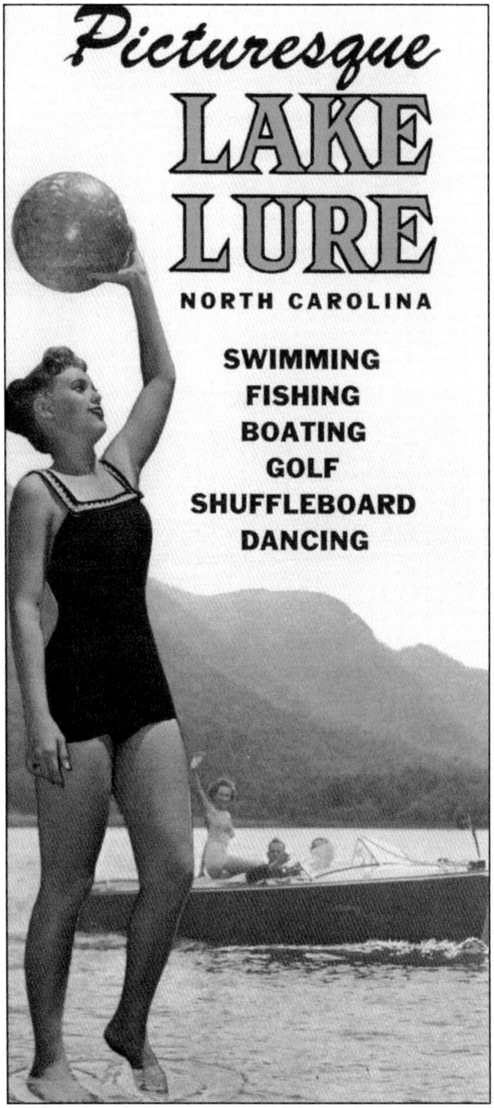

Before the Hickory Nut Gorge Chamber of Commerce was formed, the Town of Lake Lure used municipal funds to advertise the lake. Here is a brochure published by the town in the early 1960s. (Author's collection.)

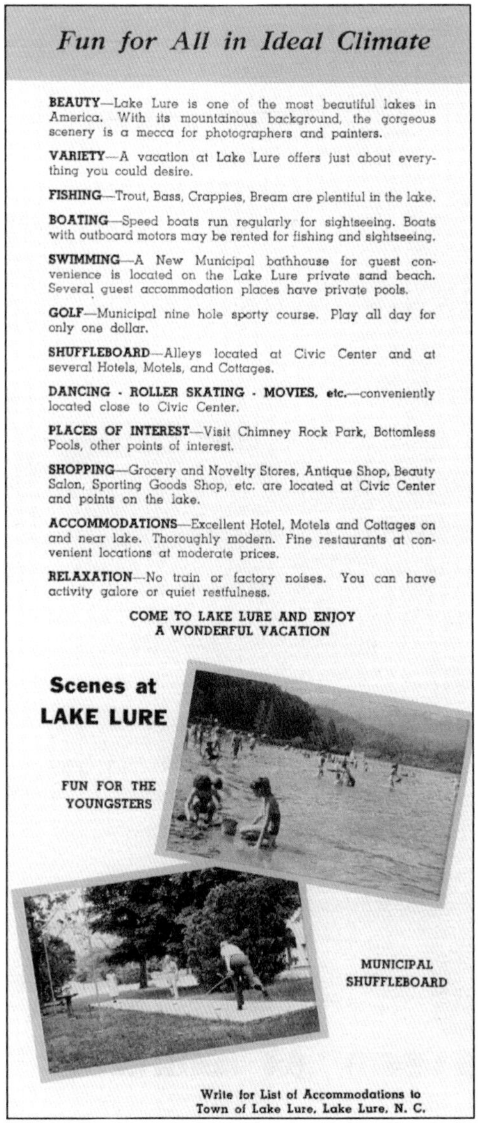

Fun for All in Ideal Climate

BEAUTY—Lake Lure is one of the most beautiful lakes in America. With its mountainous background, the gorgeous scenery is a mecca for photographers and painters.

VARIETY—A vacation at Lake Lure offers just about everything you could desire.

FISHING—Trout, Bass, Crappies, Bream are plentiful in the lake.

BOATING—Speed boats run regularly for sightseeing. Boats with outboard motors may be rented for fishing and sightseeing.

SWIMMING—A New Municipal bathhouse for guest convenience is located on the Lake Lure private sand beach. Several guest accommodation places have private pools.

GOLF—Municipal nine hole sporty course. Play all day for only one dollar.

SHUFFLEBOARD—Alleys located at Civic Center and at several Hotels, Motels, and Cottages.

DANCING · ROLLER SKATING · MOVIES, etc.—conveniently located close to Civic Center.

PLACES OF INTEREST—Visit Chimney Rock Park, Bottomless Pools, other points of interest.

SHOPPING—Grocery and Novelty Stores, Antique Shop, Beauty Salon, Sporting Goods Shop, etc. are located at Civic Center and points on the lake.

ACCOMMODATIONS—Excellent Hotel, Motels and Cottages on and near lake. Thoroughly modern. Fine restaurants at convenient locations at moderate prices.

RELAXATION—No train or factory noises. You can have activity galore or quiet restfulness.

COME TO LAKE LURE AND ENJOY A WONDERFUL VACATION

Scenes at LAKE LURE

FUN FOR THE YOUNGSTERS

MUNICIPAL SHUFFLEBOARD

Write for List of Accommodations to Town of Lake Lure, Lake Lure, N. C.

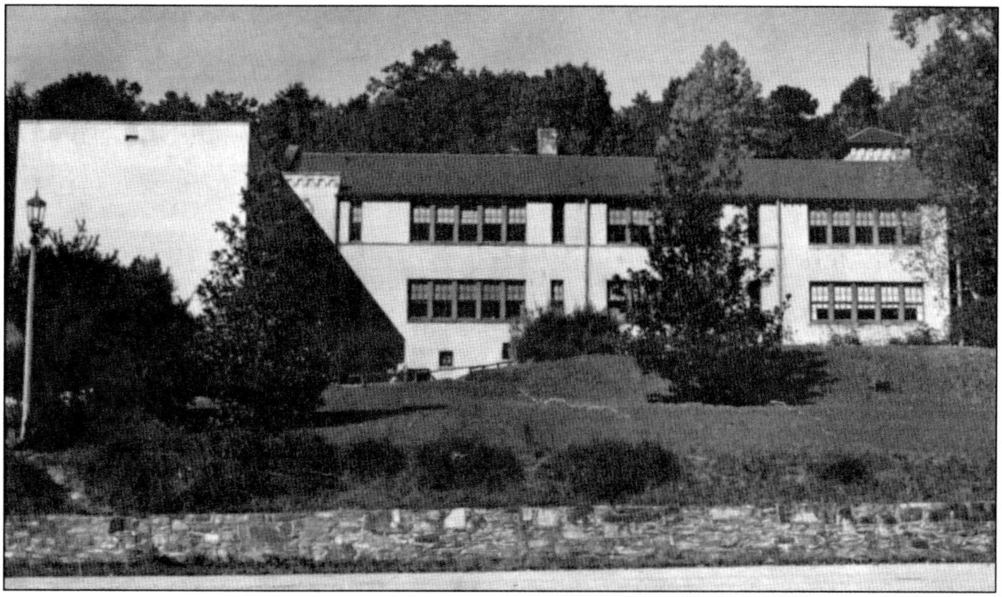

The old Lake Lure School was built by Chimney Rock Mountains, Inc., in the 1920s and operated until 1961, when Rutherford County decided to shut down the local school. The image below is from a PTA fashion show and includes, from left to right, Jane Noblitt Melton, Lucy McDaniel, Betty Jo Meliski, Helen Washburn, Addie Foster, Deloris Hernandez, and Daisy Noblitt. (Both, courtesy of Jane Noblitt Melton.)

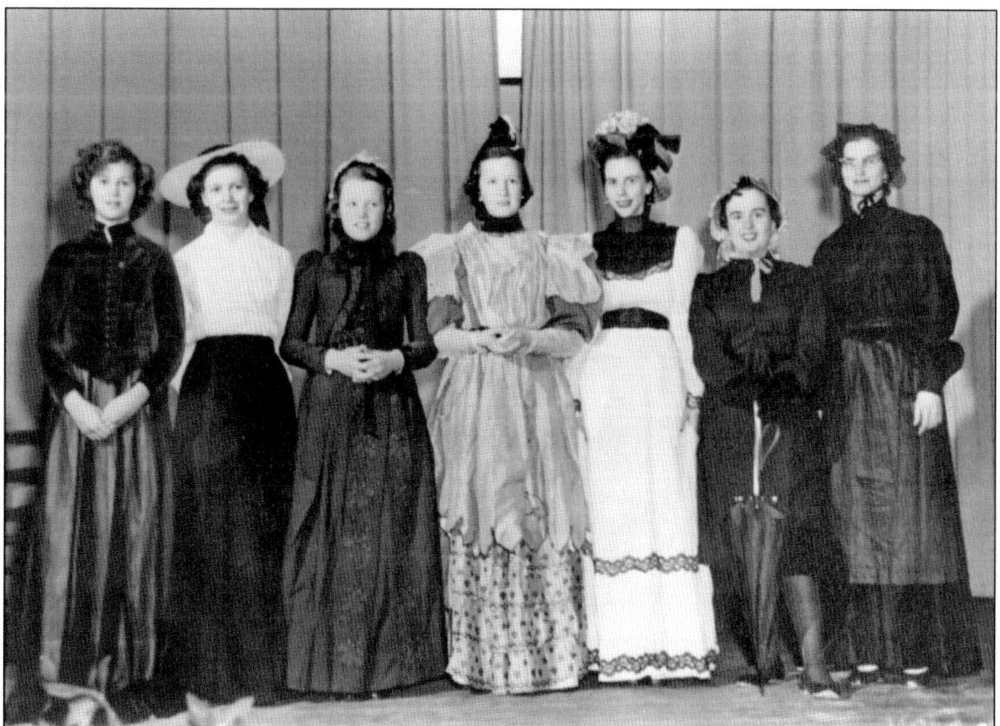

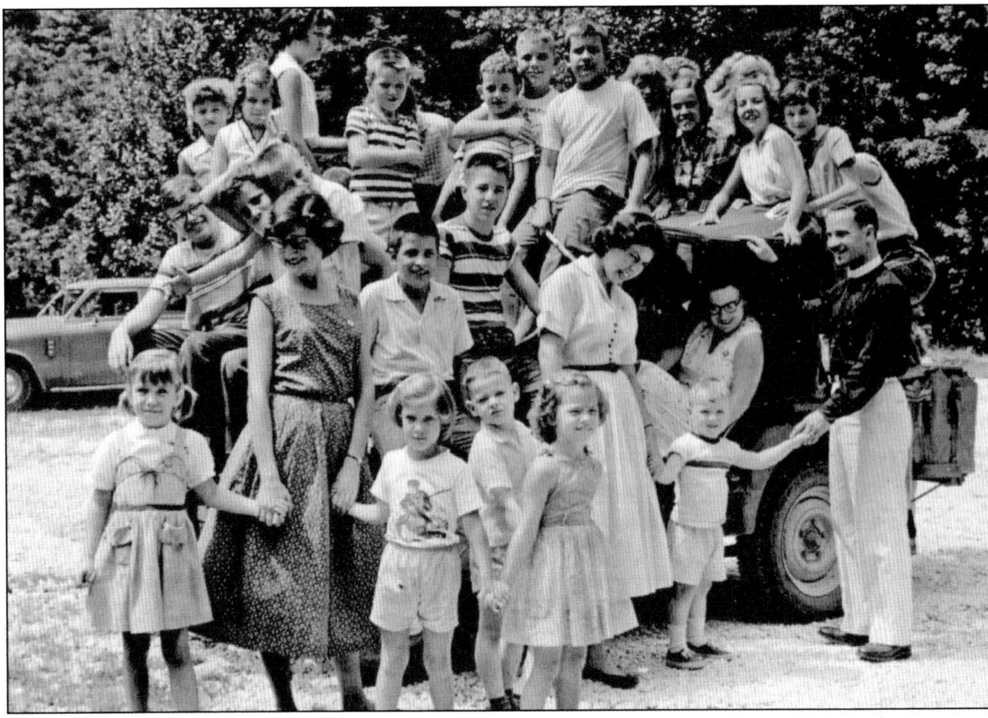

Fr. Jim Hindle was the minister at the Church of the Transfiguration, located in nearby Bat Cave, North Carolina. He is seen here overseeing summer vacation Bible school in the 1960s. (Photograph by Norman Greig; courtesy of the Greig family.)

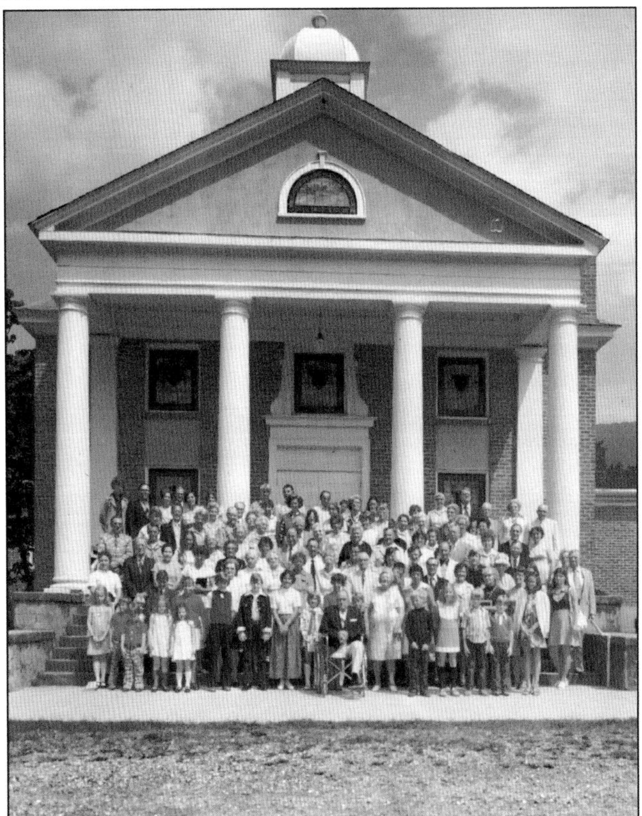

The Chimney Rock Baptist Church was originally organized in July 1872. It was disbanded about 1902. Many of its members then went to the Whiteside Valley Baptist Church. In May 1926, the church property was sold to Carolina Mountain Power Company to make way for the impoundment of Lake Lure. On August 29, 1928, the Whiteside Valley Baptist Church became Chimney Rock Baptist Church and is now located on Boys Camp Road. (Photograph by Norman Greig; courtesy of the Greig family.)

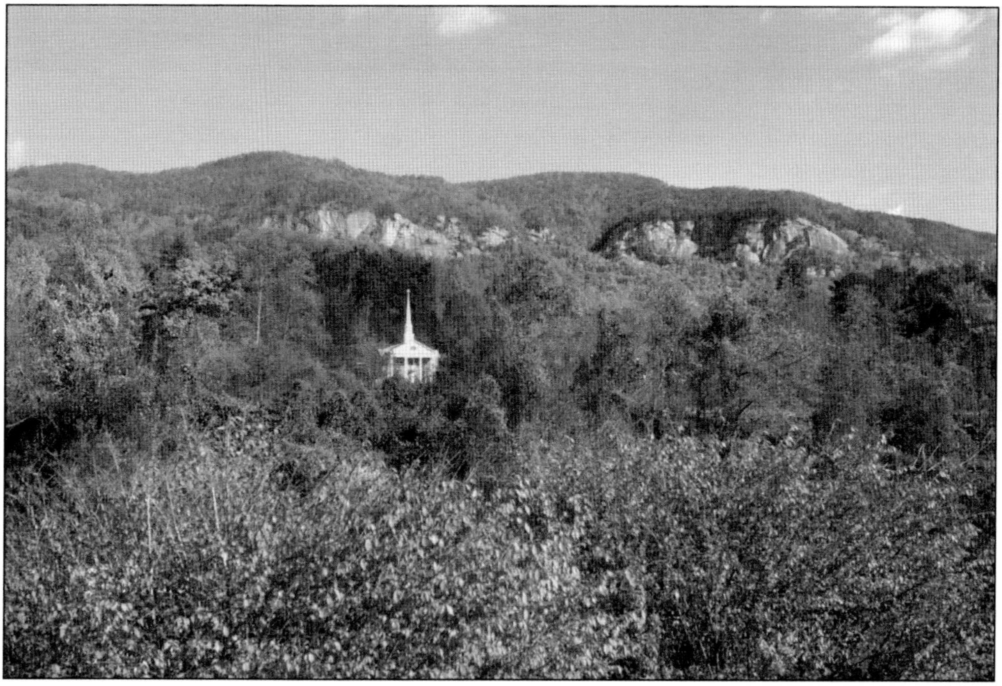

The Chimney Rock Baptist Church sits below the majestic Rumbling Bald Mountain. Note that the original round steeple has been replaced with a tall pointed one. (Author's collection.)

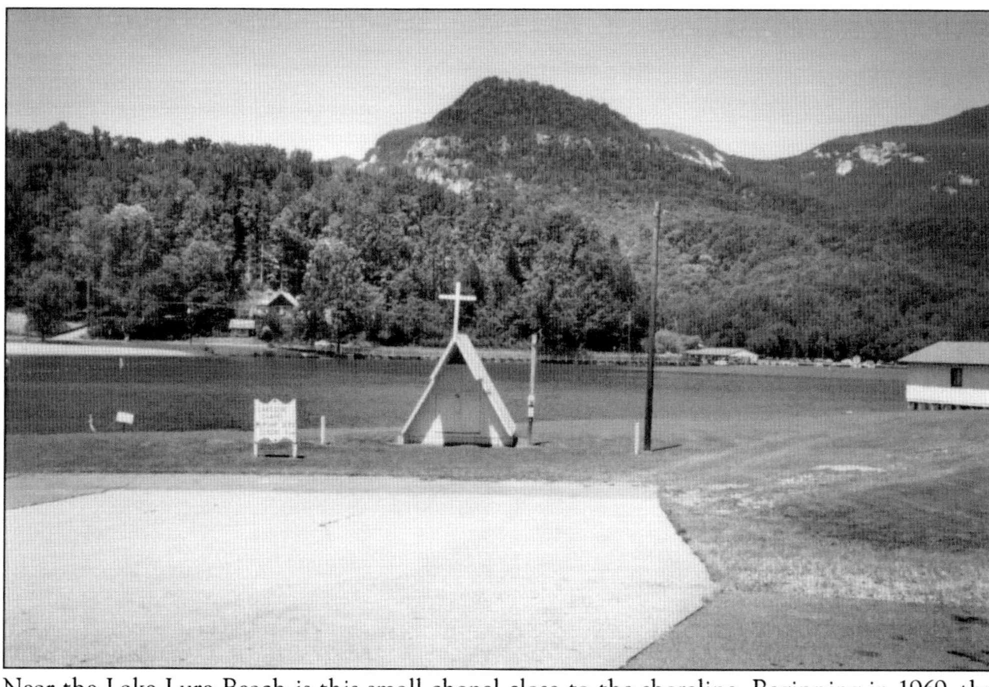

Near the Lake Lure Beach is this small chapel close to the shoreline. Beginning in 1969, the Chimney Rock Baptist Church has operated Lakeside Services. The services begin on the first Sunday in May and continue until the second Sunday in October. The service starts at 9:00 a.m. and is open to everyone. (Author's collection.)

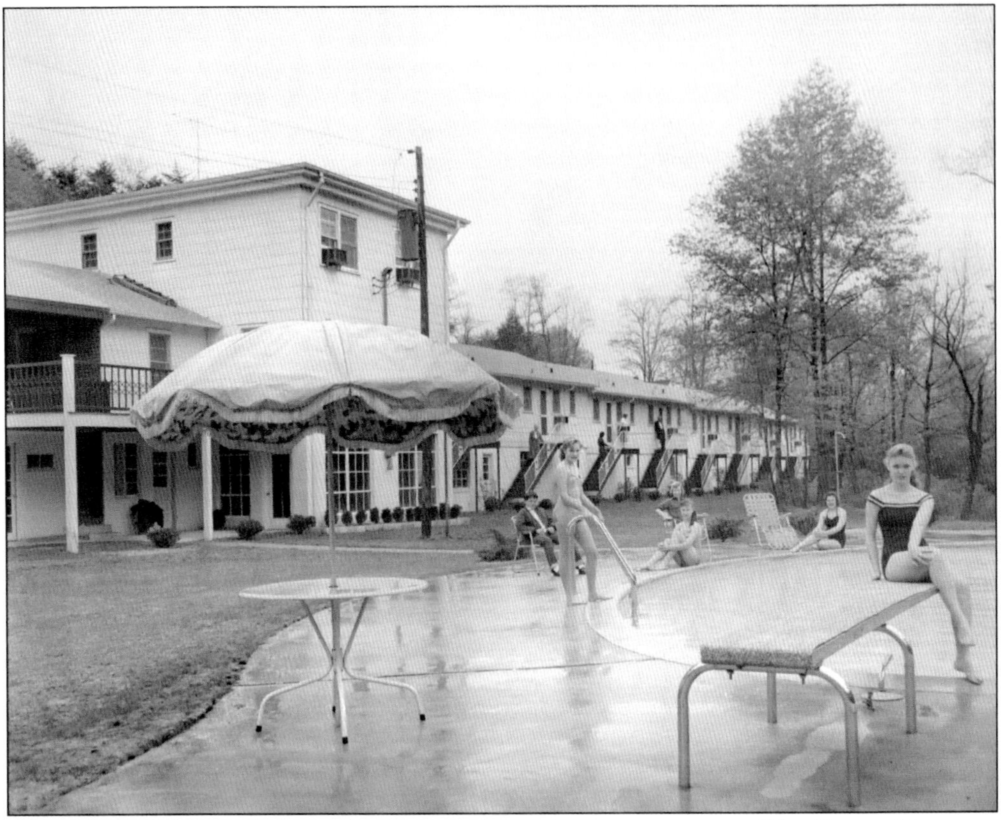

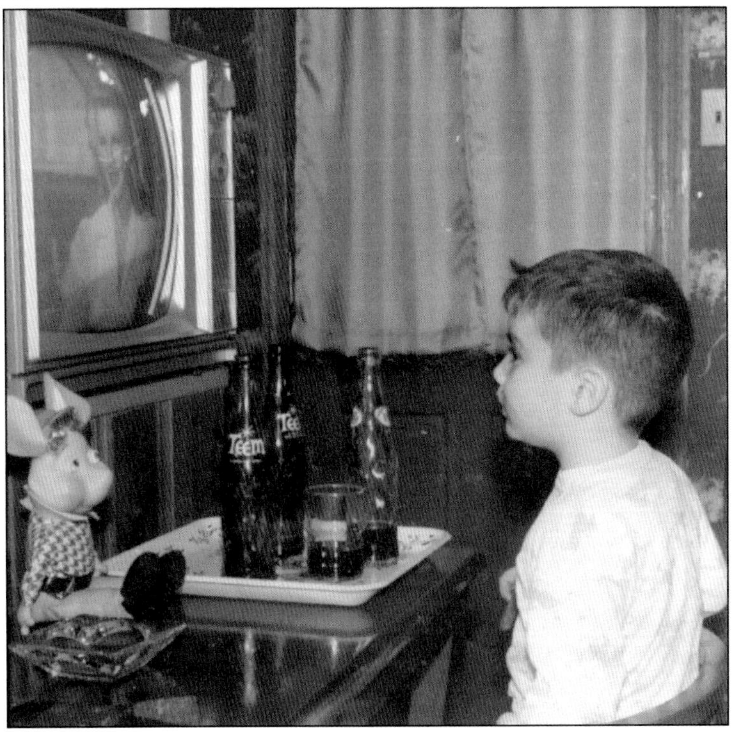

The Geneva Motor Court was built by Geneva Chapman. This photograph is from the early 1960s. (Photograph by Norman Greig; courtesy of the Greig family.)

Norman Greig's grandson Randy Balot watches television at his grandfather's home in Chimney Rock. (Photograph by Norman Greig; courtesy of the Greig family.)

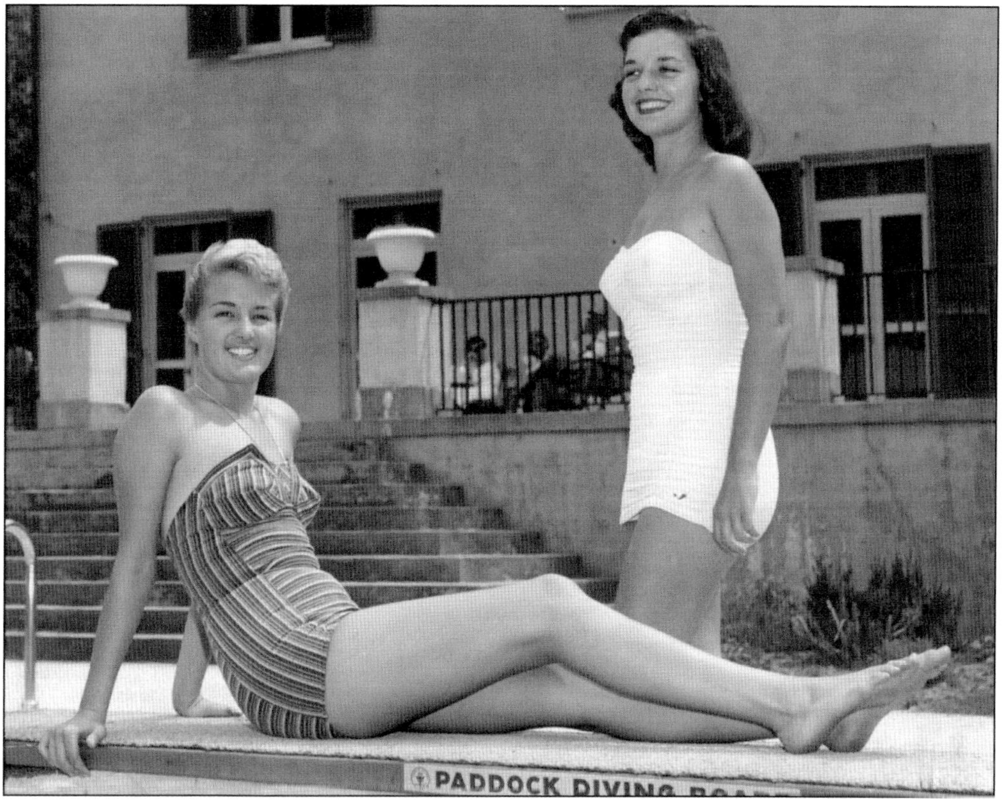

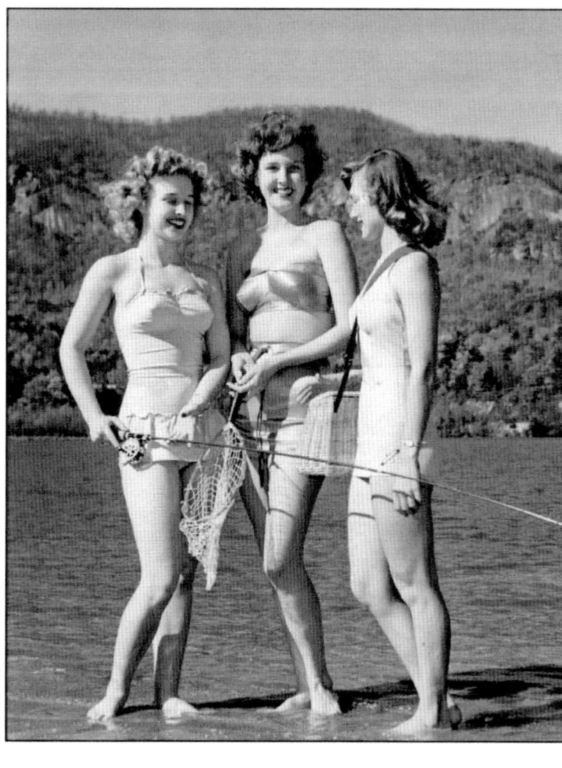

Lake Lure has always been a favorite backdrop for movies and advertisements. Here, models pose at the Lake Lure Inn and the Lake Lure Beach. (Both, photograph by Norman Greig; courtesy of the Greig family.)

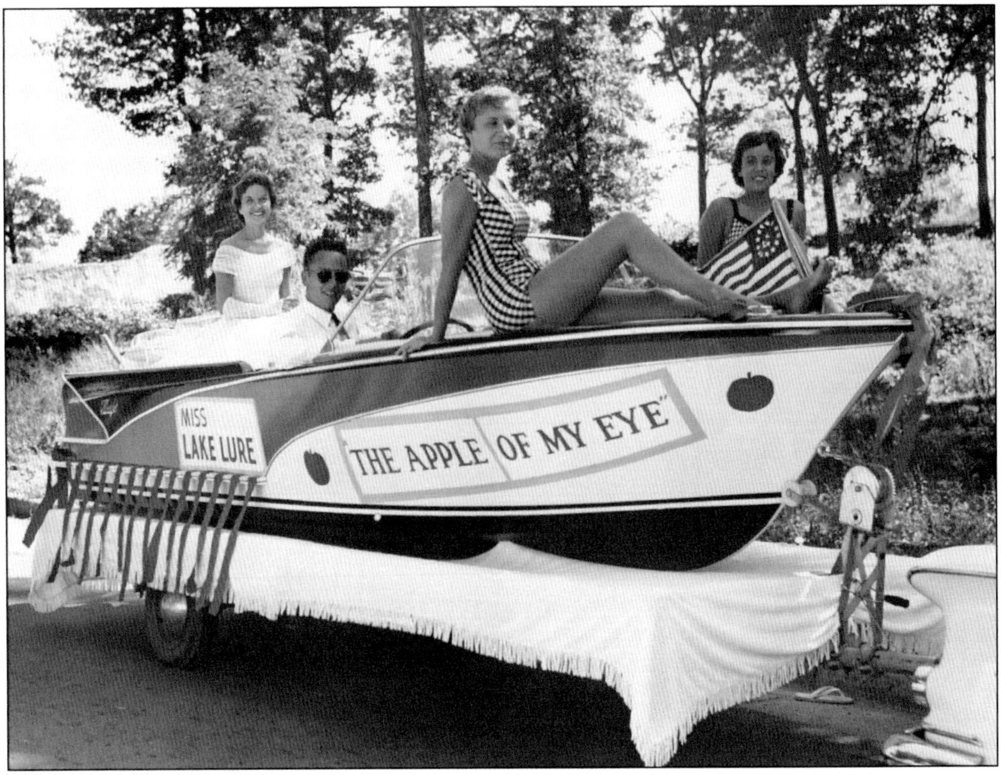

"Miss Lake Lure" Barbara Cranford is pictured above and below with unidentified drivers, Sandra Dean, and Pat Wilson. Below, the girls wave at the camera. (Both, photograph by Norman Greig; courtesy of the Greig family.)

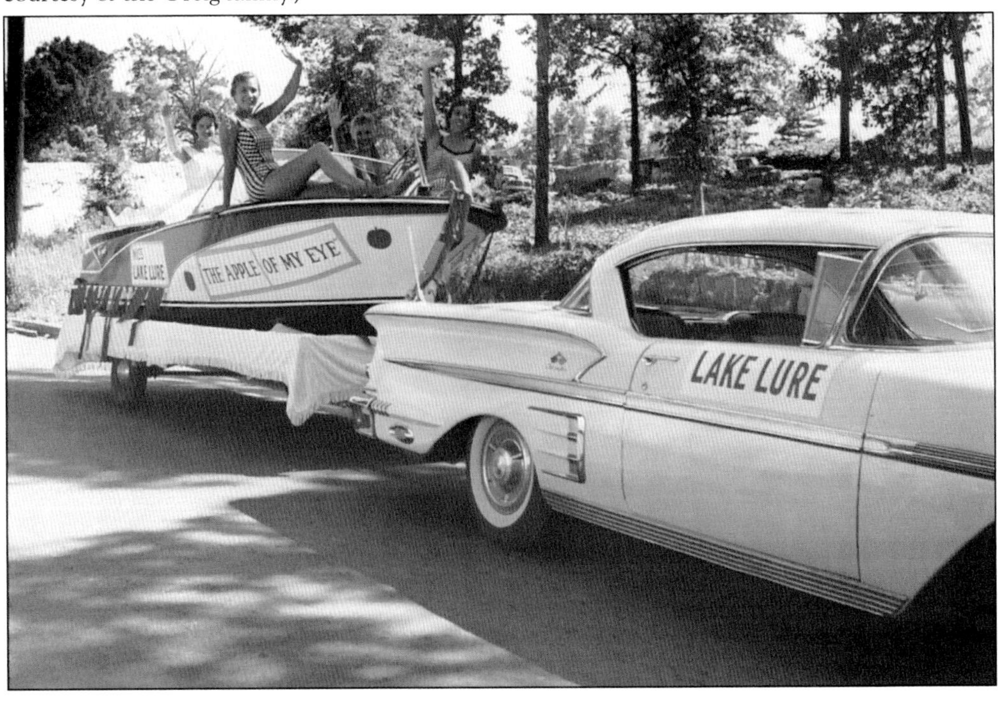

In this photograph, from left to right, "Pop" Hacket, Paul Wilson, and Lee Powers are hard at work remodeling a home. (Photograph by Norman Greig; courtesy of the Greig family.)

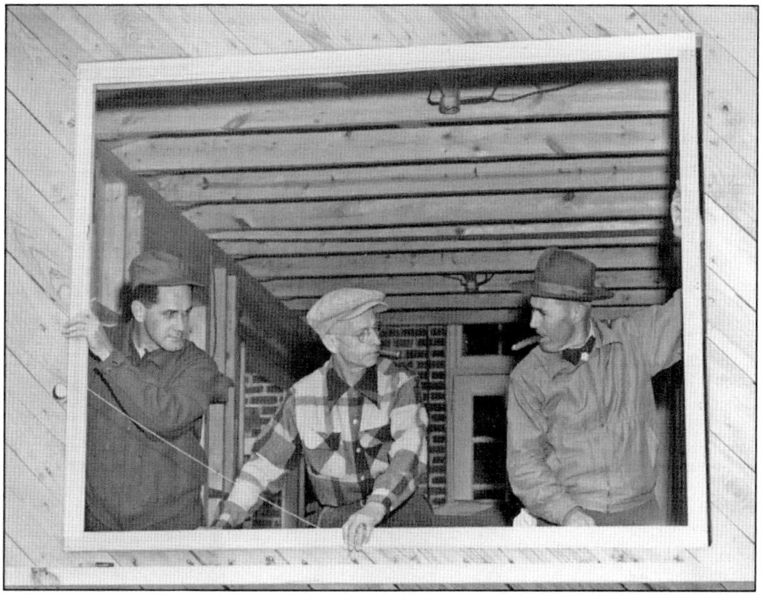

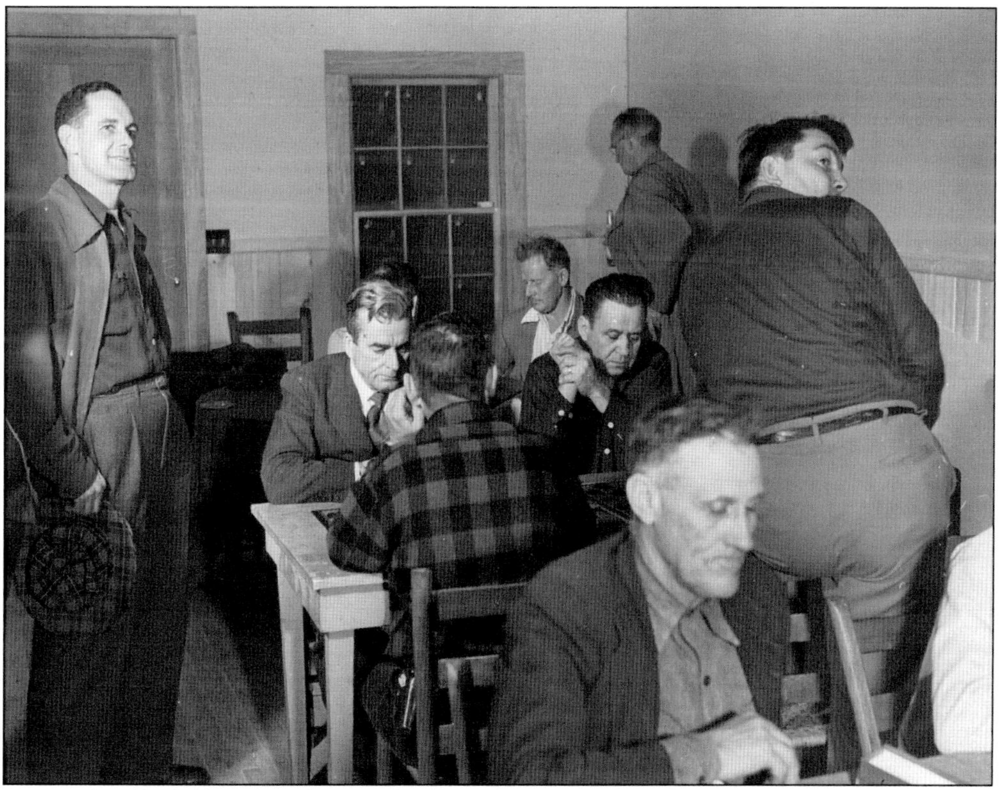

Pop Hacket (far left) and William Keller (far right with back to the camera) enjoy an evening at the Lake Lure American Legion Post 437, located on Boys Camp Road. (Photograph by Norman Greig; courtesy of the Greig family.)

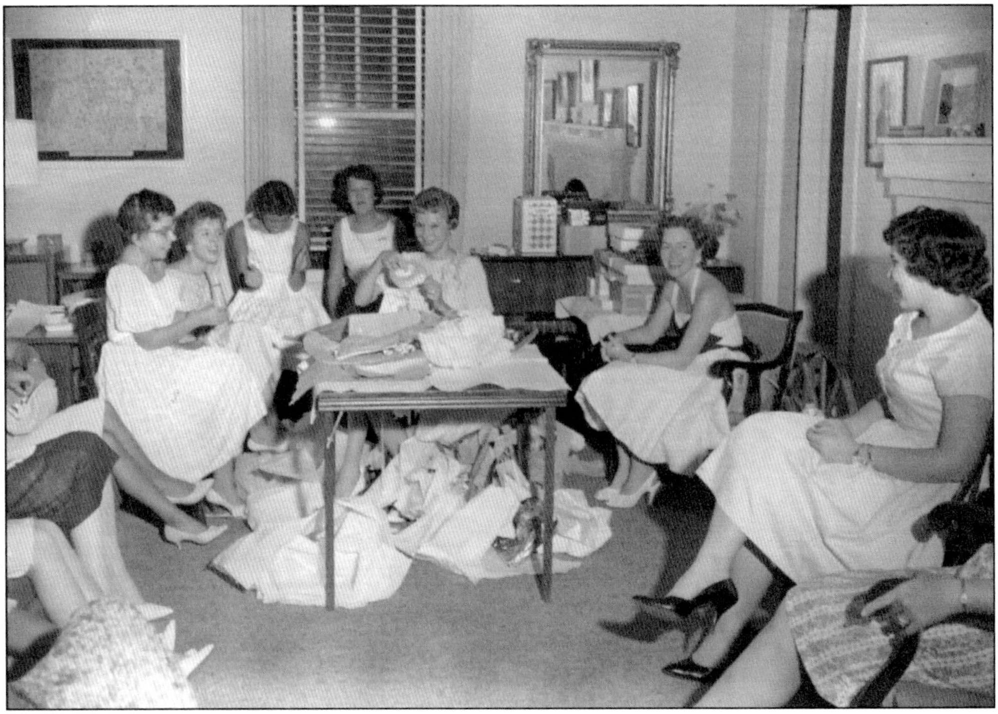

This scene is from one of many parties hosted by Norman and Beth Greig at their home, situated just off the road to Chimney Rock Park. Among those in attendance were Martha Jane Powers, Helen Washburn, Cherry Caudle, and Barbara Cranford. (Photograph by Norman Greig; courtesy of the Greig family.)

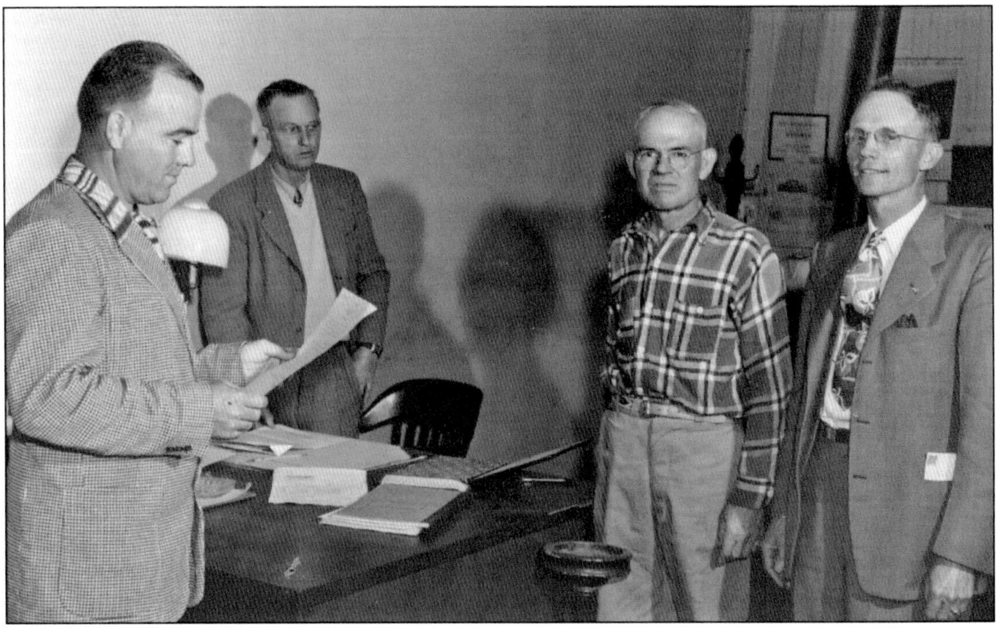

The Lake Lure Town Office was, for many years, located in the Lake Lure Arcade Building. Pictured here are, from left to right, Lake Lure mayor L.M. Pearson, unidentified, Dick Riddick, and C. Roy Cooper. (Photograph by Norman Greig; courtesy of the Greig family.)

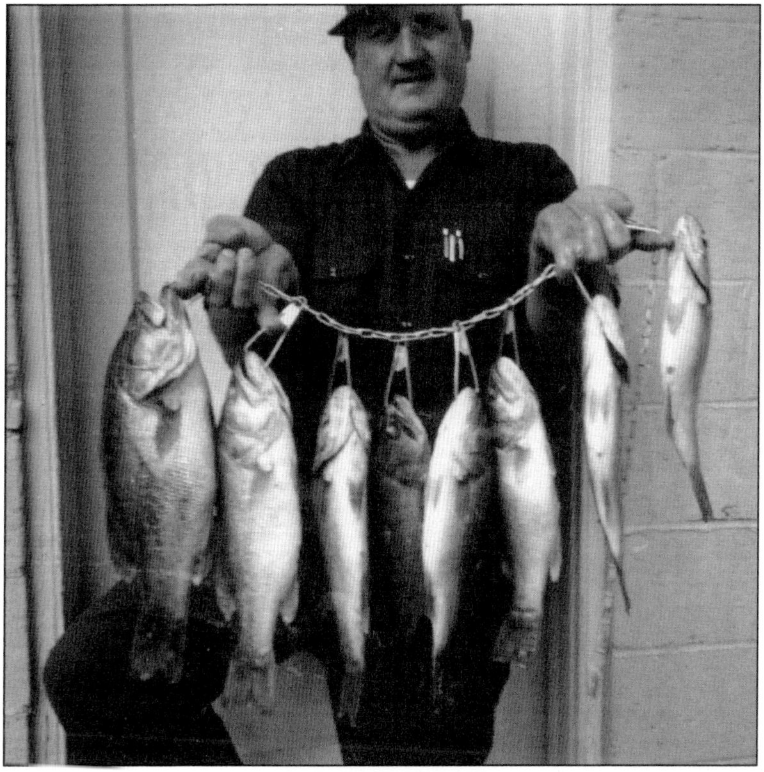

Sidney Nelon and his wife, Hazel, operated the Lake Lure Hardware Store for several decades. Sidney was a Lake Lure town commissioner, and he and Hazel were very active with the Hickory Nut Gorge Civic Club. As seen here, Sidney was also famous for his fishing skills. (Both, courtesy of the Town of Lake Lure.)

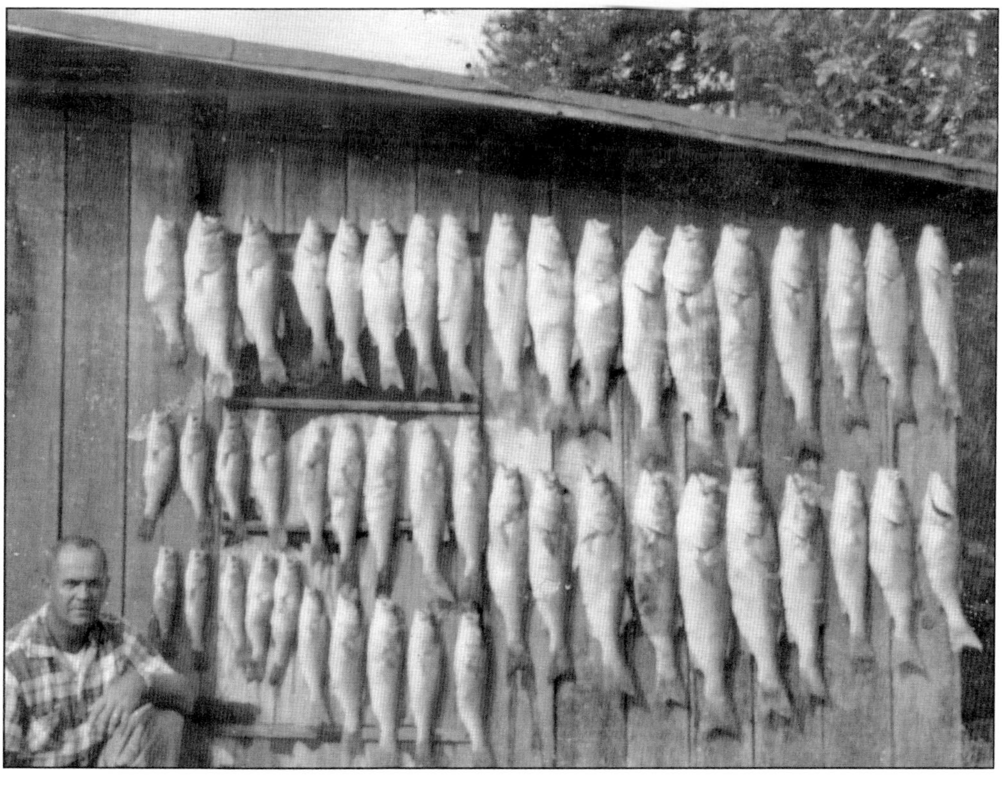

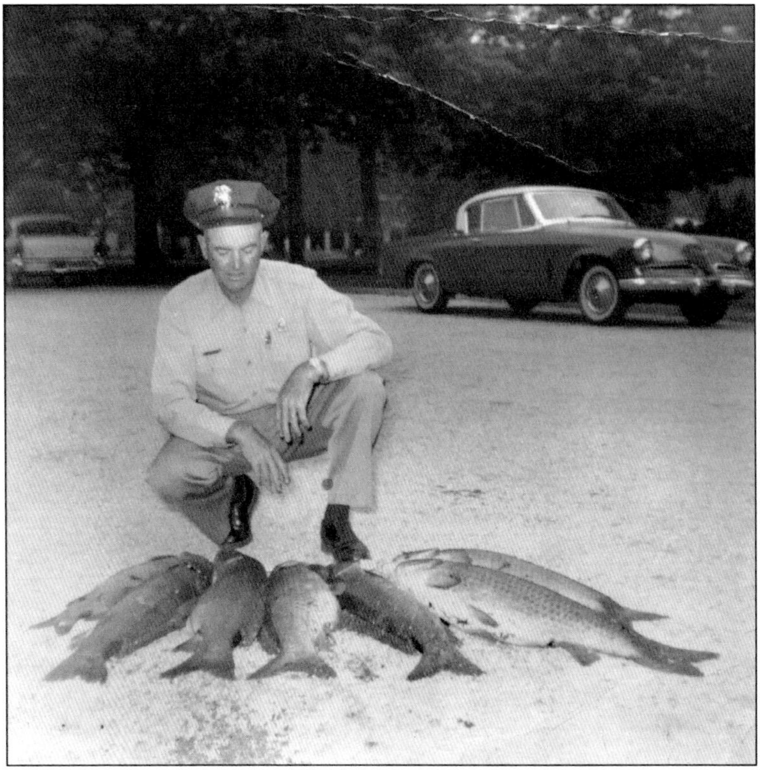

Police chief Walter Lee Pye was as famous for his fishing prowess as his policing. He spent many hours patrolling the lake and knew all the best places to apprehend his foes. (Courtesy of the Town of Lake Lure.)

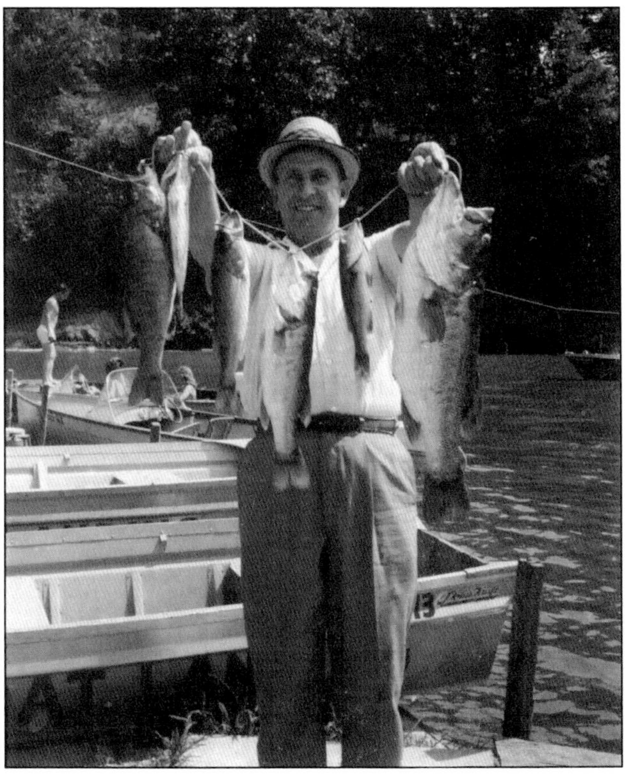

The image was captured after another great day of fishing on Lake Lure. (Courtesy of the Town of Lake Lure.)

Lake Lure has always been a fisherman's paradise. The fish varieties found in Lake Lure and the Rocky Broad River include largemouth and smallmouth bass, trout, bream/bluegills, crappie, perch, white bass, carp, and several species of catfish. (Courtesy of the Town of Lake Lure.)

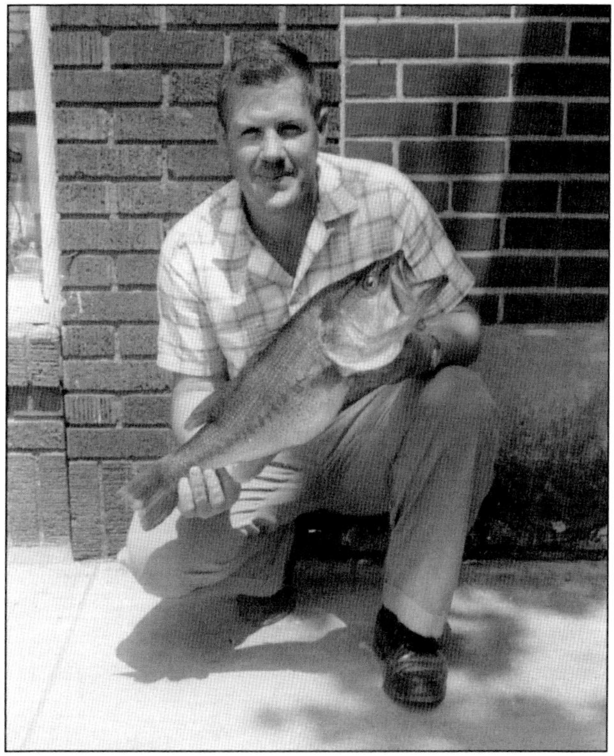

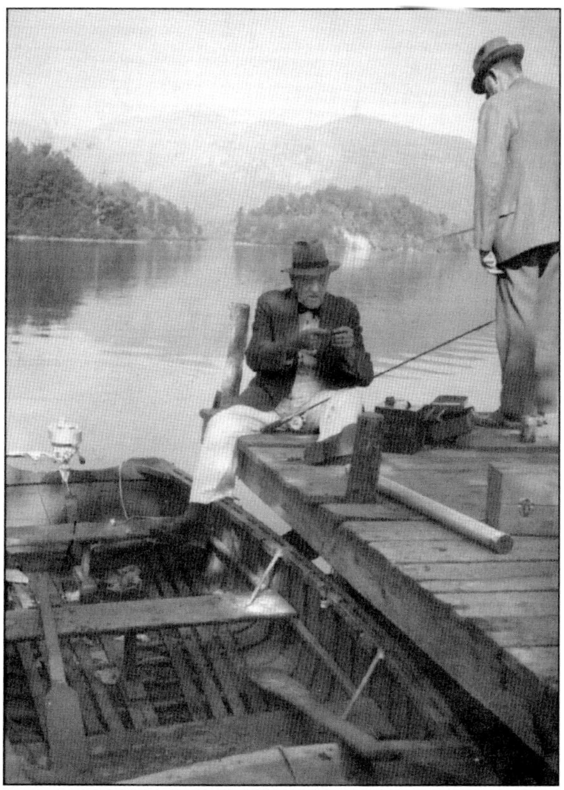

L.M. Pearson Sr. was the owner of the Log Shop Restaurant (now Point of View Restaurant) and an avid fisherman. He wore a suit every day, even when out fishing. (Courtesy of Jane Noblitt Melton.)

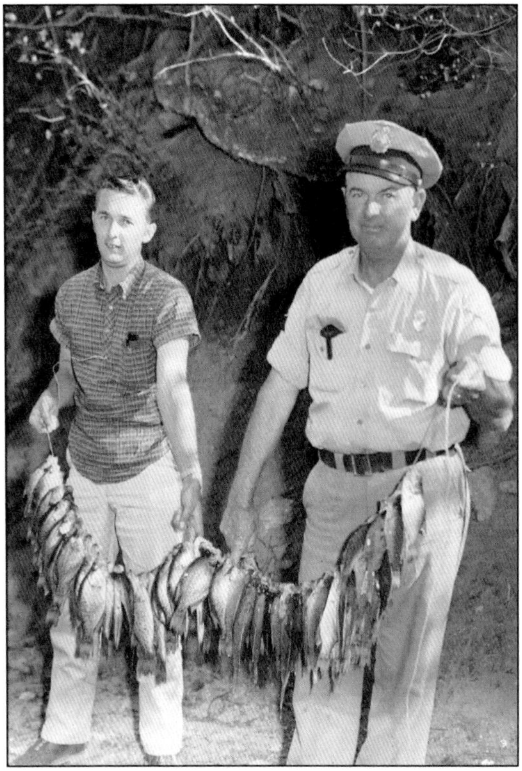

This remarkable photograph shows Lake Lure police chief Walter Lee Pye (right) and S.R. Swaringen, who grew up to also become a Lake Lure police chief. Just like his mentor, Swaringen was often found patrolling the lake with at least one fishing rod. (Courtesy of the Town of Lake Lure.)

Fishing tournaments were often sponsored to attract boaters and fishermen from around the region. (Photograph by Norman Greig; courtesy of the Greig family.)

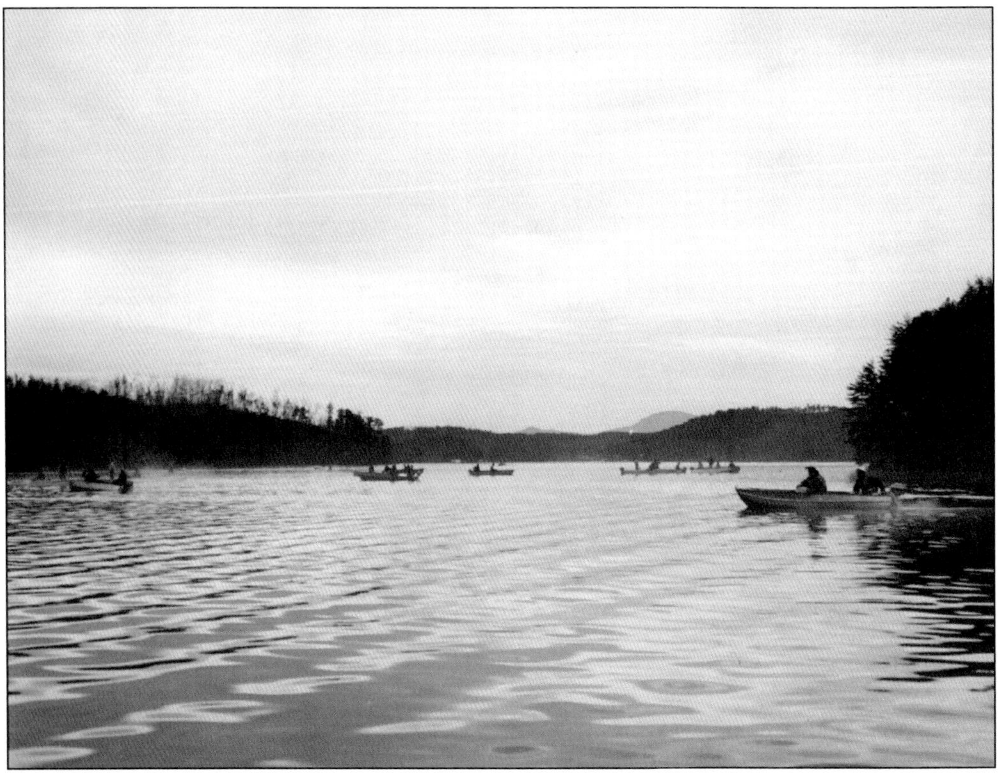

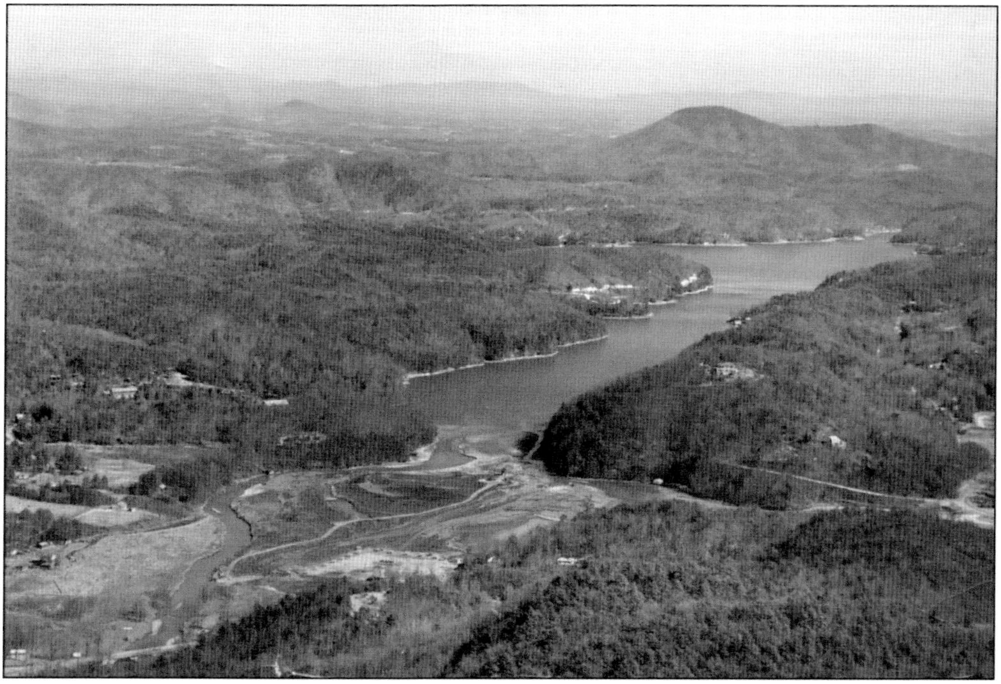

Before extensive dredging by the Town of Lake Lure, the river was narrow all the way to the main channel. (Courtesy of the Morse family.)

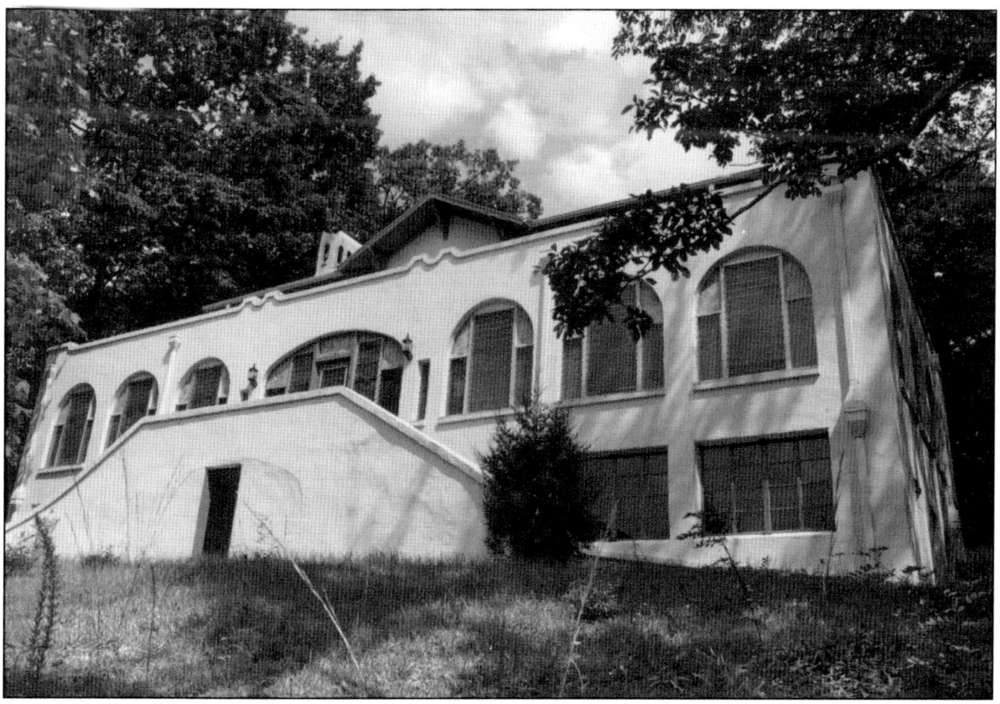

The Ward House was the first mansion built in Lake Lure. It was later bought by the family that owned the Haynes Hosiery Company and was, for many years, known as the Haynes Hill House. (Author's collection.)

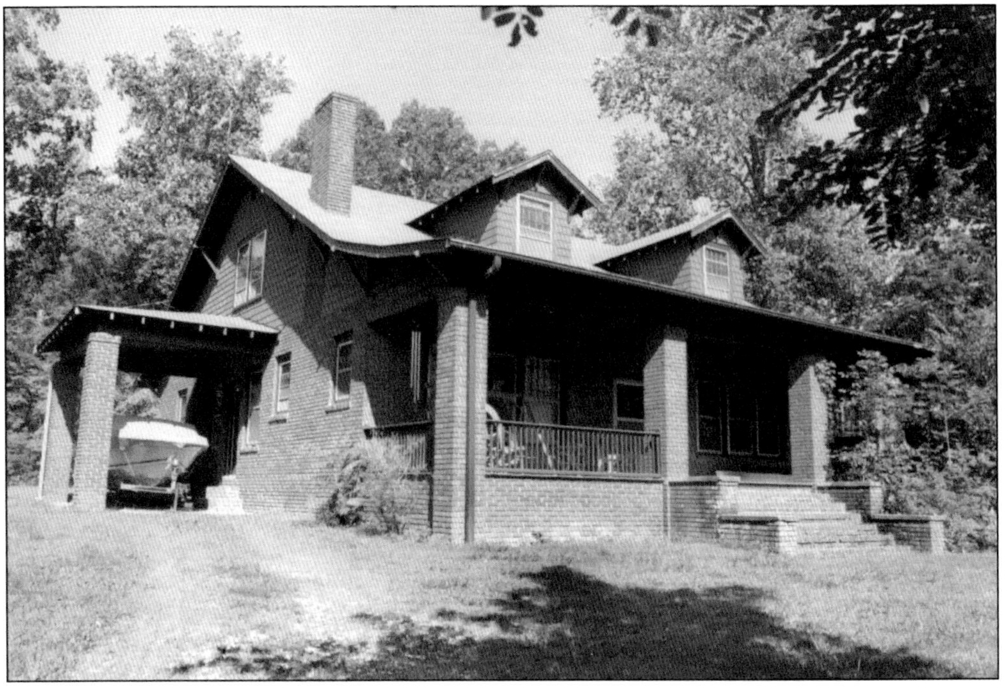

The Logan family sold the Logan House to Chimney Rock Company in 1924 and built this lovely brick home just a quarter mile to the east of the inn on Boys Camp Road. (Author's collection.)

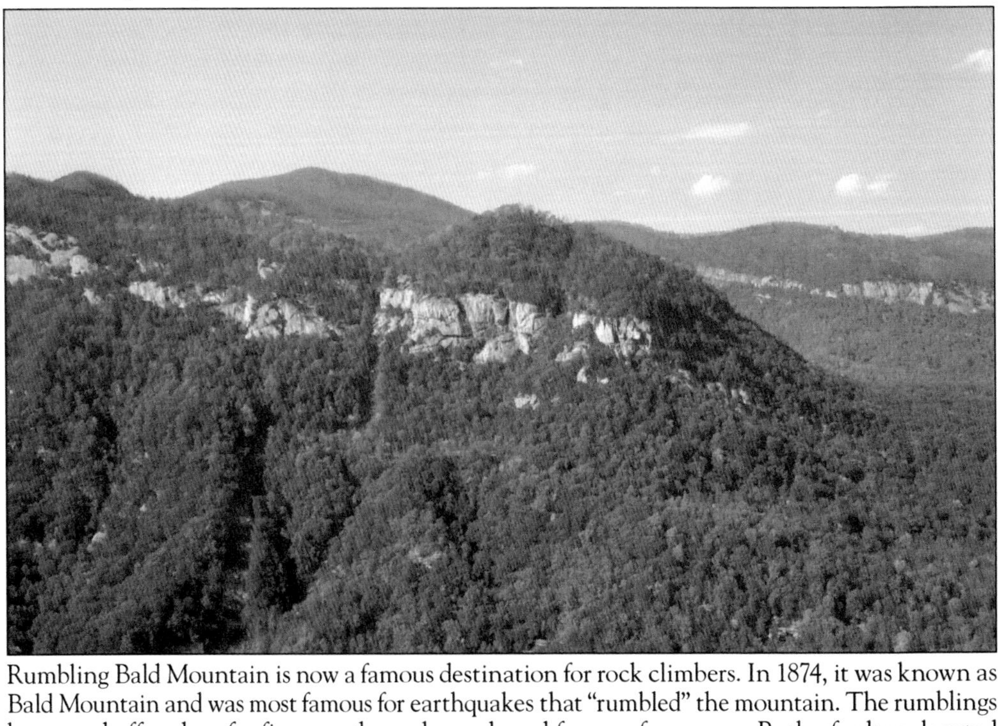

Rumbling Bald Mountain is now a famous destination for rock climbers. In 1874, it was known as Bald Mountain and was most famous for earthquakes that "rumbled" the mountain. The rumblings happened off and on for five months and were heard from as far away as Rutherfordton, located 23 miles away. The name of the mountain was eventually changed to Rumbling Bald Mountain. (Author's collection.)

Rock climbing has been in the Hickory Nut Gorge since the workers at Chimney Rock Park first started installing walkways on the rock cliffs. As a sport, rock climbing first took off in the early 1970s in an area climbers call Flakeview Area at Rumbling Bald Mountain with notable first assents by G. Jacobsohn, J. Ferguson, T. Ferguson, and A. Williams. In the mid-1970s, route development began at the Cereal Buttress with first ascents by Jeep Gaskin, Brad Shaver, and others. The 1980s were a time of many first assents with the Hanging Chain Wall route, the hardest climb in North Carolina at that time. Land purchases by the Chimney Rock State Park and the Carolina Climbers Coalition have expanded access to the many climbs at Rumbling Bald Mountain. This photograph shows Peter White at Rumbling Bald Mountain. (Author's collection.)

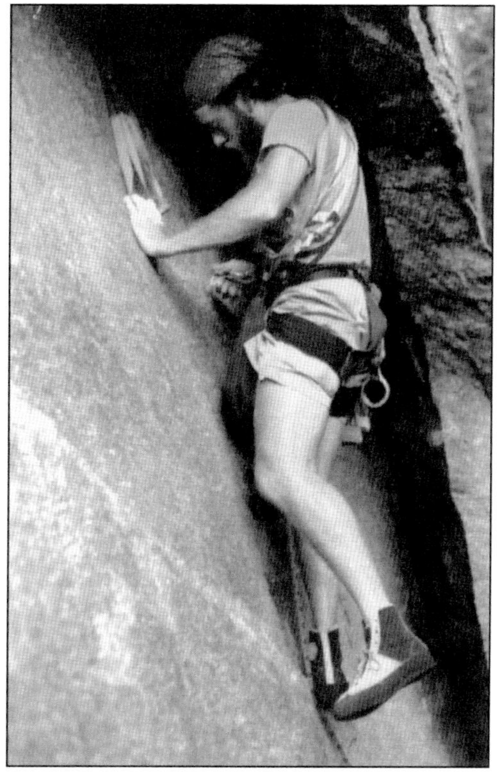

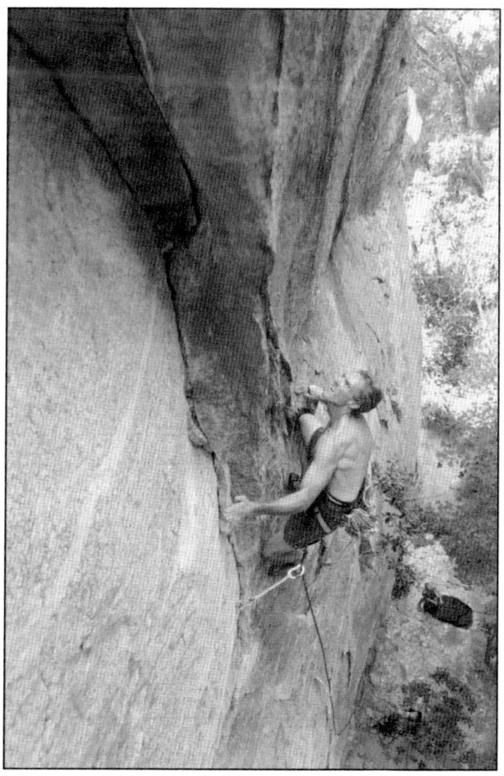

Tim Snyder is shown here climbing Arch Rival at Rumbling Bald Mountain. (Photograph by Ben Butler.)

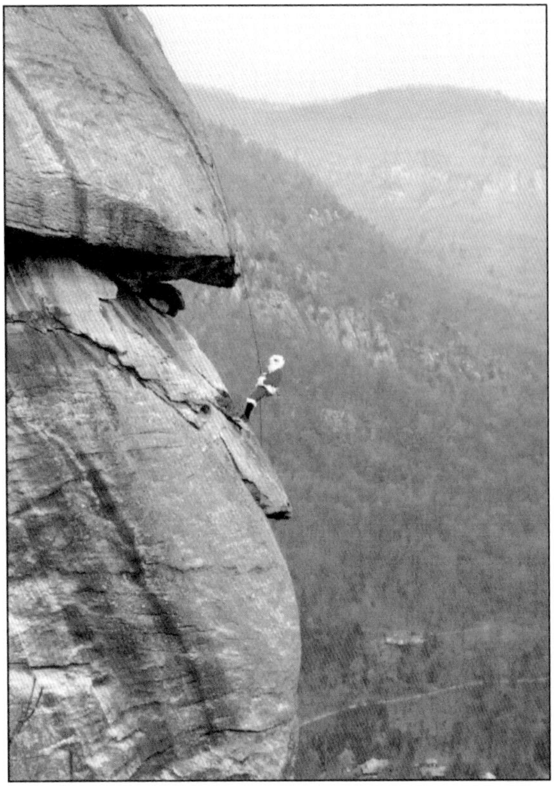

Even Santa Claus has been seen enjoying rock climbing at Chimney Rock Park. (Author's collection.)

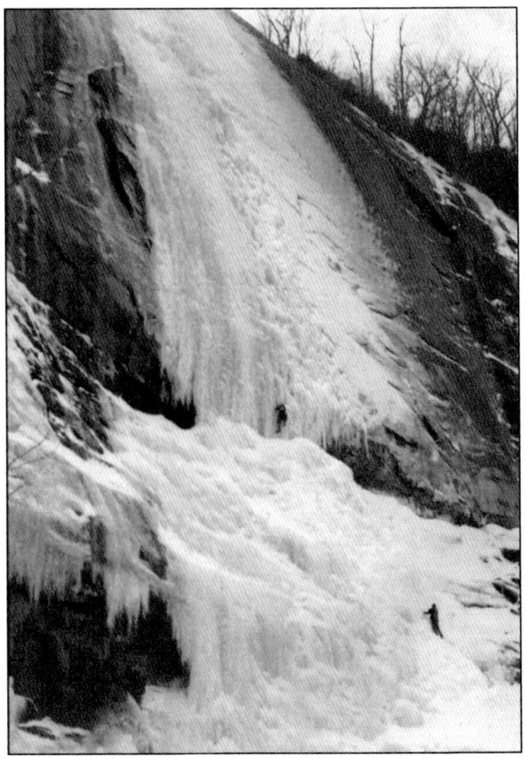

It is rare to see Hickory Nut Falls frozen hard enough to allow ice climbing, but 1981 was one of those years. Peter White and Mat Hodges were the first ever to ice climb the Hickory Nut Falls from bottom to top. Please note that ice climbing is potentially dangerous and not allowed without specific permission from the property owner. (Author's collection.)

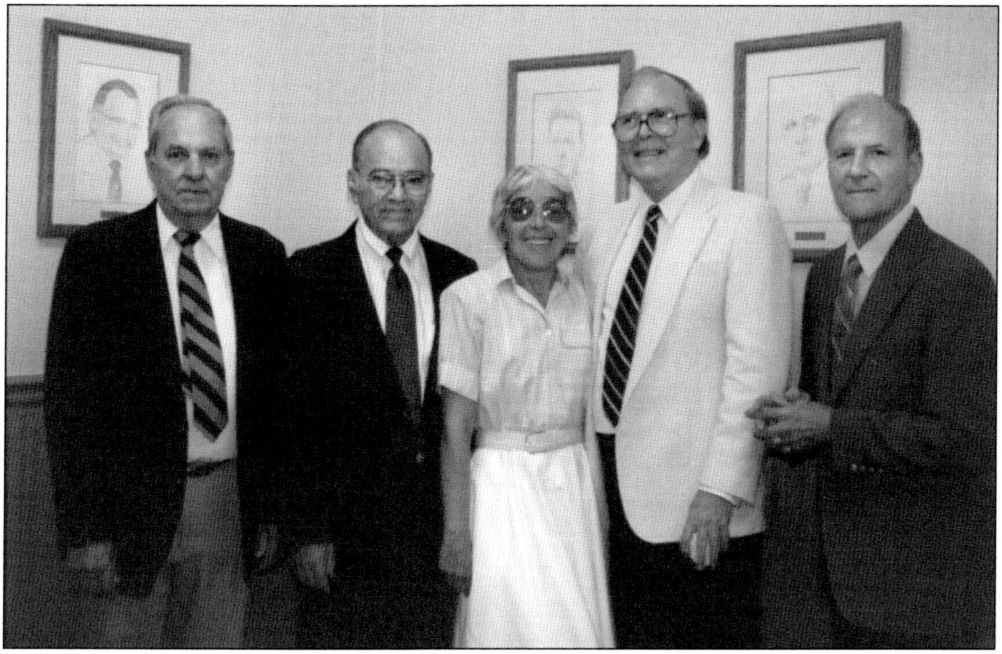

Pictured here are the mayors of Lake Lure. From left to right are Paul Wilson, L.M. Pearson, Priscilla Doyle, Charles Hicks, and Gene Michelin. There are portraits of all the past and current mayors in the foyer of the Lake Lure Municipal Building. (Courtesy of the Town of Lake Lure.)

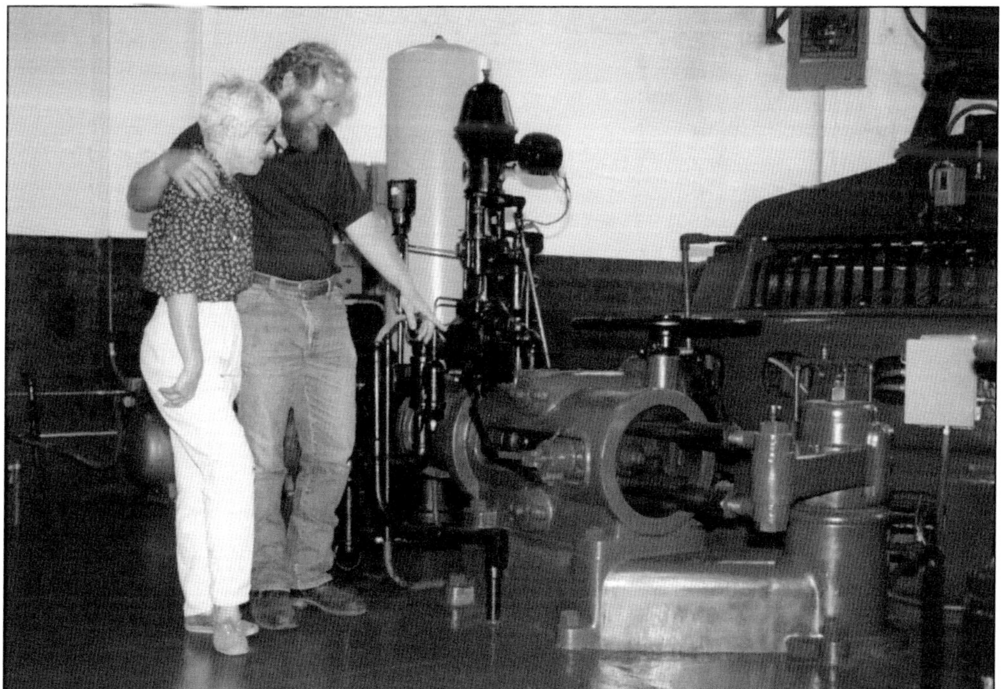

On the 65th anniversary of the town of Lake Lure's incorporation, the hydro plant had a makeover. Pictured here are Mayor Priscilla Doyle and plant director William Grimes. These are the same turbines installed in 1925. (Courtesy of the Town of Lake Lure.)

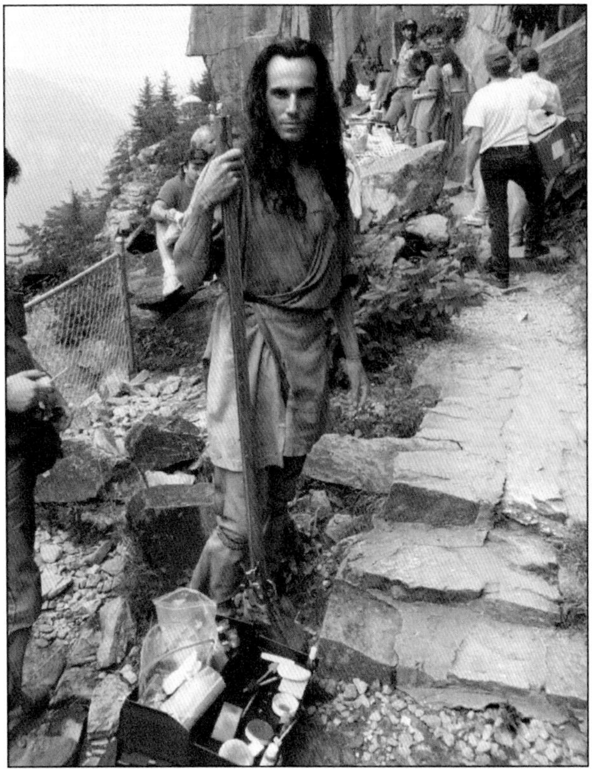

Filmmakers discovered the Hickory Nut Gorge as early as 1915. Silent movie stars such as Mary Pickford, Gloria Swanson, Douglas Fairbanks, Clark Gable, and others stayed at the Logan House and the Esmeralda Inn. Noted author Lew Wallace finished the script for *Ben Hur* while staying at the Esmeralda Inn. In modern times, several movies have used Lake Lure and Chimney Rock for film locations. These include *A Breed Apart* (1984) starring Kathleen Turner, Rutger Hauer, and Powers Boothe; *Firestarter* (1984) with Drew Barrymore and George C. Scott; *Dirty Dancing* (1987) starring Patrick Swayze and Jennifer Grey; *Last of the Mohicans* (1992) starring Daniel Day-Lewis (at left) and Madeleine Stowe (below); and *My Fellow Americans* (1996), a comedy-drama starring Jack Lemmon and James Garner. (Both, courtesy of Todd Morse.)

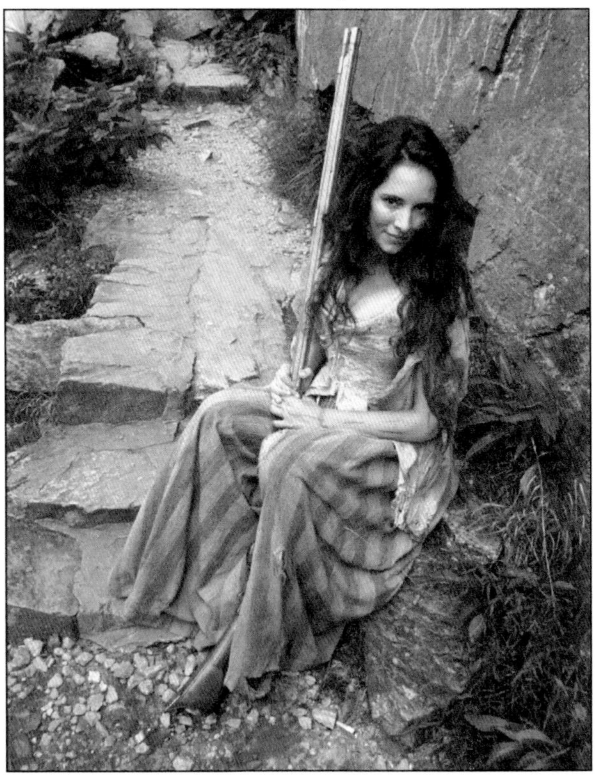

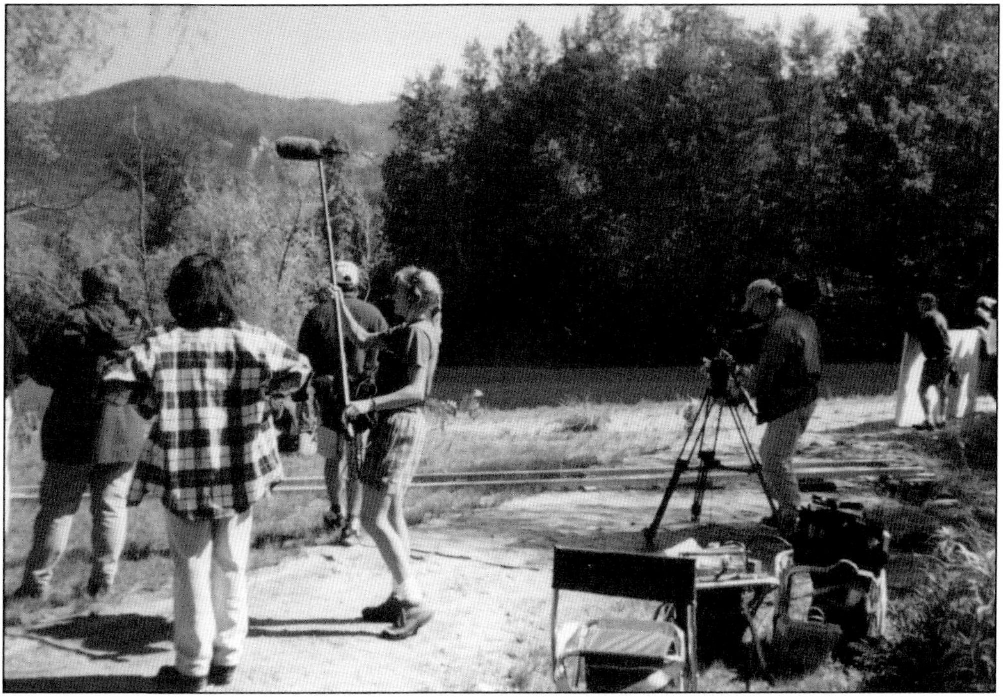

Film crews prepare to shoot a scene for the movie *My Fellow Americans*. The short scene was shot at the north side of Morse Park next to where the Rocky Broad River meets Lake Lure. (Both, courtesy of Nancy Wait.)

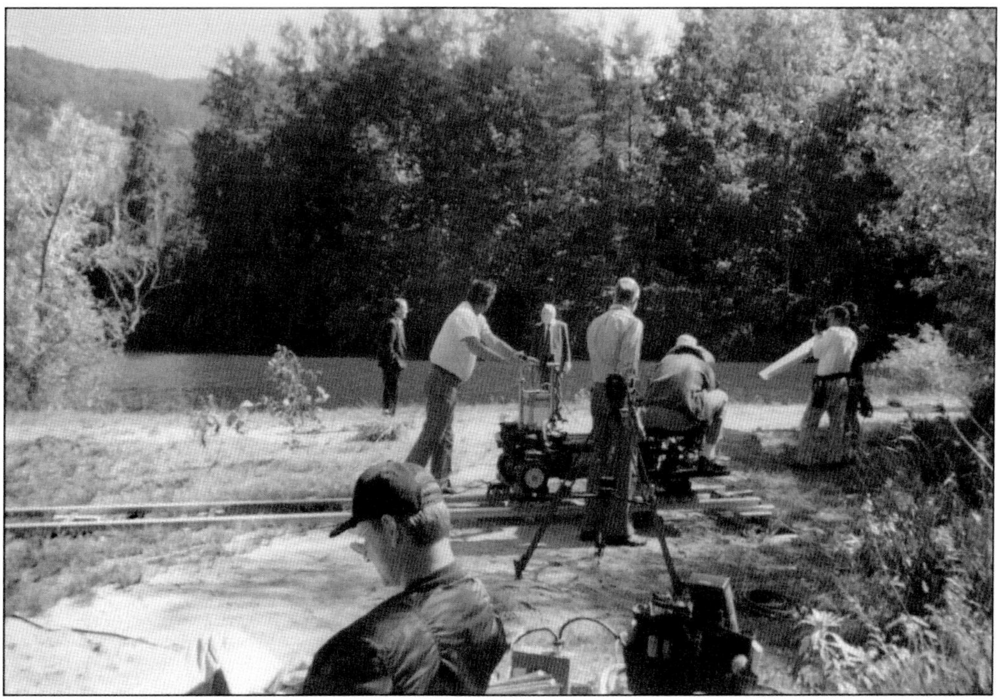

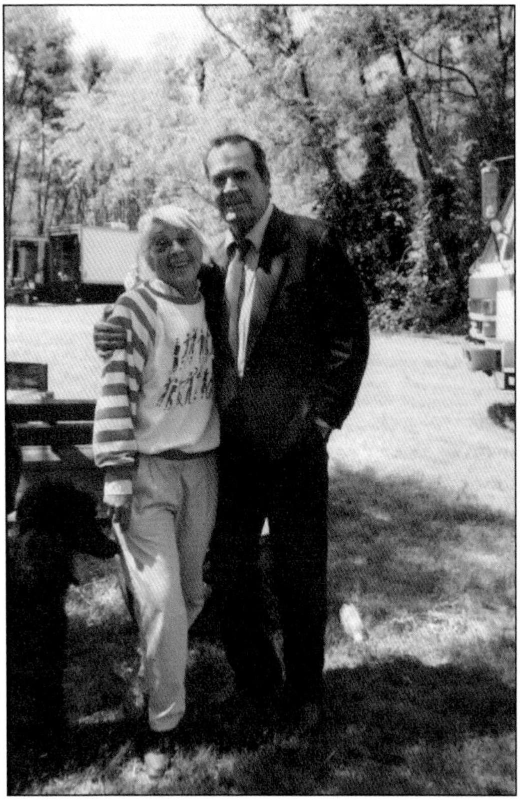

My *Fellow Americans* is a 1996 comedy-drama starring Jack Lemmon and James Garner. Jack Lemmon went to college with Mayor Priscilla Doyle. She is seen here with James Garner. (Courtesy of Nancy Wait.)

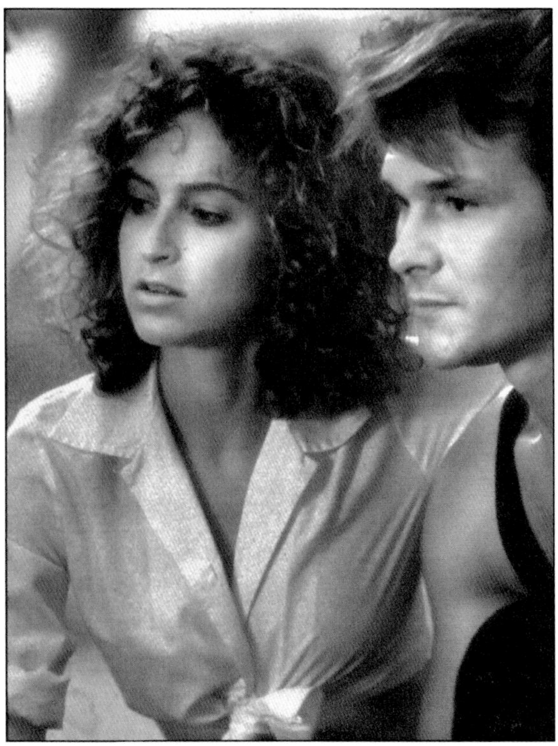

Pictured here are Patrick Swayze and Jennifer Grey while filming *Dirty Dancing*. (Courtesy of Jane Noblitt Melton.)

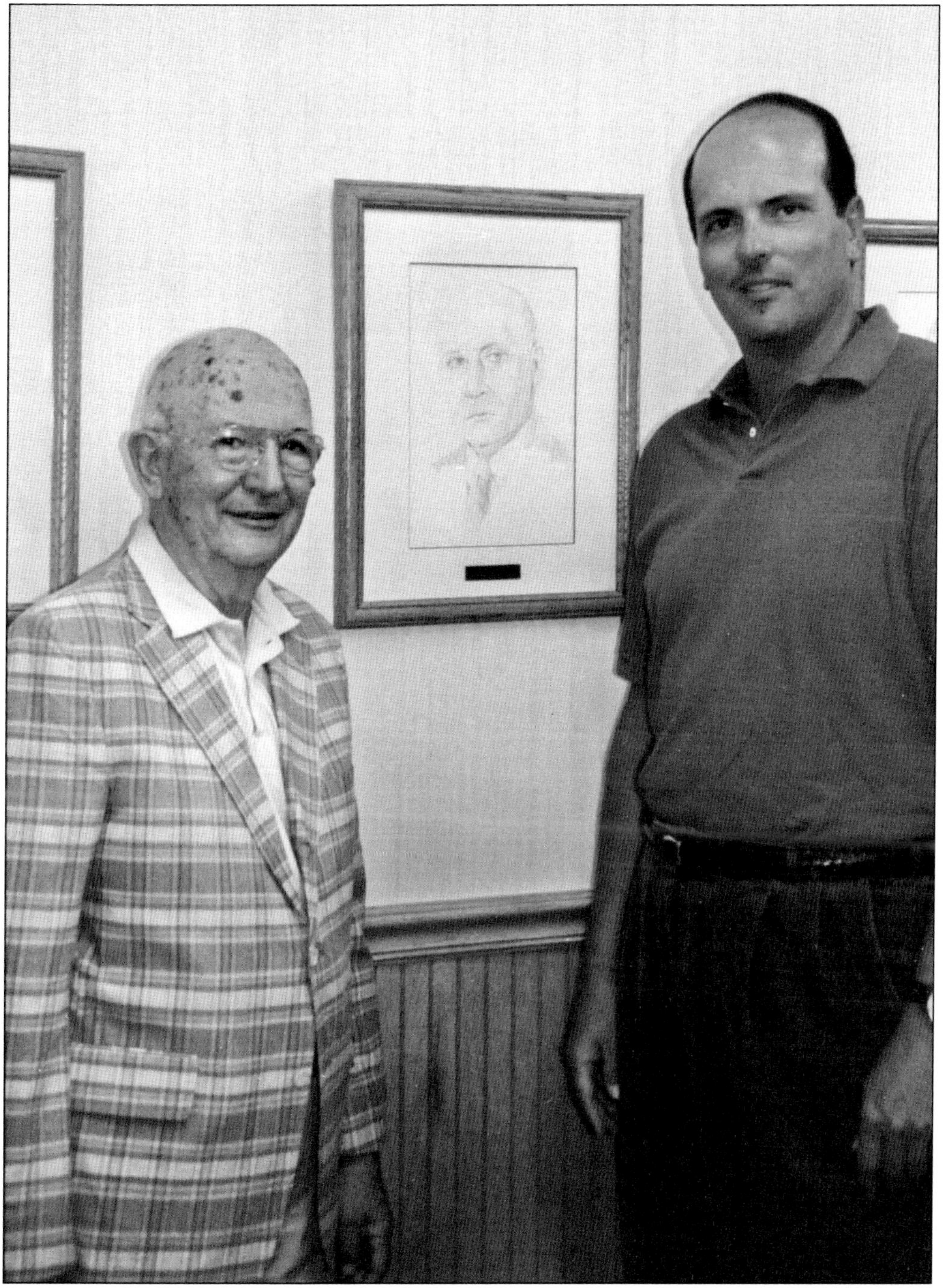

Richard "Dick" Washburn and Robert "Bob" Washburn stand on either side of a portrait of Dick's father, Dr. James Murray Washburn. Along with operating the Chalet Club, the Washburn family has always been active with the Lake Lure community. Dick served on the Planning Board from 1969 to 1979 and was chairman of the Lake Lure Zoning and Planning Board from 1979 to 2011. Bob was chairman of the Lake Advisory Board from 1992 to 2007, and Dr. Murray was mayor of Lake Lure from 1935 to 1949. (Courtesy of the Town of Lake Lure.)

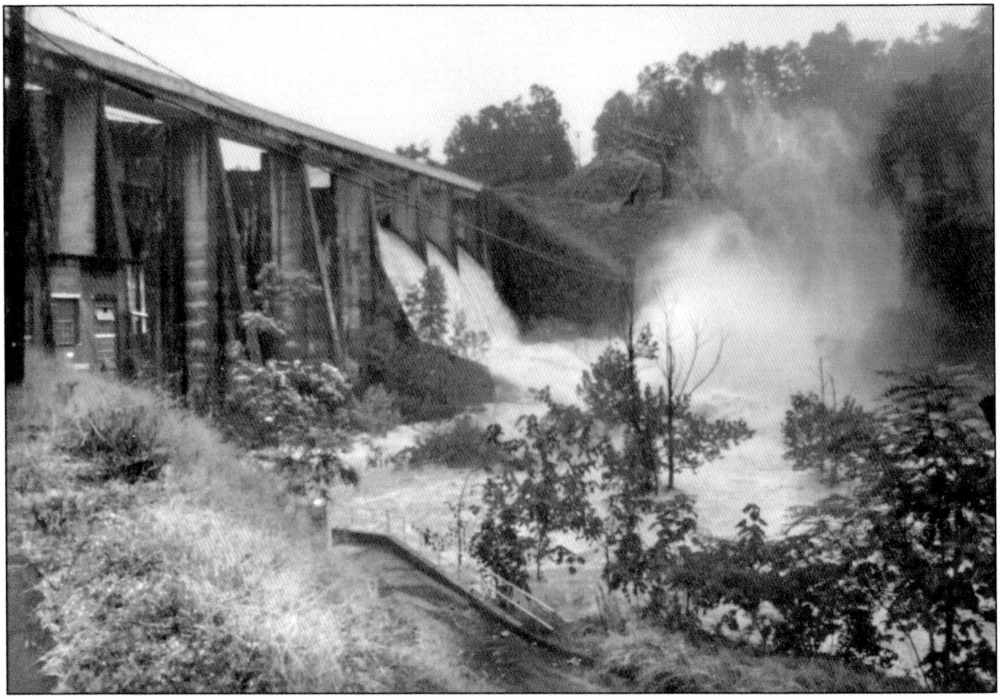

During times of large rainstorms, the floodgates are opened. The storm of 1996 created the worst flooding since the horrible flood of 1916. Below, the structure used by the Chimney Rock Baptist Church for Sunday lakeside services was inundated with floodwaters. Since the flood of 1996, sirens have been installed to warn folks downstream of the water release. (Both, author's collection.)

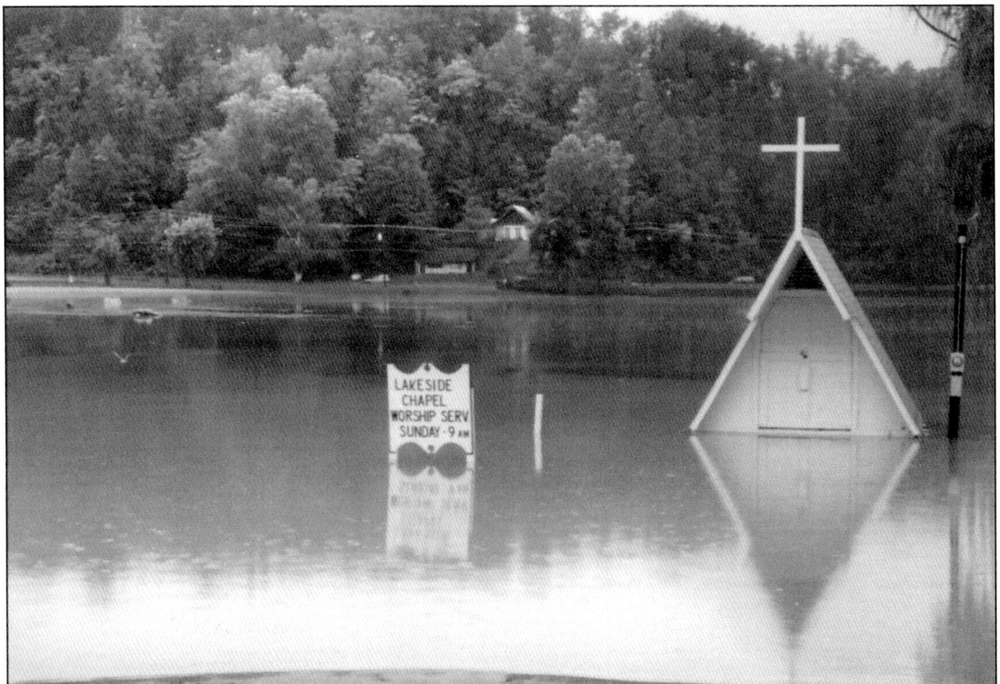

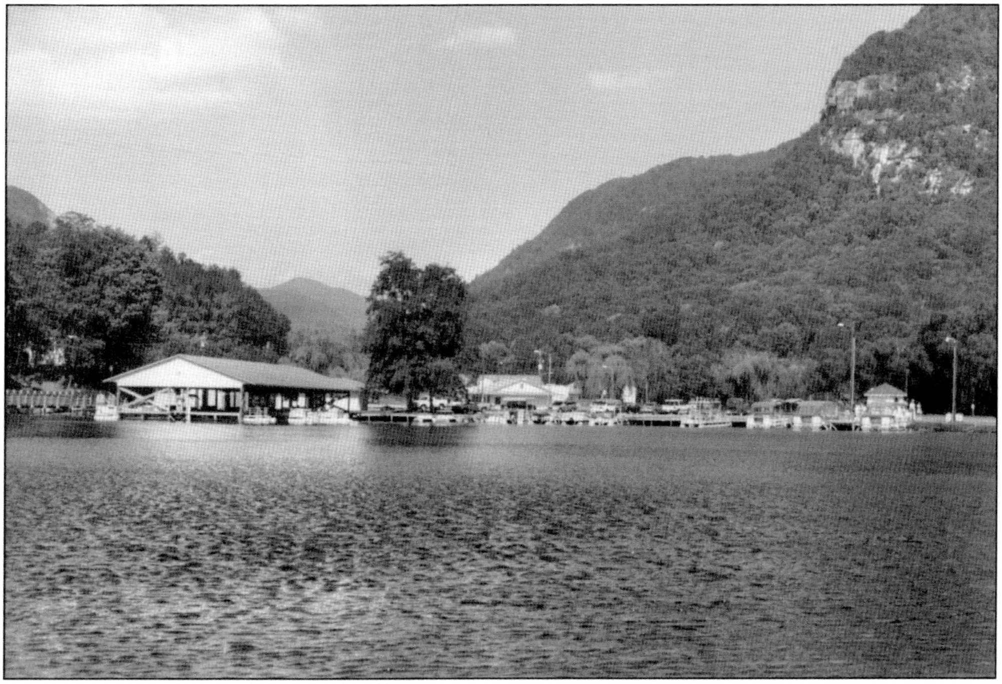

Throughout its history, Lake Lure has had several marinas. This shows the Lake Lure Municipal Marina before the covered boat slips were removed and replaced by new floating docks. (Author's collection.)

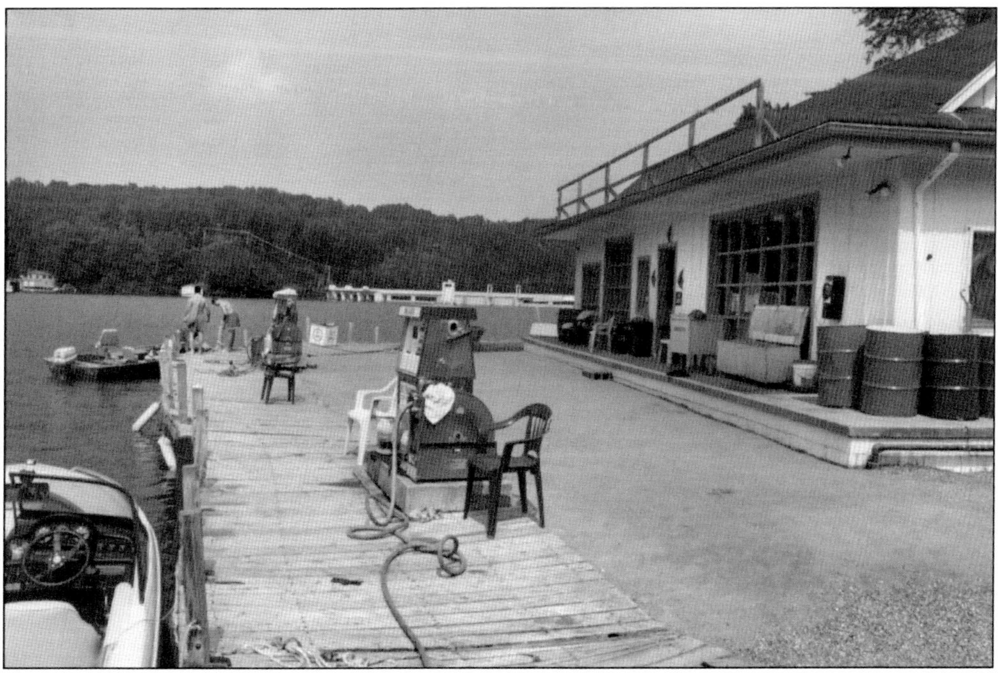

The Dam marina is located at the east end of Lake Lure near the Lake Lure Dam. It was in operation for many decades and was used in the movies *A Breed Apart* and *Firestarter*. (Author's collection.)

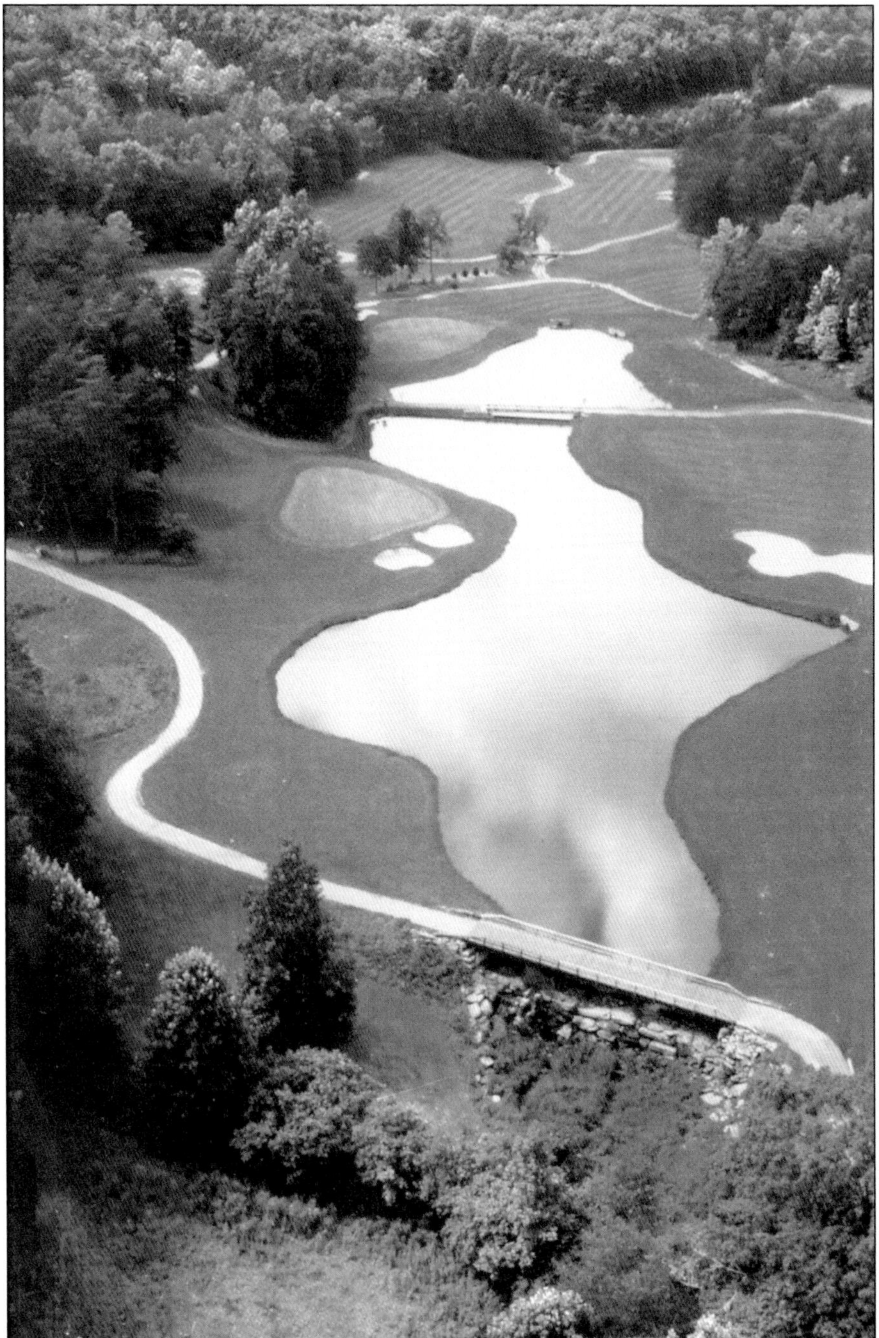

For more than a half a century, both tourists and residents have enjoyed the resort at the north end of Lake Lure. The resort, initially named The Mountains, was purchased by the Fairfield Company and called Fairfield Mountains. The property owner's association bought the resort amenities in the 1990s, and for a short time, it was known as the Lake Lure Golf and Beach Resort. The resort is now named the Rumbling Bald Resort. This photograph shows the back nine at the Apple Valley Golf Course. (Courtesy of Rumbling Bald Resort.)

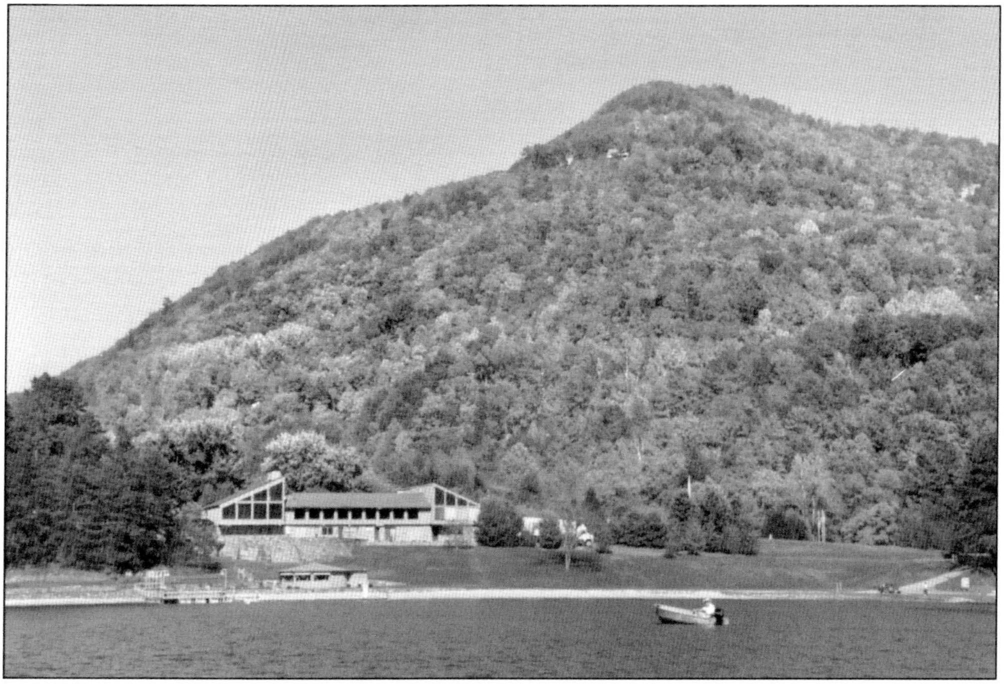

Seen here is the beach at the Rumbling Bald Resort with the Lakeview restaurant and Young's Mountain in the background. (Author's collection.)

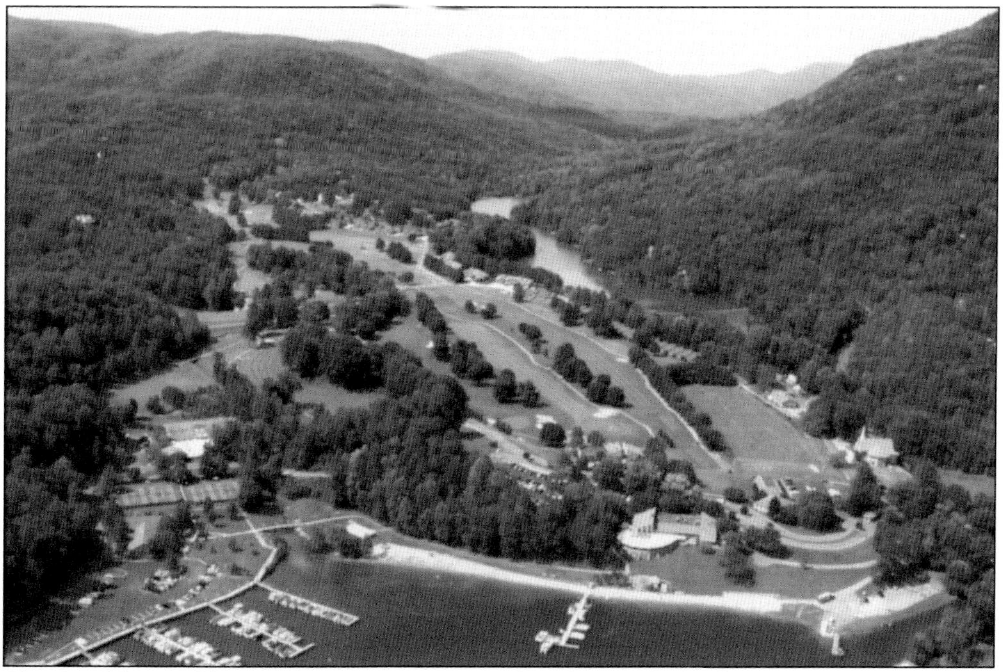

The Rumbling Bald Resort encompasses more than four and a half square miles and features two championship golf courses, tennis courts, spas, swimming pools, and boat rental. It has recently become a famous destination for weddings and family reunions. (Courtesy of Rumbling Bald Resort.)

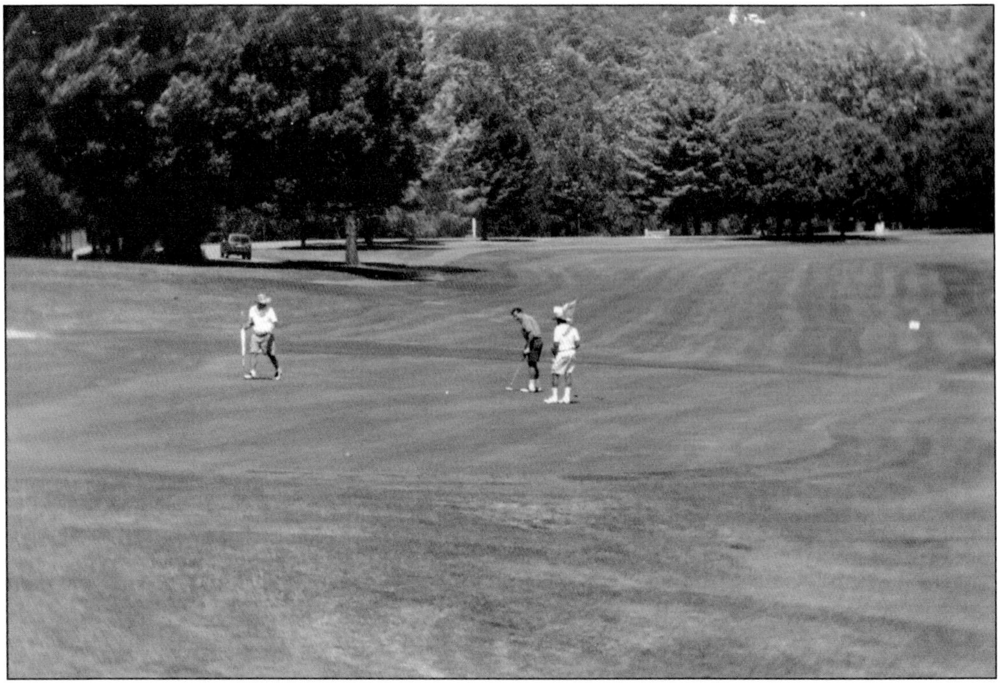

Built in 1968, Bald Mountain Golf Course was the first course constructed at Rumbling Bald Resort. The course remains popular for all ages and abilities and has received high marks from *Golf Digest* readers. This course has four sets of tees per hole and plays at 6,283 yards. (Author's collection.)

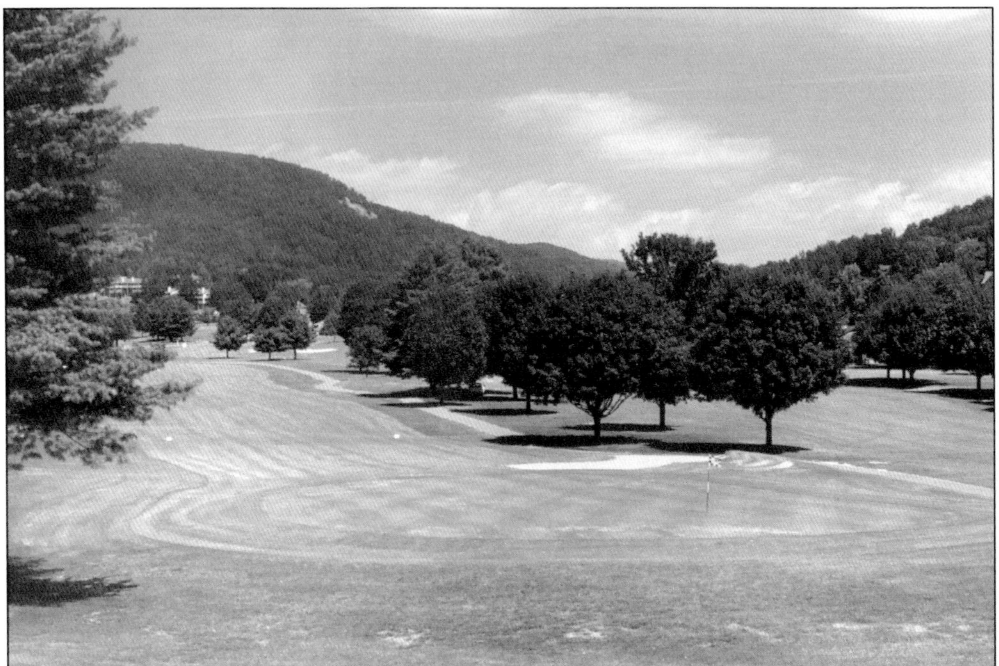

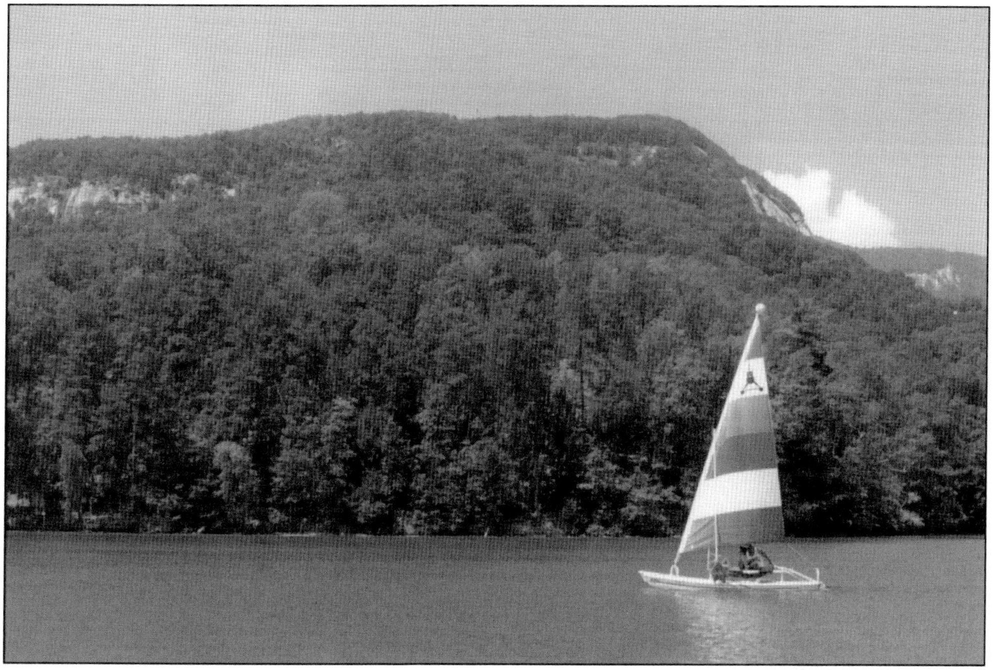

This is a view of a sailboat on Lake Lure with beautiful Rumbling Bald Mountain in the background. (Author's collection.)

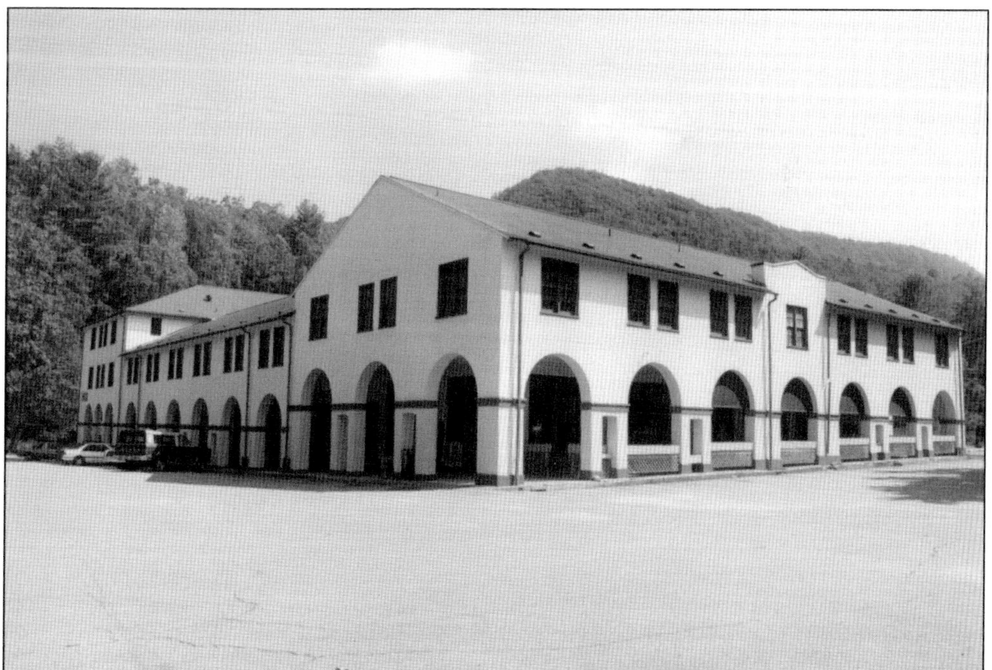

The Lake Lure Administration Building, now called the Lake Lure Arcade Building, was one of the first retail/hotel/apartment buildings in Western North Carolina. (Author's collection.)

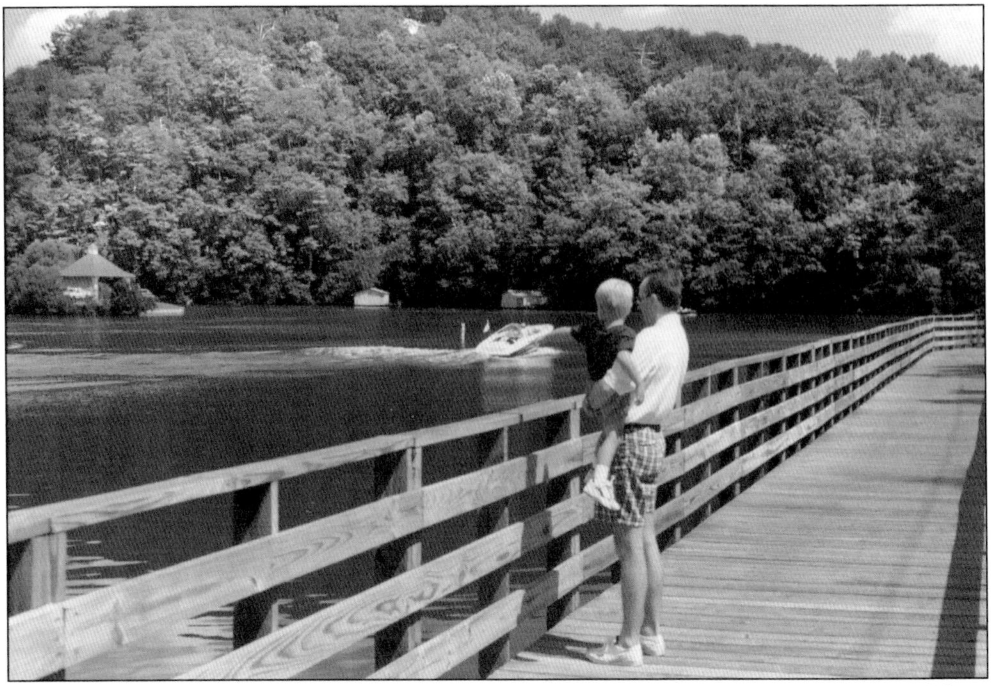

A boardwalk next to Memorial Highway was dedicated on April 23, 1991, and makes travel from the Lake Lure Marina to the Lake Lure Inn very pleasant. (Author's collection.)

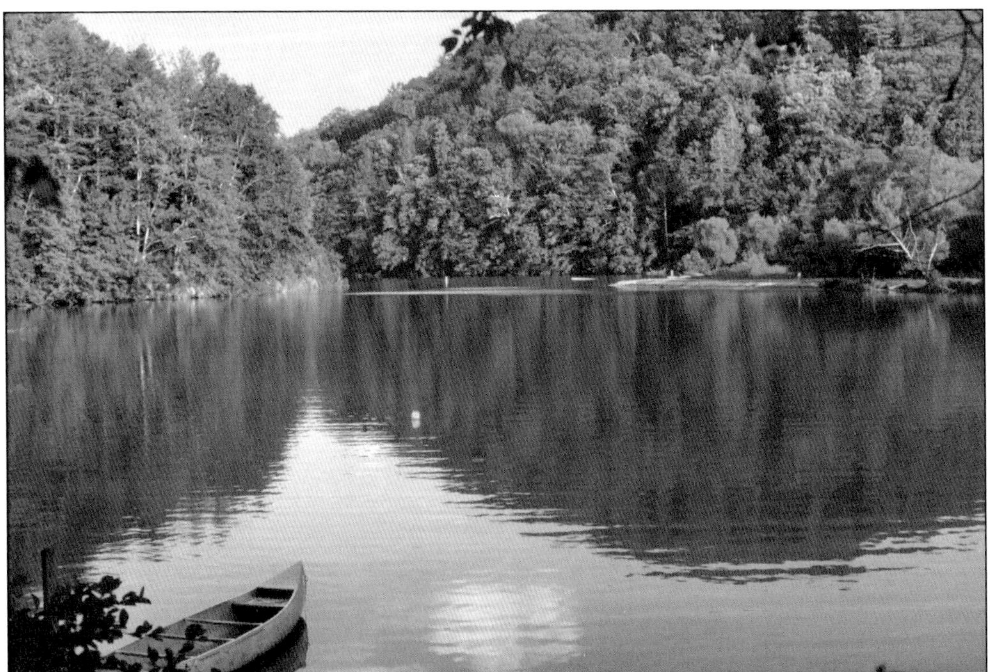

Canoeing remains a great way to explore Lake Lure. (Author's collection.)

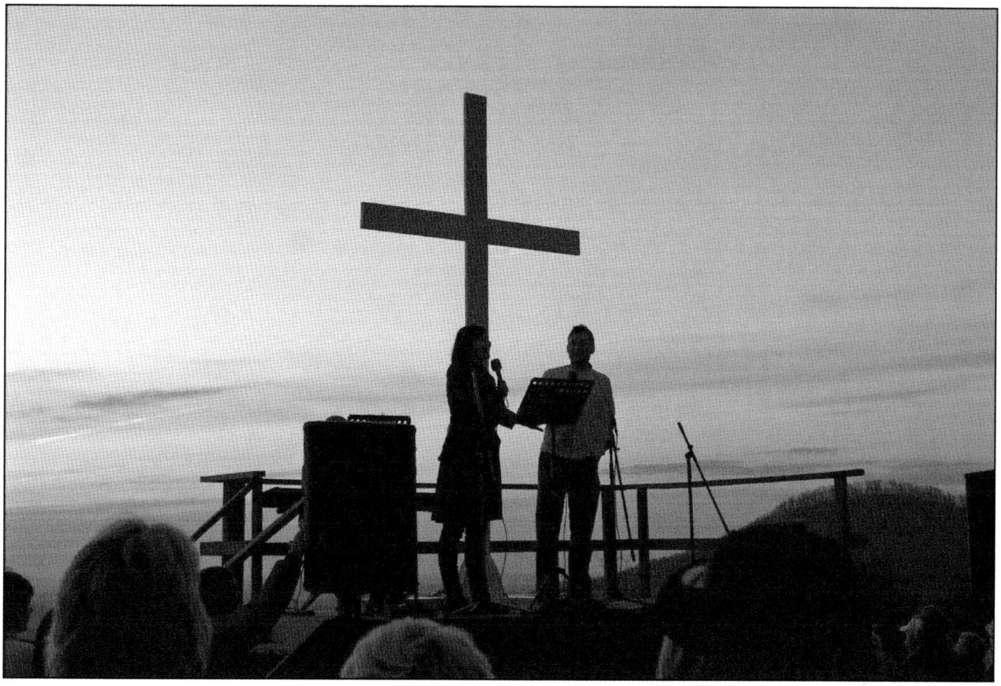

For more than 50 years, Chimney Rock Park has hosted a sunrise service at the parking lot just below the chimney. Some years it is cold, and some years it has rained, but all years are inspirational. The image below shows Ken Potter and Kathryn Proctor playing bagpipes. (Both, author's collection.)

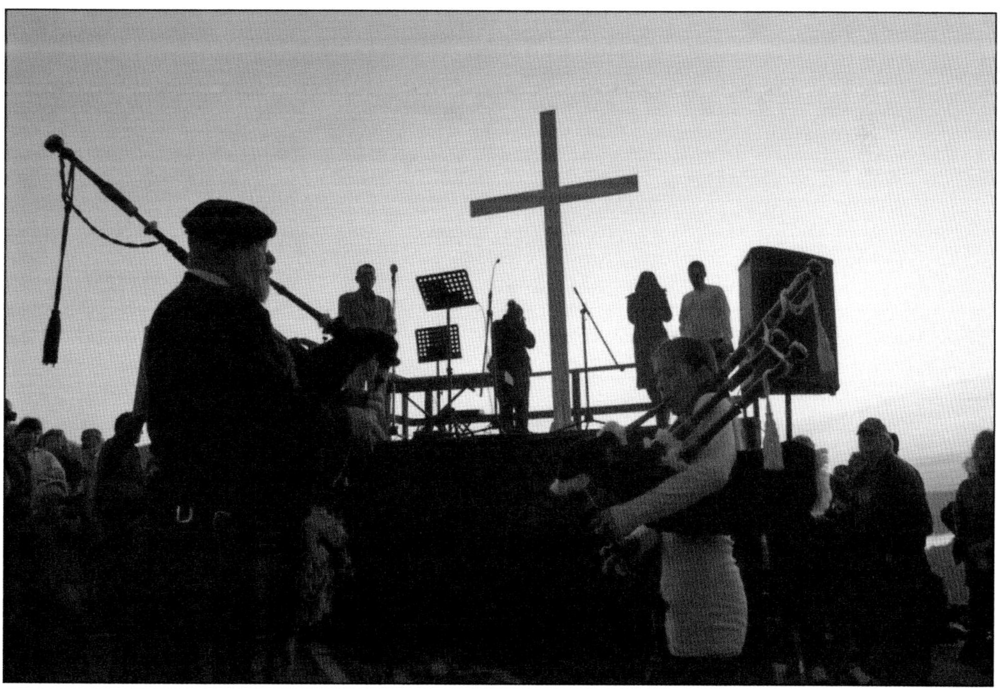

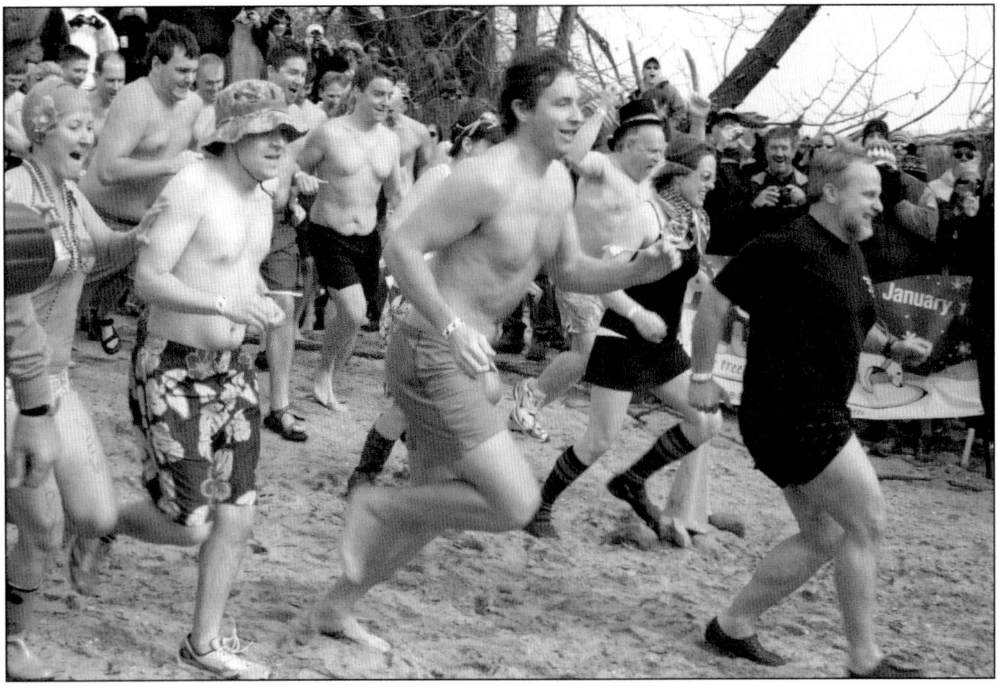

The Hickory Nut Gorge Chamber of Commerce often hosts events to bring more tourists to the valley. This photograph shows a large group of very brave folks participating in the annual Polar Plunge on New Year's Day. (Both, author's collection.)

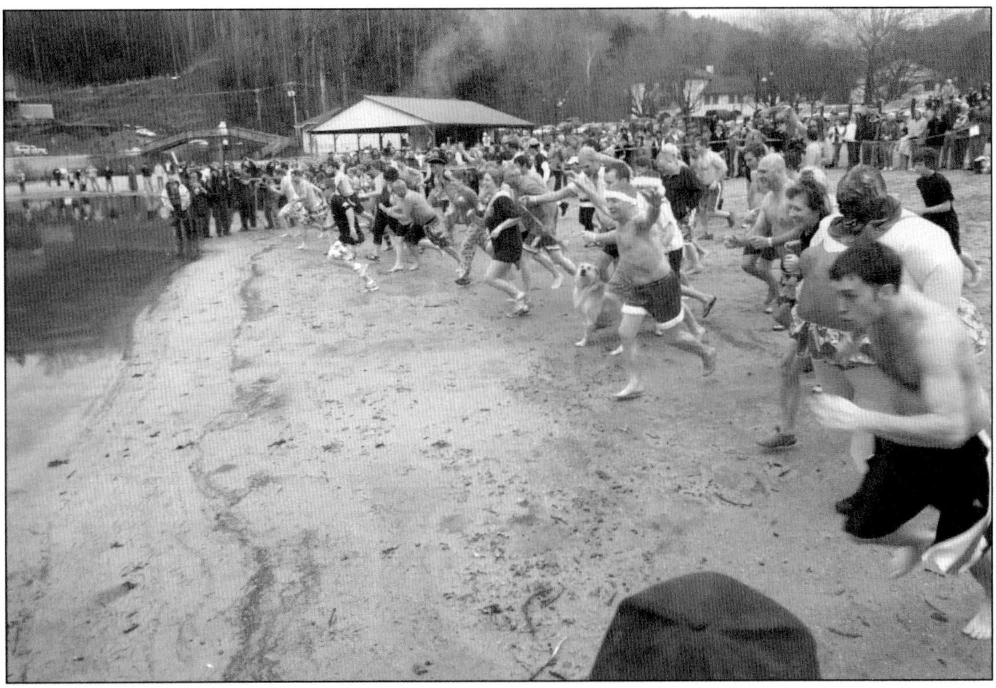

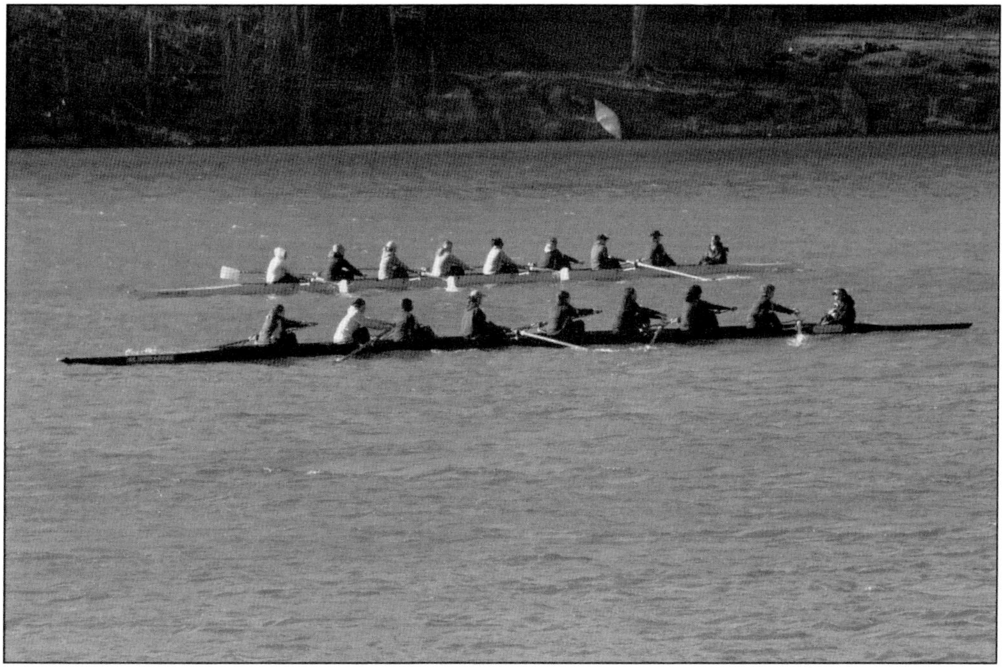

Lake Lure is an exceptional place for rowers. Several collegiate rowing teams take advantage of the area's mild winters for training. (Author's collection.)

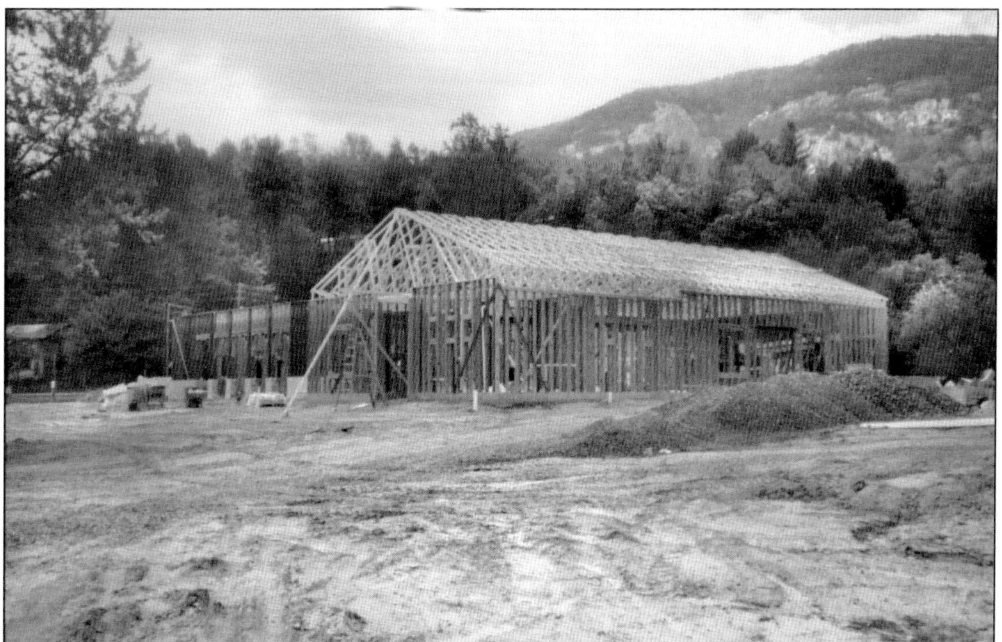

The Town of Lake Lure renegotiated its hydropower-producing contract with Duke Energy in the 1990s and, with the extra income, decided to build a new town hall. The town's offices moved from the very cramped space within the building where the town's ABC store is today. (Courtesy of the Town of Lake Lure.)

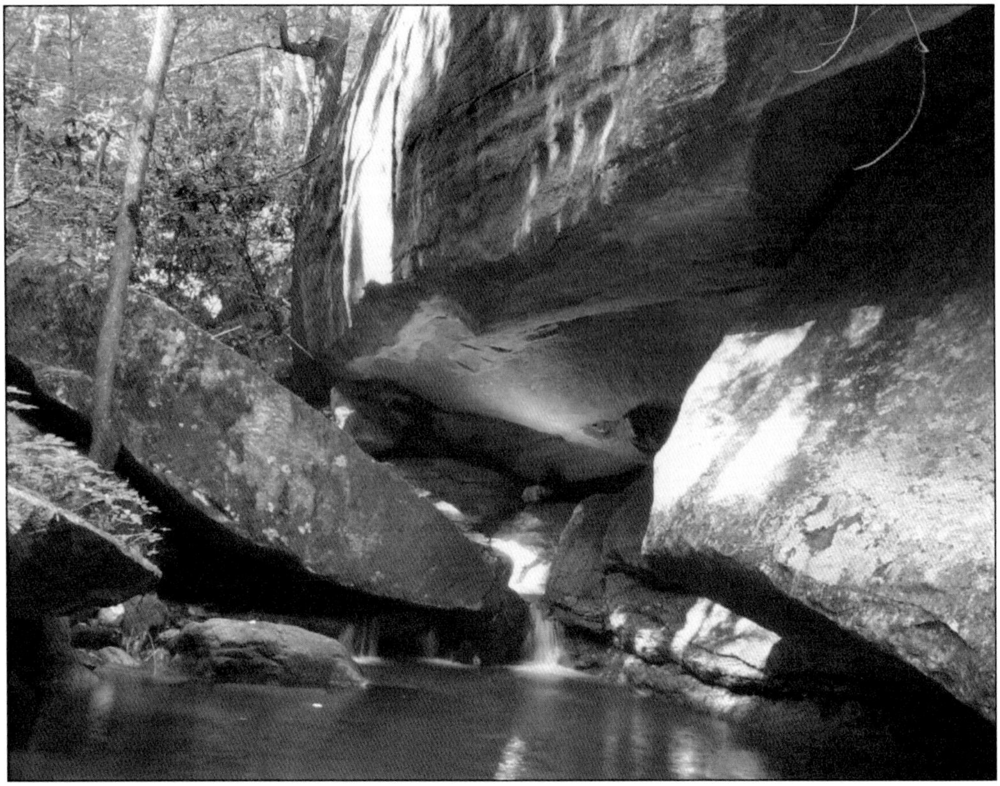

Originally named Hickory Nut Gorge State Park, Chimney Rock State Park was established in 2002 by the North Carolina Division of Parks and Recreation. In 2005, with tremendous public support, the North Carolina General Assembly authorized the creation of the state park. Early acquisitions for the new state park included a 1,568-acre tract known as World's Edge, land on Rumbling Bald Mountain, and land near the Bat Cave region. Along with diverse plant populations, the Hickory Nut Gorge has a number of pristine mountain streams and the Rocky Broad River. This image shows a remote section of Pool Creek. (Author's collection.)

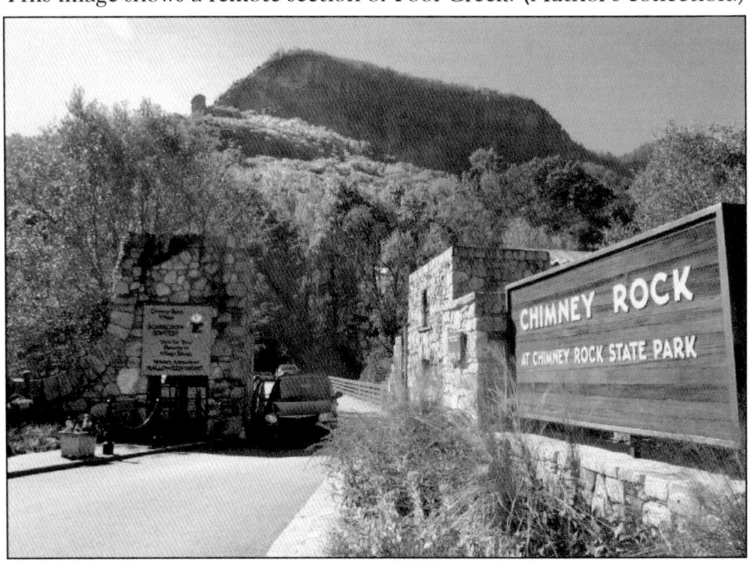

Pictured here is the entrance to Chimney Rock at Chimney Rock State Park. (Author's collection.)

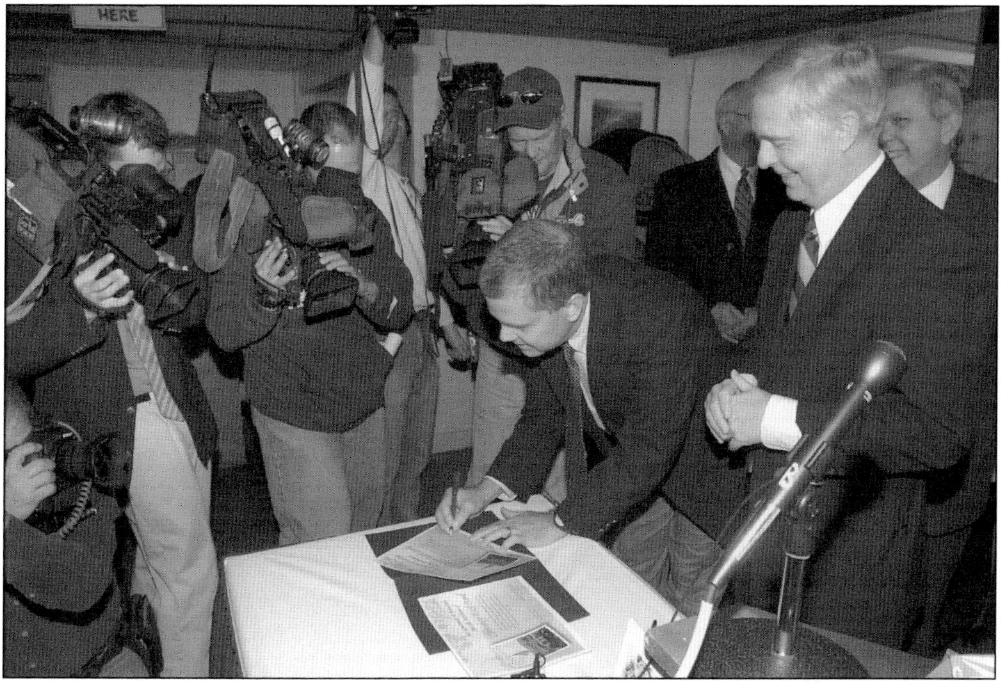

In 2006, the Morse family, owners of Chimney Rock Park for 105 years, offered their 996-acre park for sale. Shortly thereafter, the State of North Carolina began negotiations to purchase the private park and in May 2007 completed the purchase as an addition to the new state park. Soon thereafter, the park name was changed from Hickory Nut Gorge State Park to Chimney Rock State Park. The photograph above shows Todd Morse signing transfer papers with Gov. Michael Easley watching. In the image below, Governor Easley signs documents with Todd Morse, North Carolina senator (later lieutenant governor) Walter Dalton, and North Carolina House representative Bobby England looking on. (Both, courtesy of Todd Morse.)

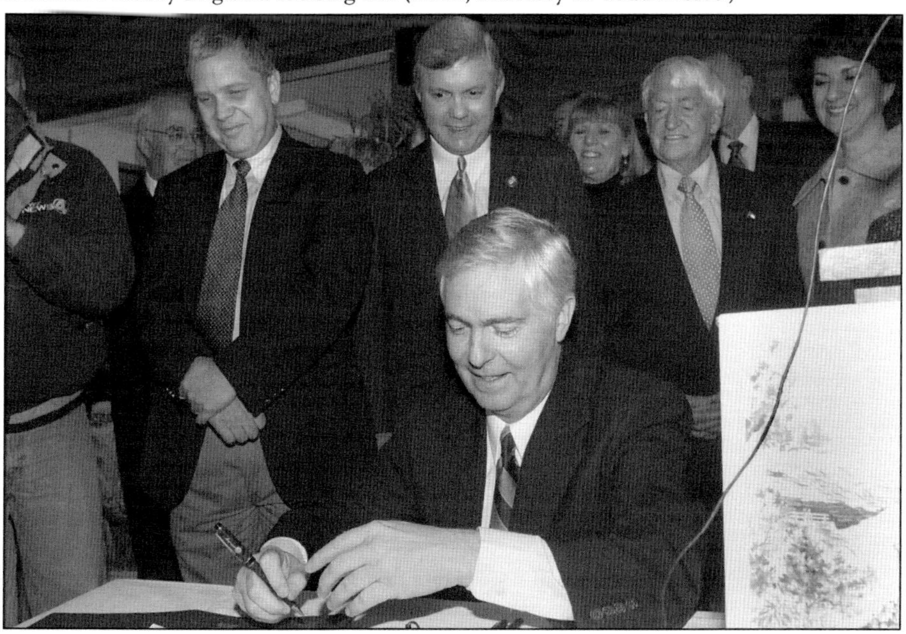

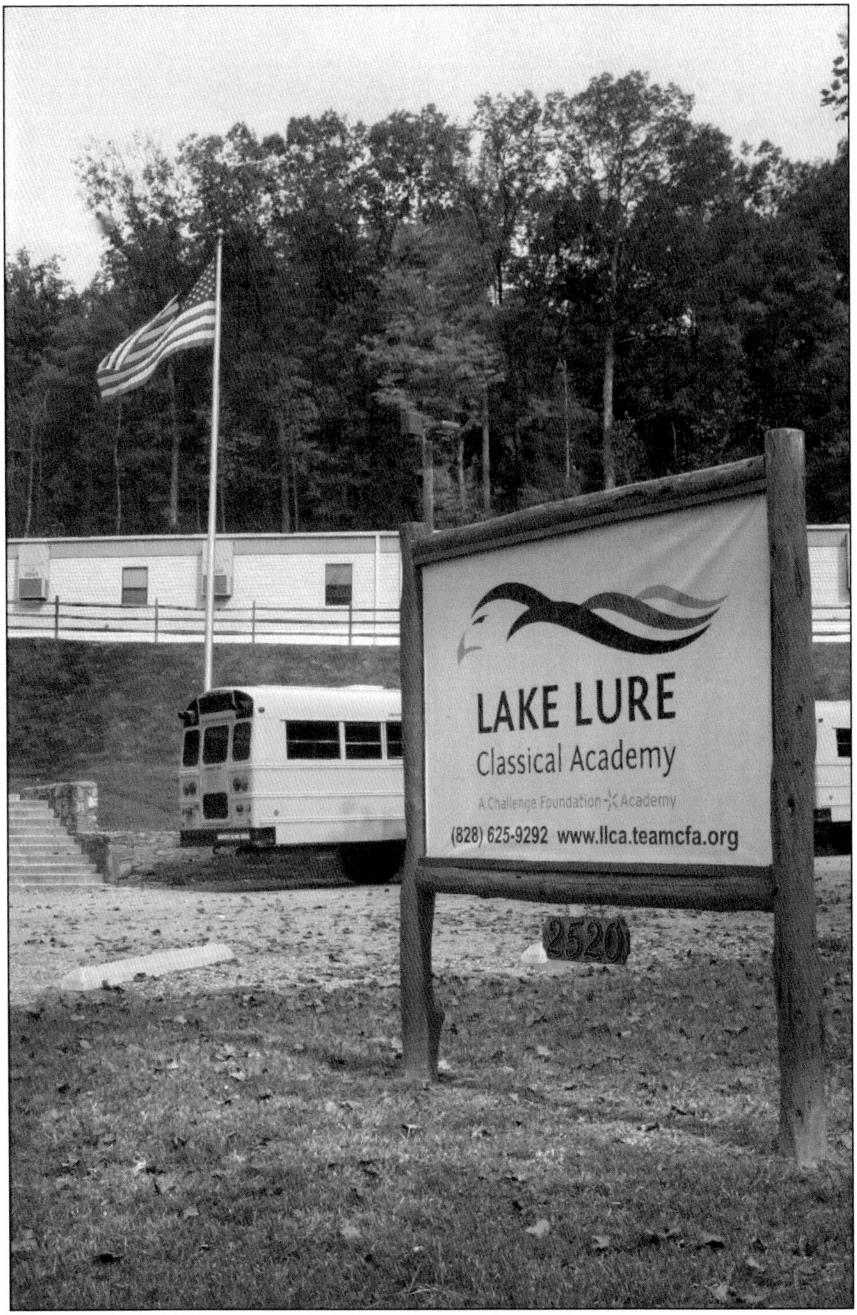

Lake Lure did not have a public school from 1961 until 2010. Local civic leaders and TeamCFA, a national nonprofit organization dedicated to charter schools, decided to create a public charter school. On August 21, 2009, the founding board of directors of the Lake Lure Classical Academy: A Challenge Foundation Academy (LLCA-CFA) was appointed. The eight board officers were Philip Byers, chairman; Jim Proctor, vice chairman; Russ Pitts, treasurer; and Chris Braund, secretary; Joan Lange; Cheryl Reinstadler; David Faunce; and Bryan King. Caroline Upchurch is the school's first director. The school is successful, drawing students from four surrounding counties. (Author's collection.)

Seen here is the sunset over majestic Lake Lure during the summer solstice. During the summer months, the sun sets behind the north end of Round Top Mountain. In the winter, the sun sets way to the south of Chimney Rock Mountain. (Author's collection.)

SELECTED BIBLIOGRAPHY

Cole, J. Timothy. *The Rumbling Mountain of Hickory Nut Gap, The Story of North Carolina's Most Celebrated Earthquakes.* Wilmington, NC: self-published, 1990.

Colton, Henry. *Mountain Scenery: The Scenery of the Mountains of Western North Carolina and Northwestern South Carolina.* Raleigh, NC: W.L. Pomeroy, 1859.

Chunn, Ida F. *The Descriptive Illustrated Guide-Book to North Carolina. Their principal resorts.* New York, NY: E.J. Hale & Son, 1881.

Griffin, Clarence W. *Western North Carolina Sketches.* Forest City, NC: Forest City Courier, 1941.

———. *Essays on North Carolina History.* Forest City, NC: Forest City Courier, 1951.

———. *The History of Old Tryon and Rutherford Counties, 1730–1936.* Asheville, NC: Miller Printing Company, 1937.

Merkel, Kimberly. *The Historic Architecture of Rutherford County.* Forest City, NC: Rutherford County Arts Council, Inc., 1983.

Price, Buddy. *Carolinas Climbing Guide.* Piedmont, SC: self-published, 1977.

Survey and Planning Unit, Division of Archives and History. *National Registry of Historic Places Inventory-Nomination Form for the Sherrill's Inn.* Raleigh, NC, 1975.

Survey and Planning Unit, Division of Archives and History. *National Registry of Historic Places Inventory-Nomination Form for Pine Gables.* Raleigh, NC, 1999.

Worley, Margaret W. *The Carolina Mountains.* Boston and New York: Houghton Mifflin Company, 1913.

Index

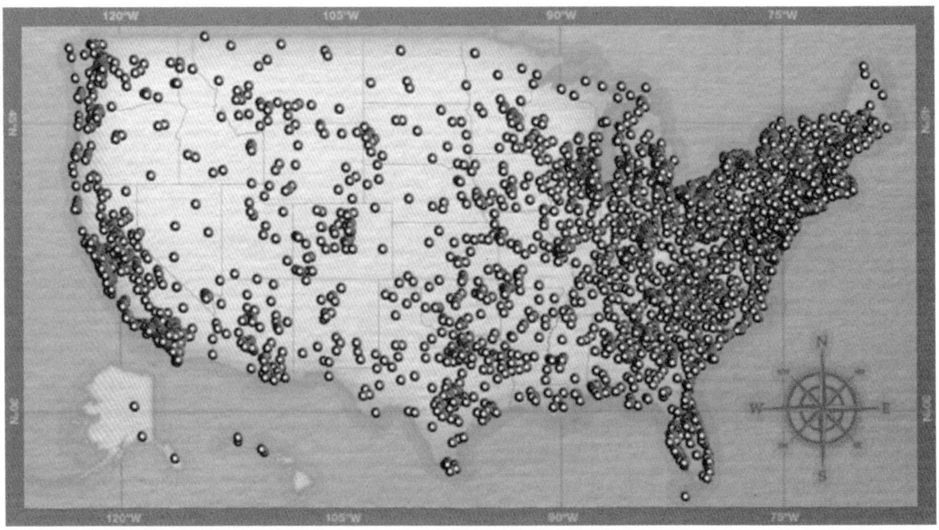